talking

the

TALK

French

DANIÈLE BOURDAIS
& SUE FINNIE

Series Editor: Alwena Lamping

Published by BBC Active, an imprint of Educational Publishers LLP, part of the
Pearson Education Group, Edinburgh Gate, Harlow, Essex CM20 2JE, England.

© Educational Publishers LLP 2017

BBC logo © BBC 1996. BBC and BBC ACTIVE are trademarks of the British
Broadcasting Corporation.

First published 2017.
5 4 3 2 1

ISBN 978-1-4066-8467-4

Publisher: Debbie Marshall
Development editor: Jenny Ollerenshaw
Layout: Reality Premedia Services
Cover design: Two Associates
Cover photograph: © iStock.com/oksix
Illustrations: © Mark Duffin
Project editor: Emma Brown
Proofreading: Florence Bonneau
Contributor: Siân Stratton-Brown
Audio producer: Colette Thomson, Footstep Productions Ltd.

Printed and bound by Neografia, Slovakia.

The Publisher's policy is to use paper manufactured from sustainable forests.

contents

introduction   5
the basics   7

how to sound French   9

un
first impressions   13

choosing between tu and vous   14
meeting and greeting   15
greeting people with confidence   16
farewells   17
wordbank: time expressions   18
introductions   19
wordbank: family   20
spelling names   21
basic courtesies   22
talking the talk   23
checkpoint 1   24

deux
getting to know people   25

breaking the ice   26
asking questions   27
sharing information   28
avoir to have   30
describing people   32
wordbank: adjectives: people   33
talking about places   34
wordbank: adjectives: places   36
how to remember words   37
talking the talk   38
verb practice 1   39
checkpoint 2   40

trois
what you do in life   41

saying what you do   42
wordbank: occupations   42
how French verbs work   44
reflexive verbs   45
wordbank: reflexive verbs   45
discussing work   46
faire to do, to make   48

talking the talk   50
verb practice 2   51
checkpoint 3   52

quatre
the art of conversation   53

following what's being said   54
making yourself understood   55
educated guesswork   56
prompting   57
showing empathy   58
unexpected meanings   59
commenting   60
wordbank: adjectives:
commenting   61
adding structure and fluency   62
talking the talk   63
checkpoint 4   64

cinq
been there, done that   65

saying what you have done   66
past participles   67
saying where you have been   68
conversation starters   70
wordbank: time expressions   71
coping in a crisis   72
saying something had taken place   73
talking the talk   74
verb practice 3   75
checkpoint 5   76

six
how things were   77

talking about what you used to do   78
saying how things were   80
wordbank: time expressions   81
reminiscing   82
chatting about the past   83
talking the talk   84
verb practice 4   85
checkpoint 6   86

sept

lifestyle choices   87

saying what you do and don't like   88
saying what you liked   89
adding nuance   90
saying what interests you   91
wordbank: interests   92
wordbank: household jobs   94
using **on**   95
expressing a preference   96
talking the talk   97
checkpoint 7   98

how to use a dictionary   99

huit

making plans   103

when?   104
what time?   105
suggesting things to do   106
wordbank: activities   107
accepting and declining
graciously   108
talking about the future   110
saying what you're going to do   111
weather permitting   112
saying what you would do   114
offering good wishes   115
talking the talk   116
verb practice 5   117
checkpoint 8   118

neuf

needs must   119

want   120
must, have to, need to   122
wish lists   124
... and to-do lists   125
can, could   126
knowing someone or something   128
le vouloir, le devoir, le pouvoir   129
talking the talk   130
verb practice 6   131
checkpoint 9   132

dix

sharing opinions   133

asking someone's opinion   134
saying what you think   135

the subjunctive   136
agreeing and disagreeing   138
making a case   139
what do *you* think?   140
wordbank: topical issues   140
numbers and statistics in
conversation   141
more or less   143
talking the talk   145
checkpoint 10   146

onze

inside information   147

finding out what's available   148
saying someone or
something's missing   149
finding out how to do something   150
asking for advice and
information   151
giving advice and instructions   152
everyday instructions   154
talking about food   155
health matters   156
wordbank: food   158
talking the talk   159
checkpoint 11   160

douze

keeping in touch   161

le franglais   162
saying thank you   164
keeping in touch   165
phonecalls and emails   166
shortcuts   167
wordbank: computer talk   168
talking the talk   169
checkpoint 12   171

grammar terminology   172

grammar summary   175

numbers   190

answers
   checkpoints   193
   verb practice   197

vocabulary builder   200

introduction

Talking the TALK French is BBC Active's latest addition to the bestselling **TALK** series. It is about social conversation: not just small talk but getting to know people and their lives, sharing information, opinions and anecdotes, making plans, talking about aspirations and obligations — and more.

An **audio component** complements the book. It is available for you to download from www.bbcactivelanguages.com/TTF.

Who is it for?

It's for people of all ages who are learning French or who are familiar with the basics, and whose ambition is to be able to chat to people in French, whether someone they've met on holiday, a business contact, extended family, a fellow enthusiast, a neighbour or anyone else.

The contents are also ideal for someone who has followed a course but would like to update their French and extend the range of what they can say.

How does it work?

It is based on the principles of successful conversation.

Everyday conversation hangs on a relatively small number of **core linguistic structures** which provide the framework for what we want to say.

The potential of this framework is realised by building on it, so **personalised vocabulary building** is a priority. This book contains hundreds of examples, using **varied and contemporary language**.

Conversation works better if you have the **strategies to keep it flowing**. And it's easier when you're confident that what you're saying sounds **natural and up to date**, and when you know that you'll be **readily understood**.

Is it easy to use?

The approach is hands-on, to enable you to adapt what you're learning so that it's **personal and relevant** to you.

Content is presented in **manageable steps**, with page headings showing clearly what the focus is. Core linguistic structures are generously illustrated and explained with the hallmark TALK clarity. Focused wordbanks, placed just where you need them, allow you to practise, adapt and **personalise the language structures**: there are frequent suggestions on how you might do this.

The design allows learning French to fit into a busy lifestyle: this is a book that can be dipped into a page or two at a time. The pages are grouped into 12 chapters, each of which ends with conversations that bring the language you're learning to life and a checkpoint which serves as revision and as an aid to remembering the contents.

How does the audio fit in?

The French presenters of the audio have clear aims:

- **helping you to pronounce French correctly**, since conversation is more enjoyable when both sides understand each other without endless repetition. They guide you through the sounds of French, focusing on the ones that English speakers often struggle with. They do this with material selected from each chapter, **reinforcing the core language structures**. They're supported in the book by how to sound French, a guide to the sounds and stress patterns of French.

- **developing your listening skills**, since conversation is as much to do with listening as talking. Each chapter ends with informal conversations between the presenters; these are printed in your book on the Talking the TALK page, and the Audio Support Pack offers suggestions on how to make the most of them.

How do I access the audio?

To download the audio, go to www.bbcactivelanguages.com/TTF.

For maximum flexibility, you can download the complete script including the conversations and you can download the conversations separately, entirely in French, for intensive listening.
The Audio Support Pack is also available from www.bbcactivelanguages.com/TTF. It includes full transcripts plus guidance and activities on how to make the most of the conversations.

> BBC Active would like to thank all the language tutors who contributed to the planning of Talking the TALK. The concept is based on your suggestions and feedback.

the basics

To get to the point when you can hold your own in a conversation, you don't need to know complex and detailed grammatical terminology. But familiarity with the basic terms can fast-track you to that point because it allows you to make sense of explanations of how French works.

The ten definitions on this page will take you a very long way. You don't have to learn them all now: just remember they're here for quick reference. If you decide you'd like to know more, there's a fuller list on pages 172–174.

Nouns are the words for living beings, things, places and abstract concepts: *boy, Rachel, engineer, mosquito, computer, house, Provence, time, strategy*.

Articles are *the, a/an* and *some*.

A **pronoun** is used instead of a noun, and saves having to repeat that noun. *Where's Theo? He's with a friend, I saw them earlier.*

Adjectives are words used to describe a noun or a pronoun: *good wine; strong red wine; my wine; that wine; It is French; It was superb.*

Verbs are words like *eat, live, sleep, go, listen, have, want, be, die*, that relate to doing and being. In English you can put *to* in front of a verb: *to eat.*

In a dictionary, French verbs are listed in the **infinitive**, the equivalent of *to eat*. Nearly all French infinitives end in **-er**, **-ir** or **-re**: **arriv**er *to arrive*, **fin**ir *to finish*, **vend**re *to sell*.

The **-er**, **-ir** and **-re** at the end of infinitives are called – understandably – **verb endings**. They're significant in French: they change to carry a variety of information.

The **tense** of a verb refers to when it's happening, e.g. present tense, future tense. The perfect and imperfect tenses refer to the past.

Most verbs, nouns and adjectives follow patterns: these are defined as **regular**. Ones that deviate from the patterns are called **irregular** and have to be learnt separately. English too has irregularities, e.g. *boy/boys* but *child/children*; *work/worked* but *speak/spoke*.

the main differences between French and English

There are many similarities between French and English, and some essential differences too. It helps to be prepared for them.

- One conspicuous contrast is the way adjectives often come after nouns in French: **parc national** *national park*, **intelligence artificielle** *artificial intelligence*. Also, words like *me, it, us, her, them* usually come before a verb not after it: **je les respecte** *I respect them*.

- Every single French noun — not just the words for people and animals — is either **masculine (m)** or **feminine (f)**. There's no sense of *it*, not even for things like cars, food, sport or days of the week.

- Words linked to a noun have to be masculine or feminine to **agree** with it: **le menu** (m) *the menu*, **la musique** (f) *the music*, **les villages** *the villages* (m pl), **les idées** *the ideas* (f pl). An adjective in a dictionary has the masculine singular ending, but it changes to agree: **un menu important, la musique importante, les villages importants, les idées importantes.**

- French has two words for *you*, **tu** and **vous**, depending on who you're talking to. So every sentence or question containing *you* has two possible versions. French often uses **on** *one* rather than **tu** or **vous** when *you* is used in a general rather than a personal way, as in *You never can tell* or *You pay at the door.* **On** is also frequently used instead of *we*.

- In the English *Do you speak other languages? Yes, I speak Russian*, the verb *speak* in the question is repeated in the answer. In the French equivalent **Vous parlez d'autres langues? Oui, je parle russe**, the verb has a different ending in the answer because the ending of a verb depends on who is carrying it out.

- You generally need two words to say *not* in French: **ne** and **pas**, which sandwich the verb between them: **Je ne suis pas en retard** *I am not late.* Other negative words also require **ne** and aren't like an English double negative: **Je ne suis jamais en retard** *I am never late.*

- Pronunciation is markedly different. French and English have many hundreds of words that are identical or nearly identical in writing, and they're a great boost to vocabulary. But they don't sound a bit the same, so to ensure that you'll be readily understood, you need to know where the differences lie.

how to sound French

Hundreds of French words are identical to their English equivalent — when you see them written down. But they don't sound the same: the two languages have their own distinct sounds and rhythms.

Even if your French accent isn't perfect, there are ways of ensuring that French people understand you more easily. The key lies in:

- **knowing** how to pronounce the letters and the key combinations of letters — which are more consistent in French than in English.

- **listening** to as many different voices and accents as possible. There are different levels of listening: more often than not you're listening in order to understand *what* is being said, but you can also listen in order to hear *how* something is being said. It doesn't matter that you don't understand everything: what you're doing is getting a feel for the rhythm and overall sound of French.

- **practising** until what you say is what you hear. It's not enough to say things in your head; you need to say them out loud so that your jaw, facial muscles, mouth, tongue, vocal cords and lips are all working to produce the French sounds.

The **Talking the TALK audio download**, available from www.bbcactivelanguages.com/TTF, is there to support you. But before sampling the audio, have a look at the next few pages, which summarise the fundamentals of pronunciation, stress and rhythm.

vowels

a à	as in *cat*	Paris, parc, la, là, voilà
â	as in *cart*	pâtes, tâche
e	as in *mother*	je, le, petit
	as in *hey*	ballet, béret, poulet
è ê ë	as in *bed*	père, mère, fête, forêt, Noël,
é	as in *hey*	café, fiancé, soufflé, rosé, liberté
i î ï	as in *machine*	Nice, Nîmes, gîte, naïve
o	as in *pot*	homme, bonne
	as in *over* at the end of a word: **métro, vélo**	
ô	as in *over*	Jérôme, hôtel
y	as in *machine*	rallye
	y as in *yes* when between vowels: **voyage, payer**	
u û	u is often wrongly pronounced *oo*. To produce the right sound, position your lips to say *oo* and, without moving them, say *ee*. Try it with **tu, du** *some*, **duvet, jus** *juice*, **déjà vu, mûr** *ripe*, **dû** *had to*.	

combinations of vowels

The vowels sound different in combination with others:

ai/ei	as in *day*	maison, beige
au/eau	as in *over*	sauce, Bordeaux
eu/œu	*uh* as in *girl*	beurre, sœur, bœuf
	like *uh* but with your mouth not as open: **deux, bleu, jeu**	
oi	*wa* in *wag*	moi, noir, croissant
ou	as in *cool*	mousse, route, Louvre
oui	*ooee*	oui, Louise
ui	as in *cuisine*	lui, minuit

These pages are intended to complement and support the Talking the Talk audio, which focuses on pronunciation. The English examples above are very close to the French sounds, but by far the best way of getting the sounds right is to listen to the native French speakers on the audio and imitate them.

nasal vowels

Barring a few exceptions, vowels before **m** and **n** are **nasal** vowels, which don't occur in English. Air is expelled through the nose as well as the mouth; **m/n** aren't actually sounded. The French words given below all need the addition of this nasal sound when saying them:

an/am/en/em as in *aunt* without the *t:* **blanc, flambé, vent, décembre**
in/im/ain/ein as in *sang* without the *ng:* **vin, timbre, train, faim, plein**
on/om as in *song* without the *ng:* **maison, tombe**
un/um as in *sung:* **un, lundi, parfum**
oin as in **ou** + **un**: **loin, moins**

Vowels before **m** and **n** are *not* nasal when there's another vowel immediately after **m/n** as in **une, énergie, vinaigre** *vinegar,* **plume** *feather;* or if the **m/n** is doubled as in **flamme** *flame* or **Cannes**.

consonants

Most consonants sound similar in French and English, but a few are different.

c as in *cat/kitten* before most letters	**c**afé, **c**ulture, **c**rèche
ss before *e, i, y*	**c**itron, **c**entral, **c**yber
ç *ss*	fran**ç**ais, salade ni**ç**oise
ch *sh* as in *shoe*	**ch**âteau, **Ch**ampagne
g as in *golf*	**g**arage, é**g**alité, ba**g**uette
jh as in *leisure* before *e* or *i*	**g**ara**g**e, **g**énial, **g**irafe
gn *ny* as in *canyon*	campa**gn**e, champi**gn**on
j *jh* as in *leisure,* **not** *j* as in *jet*	**j**aune, **j**oie, ma**j**orité
h is always silent in French	
ll *ll* as in *vi*llage	vi**ll**e, e**ll**e, be**ll**e
or *y* as in *pay*	fi**ll**e, vie**ill**e, pa**ill**e
qu like *c* in *card,* not *qu* in *quit*	**qu**iche, **qu**ai, répu**bl**ique, **qu**alité
r is rather like *ch* in the Scottish *loch:*	**r**ouge, **pr**ofesseur
th *t* as in *tea,* **not** *th* as in *the* or *thing*	**th**é, **th**éâtre

Say the words out loud, paying special attention to **j**, which is a much softer sound than the English *j,* and **qu** which sounds like the English *k,* not *qu*.
Among the most commonly mispronounced French words are those containing *tion* or *ssion*. In English it's *shun* in words like atten*tion,* conversa*tion,* na*tion*al and impre*ssion,* whereas in French there's not even a hint of *sh*. Instead the sound is a clear **ss**: con·vehr·sass·sseon, nass·sseon·al.

final consonants

Most final consonants of a word are not pronounced in French. However, when the following word begins with a vowel, you usually sound that final consonant and merge the words together. This is called liaison.

les enfants	les zenfants	*the children*
vous êtes	vous zêtes	*you are*
aux États-Unis	aux zÉtatszUnis	*in the USA*
il est arrivé	il est tarrivé	*he arrived*
en avion	en navion	*by plane*

There are four consonants, **c, r, f** and **l**, which are pronounced when they occur at the end of a word – with the odd exception: for example, **avec** (pronounced); **estomac** (not pronounced).

stress

Every English word has a stress on a different syllable, and learners of English have to learn where that is. To French ears, English sounds rather jerky because of this. In French, all syllables in a word are given equal emphasis, with just a small stress on the last syllable of long words. Similarly, all words in a sentence have equal emphasis, with a little more on the last one.

This gives French a much smoother sound.

So in English the word *electricity* is pronounced *e·lec·tri·city* with the stress on *tri*; in French **électricité** is pronounced *é·lec·tri·ci·té* with a small stress on the final *té*.

Similarly the word *impossible* is pronounced *im·poss·ible* in English with the stress on *poss*. Whereas in French it's pronounced *im·po·ssible* with the stress on *ssible*. If you're able to avoid the English habit of stressing syllables other than the final one when speaking French your accent will sound much more authentic.

intonation

Pronunciation is about more than individual words: it involves the rhythm and intonation of whole sentences. In French the voice rises at the end of a question but falls at the end of a statement or an exclamation. Try it with:

Ça va? *OK?*

Oui, ça va. *Yes, OK.*

un
first impressions

French has given us the word **etiquette**, and **savoir-faire** too, and it's true that the French like to do things properly and with style. French people care about good manners and they appreciate basic courtesies from others.

Les bonnes manières permeate all aspects of life, including the language. Levels of formality are built right into the French language: it's important, for instance, to choose the right word for *you*, so that you don't unknowingly get off on the wrong foot.

French people are more **cool** (now that's a word the French have borrowed from English) and less formal than they were in the past, but there are still codes of behaviour underlying the way people communicate, affected by social context, age and hierarchy. Don't assume you should immediately **faire la bise** *air-kiss, touch cheeks* with all and sundry. As a visitor to France, it's safer not to be too informal until you're quite sure it is welcomed; that way, you'll avoid coming across as over-familiar or lacking in respect.

Take a little time to get off on the right foot (**partir du bon pied**) when you meet people in France. First impressions matter.

choosing between tu and vous

Unlike English, which has only one word for *you*, French has two: tu and vous, and they're not interchangeable.

tu   someone you know well and call by their first name, such as family members and close friends; children; sometimes people you've just met who are about your age or younger. It's to do with being casual, familiar and informal.

vous   a stranger; somebody you've already met but don't know particularly well; a person who's clearly older than you are, who's in a senior position in work or towards whom you want to appear respectful. This is the one for more formal situations.

vous   is also the word to use when you talk to **more than one person**, regardless of whether you address each individual in the group as **tu** or **vous**.

The verb changes according to whether you use **tu** or **vous**.

	Have you got a moment?	*Do you speak French?*
tu	**Tu as un moment?**	**Tu parles français?**
vous	**Vous avez un moment?**	**Vous parlez français?**

Indiscriminate use of **tu** is becoming more widely acceptable and is the norm on social media and among groups of young people. But you could unintentionally alienate someone by using it if they're expecting **vous**, particularly an older person or an official, who might perceive it as rudeness. If you're starting a conversation and you're not sure whether to use **tu** or **vous**, opt for **vous**. If **tu** is more appropriate, someone will soon suggest **On se dit tu?** or **On se tutoie?** *Shall we use **tu**?*

on
English often uses *you* to mean people in general, as in *you pay at the door*. In the past, *one* would have been used instead: *one pays at the door*. The French equivalent is **on**, which has none of the dated or affected association that *one* can have. On the contrary, it's an essential feature of everyday spoken French and is also a regular alternative to **nous** *we*: **On va a Paris?** *Shall we go to Paris?*

meeting and greeting

The safest way for you to greet and take your leave of a French person is to shake hands: se serrer la main. At a business or social meeting, you should shake hands with everyone present when you arrive and again when you leave. French people tend to shake hands with friends and work colleagues every day.

La bise *air-kiss greeting* is mainly for family and close friends, or sometimes friends of friends. The number of times you touch cheeks varies from person to person and from region to region. There are no set rules: it can be two, three or sometimes four times. In Corsica, it may even be five times. Only go for **la bise** if a French person initiates it. And it's not an actual kiss – avoid planting your lips on their cheek. Hugging is best avoided too, though a light touch on the arm or shoulder is OK.

Monsieur and Madame + name equate to *Mr* and *Mrs,* but **monsieur** and **madame** are also in everyday use without a name. It's considered a basic courtesy to add them when addressing people — something which has no equivalent in English: **Bonjour, monsieur. Merci, madame**.

Mademoiselle used to be the title for an unmarried woman, but now it's polite to use **madame** for all adult women, married or single, over the age of 18.

Monsieur and **madame** have a plural:
> **Bonjour, messieurs.** male group
> **Bonjour, mesdames.** female group
> **Bonsoir, messieurs-dames.** mixed group

Use **docteur** if you're talking to a doctor, man or woman. **Maître** is the word for those in the legal profession, e.g. solicitors and lawyers. Other professional titles can consist of **monsieur** or **madame** in front of the profession: **Monsieur le Président, Madame la Juge.**

Traditionally, you use the masculine word for a profession, whether you're talking to a man or a woman, e.g. **Monsieur le Député/Madame le Député, Monsieur le Ministre/Madame le Ministre. L'Académie française**, the official guardians of the French language, prefers this form of address. However, in the real world, and in particular in Belgium, Switzerland and Quebec, such titles are commonly changed to a feminine form: **Madame la Députée.**

greeting people with confidence

hello

Bonjour. *Hello. Good morning.*
Bonsoir. *Hello. Good afternoon. Good evening.*
Salut. *Hello. Hi.*

Bonjour is suitable for greeting anyone until mid-afternoon, when **Bonsoir** takes over. **Salut** is more casual and best reserved for friends.

Greetings tend to be followed by a title or a name.
Bonjour, monsieur/madame.
Bonjour, docteur.
Bonsoir, Monsieur le Juge.
Salut, Léa!
Salut, les gars! *Hi, guys!*
Salut, mon vieux. *Hi, mate.*

Mon vieux, literally *my old one,* is a common greeting for a male friend — but don't even think of adapting it to the feminine form!

how are you?

Comment vas-tu? Comment allez-vous? *How are you?*
Ça va? *How's it going?*
Comment ça va? *How are things going?*
Ça va bien, merci. *Fine, thank you.*
Et toi? Et vous? *And you?*

While **Ça va bien** is a perfectly adequate reply to **Ça va?**,
there are alternatives:
Oui. Ça va. *OK.*
Ça va très bien. *Very well.*
Vraiment bien. *Really well.*
Super bien, merci. *Great thanks.*
Pas trop mal. *Not too bad.*
Comme d'habitude. *As ever.*
Comme ci, comme ça. *So-so.*
Ça va mal. *Not so good.*
Ça ne va pas du tout! *Awful!*

farewells

Au revoir. *Goodbye.*
Salut!/Ciao! *'Bye.*
Bonne nuit, chéri(e). *Goodnight, darling.*
Dors/Dormez bien. *Sleep well.* **(tu/vous)**
Fais/Faites de beaux rêves. *Sweet dreams.* **(tu/vous)**

Au revoir can be used with anyone at any time of day. Its literal and original meaning is *until we see each other again.*
In casual situations, **Salut** is used to say *Goodbye* as well as *Hi.*
Bonne journée and **Bonne soirée** mean *Enjoy your day/your evening.*
Au revoir, Monsieur Leclerc.
Salut, Julie!
Bonne journée, les enfants.
Bonne nuit, chérie. Fais de beaux rêves.
Bonne nuit, madame. Au revoir.
Bonne journée à tous! *I hope you all have a good day.*
Salut, ma puce. Bonne soirée. *'Bye sweetheart. Have a great evening.*
Merci pour une soirée très sympa. *Thank you for a lovely evening.*

see you …

À **demain.** *See you tomorrow.*
À **plus (tard).** *See you later.*
À **bientôt.** À **tout à l'heure.** *See you soon.*
À **la prochaine.** *Until the next time.*
Rendez-vous lundi au bureau. *See you in the office on Monday.*
Heureux/Heureuse d'avoir fait votre connaissance. *Nice meeting you.* (m/f)

---

terms of endearment
The French equivalent of *my darling* is **mon chéri** *for a man* and **ma chérie** for a woman.

Many terms of endearment are the same for a man, woman or child. You'll hear **mon amour** *my love,* **mon trésor** *my treasure* or **mon ange** *my angel.* Slightly more unexpected is **mon chou** *my cabbage.*

Some are reserved just for women or girls: **ma puce** *my flea* and **ma biche** *my doe.* Others are used only with children: **mon poussin** *my little chick,* **mon petit lapin** *my little rabbit* and **mon chaton** *my kitten.*

wordbank

On se retrouve ... *See you ...*

> **à midi/après le déjeuner** *at/after lunch*
> **au dîner/après le dîner** *at/after dinner*
> **ce soir** *this evening*
> **demain** *tomorrow*
> **demain matin** *tomorrow morning*
> **demain l'après-midi/demain soir** *tomorrow afternoon/evening*
> **demain de bonne heure** *first thing tomorrow*
>
> **après-demain** *the day after tomorrow*
> **vendredi** *on Friday*
> **samedi prochain** *this coming Saturday*
> **la semaine prochaine** *next week*
> **ce weekend** *this weekend*
> **le weekend prochain** *next weekend*
>
> **le seize** *on the 16th*
> **le vingt-quatre** *on the 24th*
> **à huit heures** *at eight o'clock*
> **à midi** *at midday*
> time page 105; date page 104
>
> **dans cinq minutes** *in five minutes*
> **dans deux heures** *in two hours' time*
> **dans une semaine** *in a week's time*
> **dans quelques jours** *in a few days' time*
> **bientôt** *soon*
>
> **D'accord, OK.** *OK.*
> **Je serai là.** *I'll be there.*

 The **Académie française** aims to protect the French language and has tried, though without much success, to ban the use of foreign words such as **le weekend, un mail, un blog** and **un hashtag.**

introductions

Just as in English, many of the key words for introductions come from the verb **être** *to be*, which is essential to know.

je suis	*I am*	nous sommes	*we are*
tu es	*you are*	vous êtes	*you are*
il est	*he/it is*	ils sont	*they are*
elle est	*she/it is*	elles sont	*they are*
on est	*one is*		

I'm not is **je ne suis pas**, and the others work in the same way: **nous ne sommes pas** *we're not*, **elles ne sont pas** *they're not*.
Ne becomes **n'** in front of a vowel: **il n'est pas** *he's not*.

introducing yourself

Je suis Ben. *I'm Ben.*
Je suis anglais(e)/irlandais(e). *I'm English/Irish.*
Je viens de Manchester. *I'm from Manchester.*
Je suis ici en vacances. *I'm here on holiday.*
Je suis ici pour mon travail. *I'm here for work.*
Je m'appelle Amanda Richardson. *My name's Amanda Richardson.*
Mon prénom, c'est Amanda. *My first name's Amanda.*
Mon nom de famille, c'est Richardson. *My surname is Richardson.*

finding the right person

Tu es Marion? *Are you Marion?*
Vous êtes Madame Ajoux? *Are you Mrs Ajoux?*
Vous êtes Lucas Fontaine, c'est ça? *Lucas Fontaine, I believe?*
Vous êtes les MacLeod? *Are you the MacLeods?*

introducing other people

Je te présente/Je vous présente ... *Let me introduce ...*
Voici ... *This is ...*

responding

(Je suis) heureux/heureuse de faire votre connaissance.
Nice to meet you. (male/female speaking)
Enchanté/Enchantée. *A pleasure to meet you.* (male/female speaking)
Bienvenue. *Welcome.*

Voici... *This is...*

mon **mari** *my husband*	ma **femme** *my wife*
mon **grand-père** *my grandfather*	ma **grand-mère** *my grandmother*
mon **père** *my father*	ma **mère** *my mother*
mon **frère** *my brother*	ma **sœur** *my sister*
mon **fils** *my son*	ma **fille** *my daughter*
mon **beau-fils** *my stepson, my son-in-law*	ma **belle-fille** *my stepdaughter, my daughter-in-law*
mon **oncle** *my uncle*	ma **tante** *my aunt*
mon **cousin** *my cousin* (m)	ma **cousine** *my cousin* (f)
mon **beau-père** *my father-in-law, my stepfather*	ma **belle-mère** *my mother-in-law, my stepmother*

Voici mes enfants. *Here are my children.*

My is **mon** for a man or boy and **ma** for a woman or girl. For more than one person — males, females or a mixed group – you use **mes**.

Voici ma petite amie/ma fiancée, Laura. *Here's my girlfriend/fiancée Laura.*
Nick est mon petit/grand frère. *Nick is my younger/older brother.*
Je vous présente mon copain/mon ami Ali. *Let me introduce my friend, Ali.*
Voici ma meilleure amie, Aisha. *This is my best friend, Aisha.*
Je vous présente Paul Melville, un ami d'enfance/mon voisin. *Let me introduce Paul Melville, a childhood friend/my neighbour.*
Voici mon collègue Jack. *This is my colleague, Jack.*
Je vous présente ma collègue Sofia. *May I introduce my colleague, Sofia?*
Je te présente ma compagne, Helen. *Let me introduce my partner, Helen.*
Voici Chris, le compagnon de mon fils. *This is Chris, my son's partner.*

In French, there's no equivalent of the English 's: you use **de** *of* instead. So *my son's partner* becomes *the partner of my son*: **le compagnon de mon fils**; and *my wife's cousin* **la cousine de ma femme**.

Practise introductions: introduce every member of your family and circle of friends. Use mon/ma/mes as appropriate. It's much more effective if you do this out loud rather than in your head. Then write down two or three of your introductions.

spelling names

You never know when you might be asked to spell your name, or you might want to know how someone else spells theirs. The key question is **Comment ça s'écrit?**, literally *How is it written?*

When face to face with someone, you can just write your name down. Otherwise, **Je vous l'épelle** means *I'll spell it out for you.*

how to say the letters in French

a *ah*	b *bay*	c *say*	d *day*
e *euh*	f *eff*	g *jhay*	h *ash*
i *ee*	j *jhee*	k *ka*	l *ell*
m *emm*	n *enn*	o *oh*	p *pay*
q *koo*	r *air*	s *ess*	t *tay*
u *oo*	v *vay*	w *doo-bluh-vay*	x *eeks*
y *ee-grek*	z *zed*		

Moi, c'est Jack: *jhee · ah · say · ka.* I'm Jack.

When a letter has an accent, you say the letter then the accent:
à **a accent grave;** é **e accent aigu;** ô **o accent circonflexe.**

Je m'appelle Siân: ça s'écrit *ess · ee · ah* accent circonflexe · *enn.* *My name's Siân, spelt …*

For double letters, use **deux:**
Je m'appelle Harry: ça s'écrit *ash · ah ·* deux *air · ee-grek.* *My name's Harry, spelt …*

> In front of a vowel sound, the *deuh* sound of **deux** changes to *deuhz*:
> **rr** *deuhz air,* **nn** *deuhz enn.*

To make sure there's no mistake, people will often use **comme** *like* + a French first name, such as **o comme Oscar, p comme Pierre, s comme Suzanne.**

Je m'appelle Morag: c'est un nom écossais. Ça s'écrit *emm* comme Marcel · *oh* comme Oscar · *air* comme Raoul · *ah* comme Anatole · *jhay* comme Gaston. *My name's Morag; it's a Scottish name, written …*

It's well worth working out how to spell out your own name in French and committing it to memory.

> There's a town in northern France whose name is just a single letter: **Y**, pronounced *ee*.

basic courtesies

| tu | **Excuse-moi.** | *Excuse me.* |
| vous | **Excusez-moi.** | |

| tu | **S'il te plaît.** | *Please.* |
| vous | **S'il vous plaît.** | |

S'il vous plaît can also be used instead of **Excusez-moi** when you want to attract someone's attention.
S'il vous plaît, vous pouvez m'aider? *Excuse me, can you help me?*

Merci. *Thank you. Thanks.*
Merci beaucoup. *Thank you very much.*
Merci infiniment. *Thank you so much.*
Merci mille fois. *Thanks a million.*
Je te/vous remercie. *Thank you.* lit. *I thank you.*

Je vous en prie *You're welcome*, **Il n'y a pas de quoi** or **De rien** *Think nothing of it* are used in reply to **merci**.

Je vous en prie is also used in the sense of *Please do, Of course, After you*:
Je peux? *May I?* e.g. come in, squeeze past, reach over
Je t'en prie. **Je vous en prie.** *Of course.*

Pardon. *Sorry. Excuse me. Pardon.*
Désolé(e). *Sorry.*
Je suis désolé(e). *I'm sorry.*
Ce n'est pas grave. *That's all right.*

| tu | **Entre.** *Come in.* |
| vous | **Entrez.** |

| tu | **Assieds-toi.** *Do sit down.* |
| vous | **Asseyez-vous.** *Sit down, make yourself/yourselves comfortable.* |

| tu | **Fais comme chez toi.** *Make yourself at home.* |
| vous | **Faites comme chez vous.** *Make yourselves at home. Make yourselves comfortable.* |

talking the talk

The **Talking the Talk** page towards the end of each chapter sets out the transcript of the informal conversations between Nico and Sophie on the audio.

Listen to the conversation first — at least a couple of times — before you read it here. Assuming that you have worked through the chapter, you'll probably be able to get the gist and pick out some details. At the same time you'll be getting familiar with the rhythm of French.

Don't stop at that. You'll find practical ideas in your Audio Support Pack on how to make the most of these conversations, how to use them to develop your listening skills.

Nico	Salut, Sophie! Je te présente ma mère, Dominique, et mon beau-père, Vincent...
Sophie	Enchantée.
Nico	... et ma grand-mère ...
Grand-mère	Enchantée!
Sophie	Je suis heureuse de faire votre connaissance, madame. Asseyez-vous.
Grand-mère	Merci.
Nico	... et voici mon frère, Sébastien.
Sébastien	Bonjour. Et voici ma fille, Lola.
Grand-mère	Bonjour, Lola!
Sébastien	Oh là là ... excusez-moi ... À tout à l'heure! Bonne journée à tous!
Sophie	À plus tard!
Nico	Viens, je vais te présenter à mon copain Karim, et à sa compagne, Delphine.

1   What would you say if you tread on someone's toe in a crowded lift?

2   Would you use **tu** or **vous** when speaking to your new boss?

3   When talking to an elderly unmarried woman, would you call her **madame** or **mademoiselle**?

4   **Je m'appelle ...** is one way to tell someone your name. Can you think of another way to say who you are?

5   What could you add to **merci** to say *thank you very much*?

6   List two ways you might respond if someone says **merci** to you.

7   If someone replied to your **Comment ça va?** with **Ça ne va pas du tout!**, would it be more appropriate to commiserate or give them a high five?

8   What's the French for *Excuse me* when talking to more than one person?

9   **Mon beau-fils** has two different meanings in English. What are they?

10 What's the French for *See you tomorrow, See you Saturday, See you in ten minutes*?

11 How would you introduce your cousin Anna to a group of French friends?

12 What's the difference between **es** and **êtes**?

13 At what time of day do you say **Bonne nuit**?

14 Which of these is definitely younger than you? **belle-mère, fille, tante, mère, grand-mère**

15 How would you invite a couple to sit down and make themselves at home?

16 The French for *mayor* is **le maire**. Based on what you know about addressing a judge, work out how you would address a mayor.

17 How would you spell the following names in French: Brown, Smith, Jones, Green?

18 Given that **Tu es d'où?** is a way to ask one person **(tu)** where he/she is from, how would you ask the same question to more than one person?

19 If someone says **On se tutoie?**, what are they suggesting?

20 What could you say if someone has apologised for bumping into you?

deux
getting to know people

Getting to know people implies that you'll be telling them about yourself, and it's worth becoming thoroughly familiar with the words you need to do this and practising some sentences. But a conversation is a two-way process, not a scripted monologue, and to find out about the lives of the French people you meet, you're going to be asking questions.

A good conversation relies heavily on asking the right questions. Closed questions such as *Do you work here?* or *Have you been there before?* tend to lead to yes or no, at which point the conversation grinds to a halt, requiring further prompting on your part. To elicit more information, ask open questions, using words like **où** *where?*, **quand** *when?* and **pourquoi** *why?*

You'll probably need to establish early on that you're keen to speak French, otherwise people may be equally keen to practise their English on you.

J'apprends le français. *I'm learning French.*
J'étudie le français. *I'm studying French.*
Je dois m'entraîner à parler français. *I need to practise my French.*
Cela ne vous dérange pas si je parle français? *Do you mind if I speak French?*
J'aimerais parler le plus possible. *I'd like to speak as much as I can.*

breaking the ice

Ice-breakers usually involve a question, and the simplest way of forming a question in French is to make your voice go up enquiringly at the end of a statement. Try it with **Vous êtes ici en vacances** *You're here on holiday* and **Vous êtes ici en vacances?** *You're here on holiday? Are you here on holiday?*

Vous êtes ici pour le travail? *Are you here on business?*
C'est la première fois que vous venez ici? *Is this the first time you've been here?*
Ça fait longtemps que vous êtes ici? *Have you been here long?*
Il y a toujours tant de monde ici? *Are there always so many people here?*

Adding **non?** or **c'est ça?** is like adding an English question tag such as *isn't it? does she? aren't you? won't they? haven't we? didn't it?*

Vous travaillez ici, c'est ça? *You work here, don't you?*
On est dans le même hôtel, non? *We're in the same hotel, aren't we?*
C'est joli ici, non? Quelle belle vue! *It's lovely here, isn't it? What a beautiful view!*

French questions often start with **est-ce que**, which literally means *is it that* and sounds like a single word: *esker.*
Est-ce que vous êtes ici pour le match? *Are you here for the match?*
Est-ce que vous savez où se trouve le stade? *Do you know where the stadium is?*
Est-ce que je peux vous aider? *Can I help you?*

In English, the word order of a statement is reversed for a question: *She is tired, Is she tired?* This happens in French too, but these days it tends to feature more in formal situations than informal conversation.

Vous êtes ici pour l'exposition. *You are here for the exhibition.*
Êtes-vous ici pour l'exposition? *Are you here for the exhibition?*

Vous voulez voir le stand. *You want to see the stand.*
Voulez-vous voir le stand? *Do you want to see the stand?*

asking questions

Open questions are based on question words such as **qui**? *who*? or **quand**? *when*?, which are often followed by **est-ce que**.

Qui est le PDG? *Who is the CEO?*
Qui ne boit pas de vin? *Who is not drinking wine?*
À qui sont ces clés? *Whose are these keys?* lit. *To whom are these keys?*

C'est quand, son anniversaire? *When's his/her birthday?*
Quand est-ce que vous vous êtes mariés? *When did you get married?*
Quand est-ce qu'ils vont partir? *When are they going to leave?*

Où est-ce que tu es né? *Where were you born?*
Tu vas où? Vous allez où? *Where are you going?*
Tu es d'où? Vous êtes d'où? *Where are you from?*

Pourquoi est-ce que tu restes à Paris? *Why are you staying in Paris?*
Pourquoi est-ce qu'on attend? *Why are we waiting?*
Pourquoi pas? *Why not?*

Comment ça va? *How are things going?*
Comment est-ce qu'on dit ... en français? *How do you say ... in French?*
Comment est-ce qu'on mange les escargots? *How do you eat snails?*

C'est combien? *How much is it?*
Combien est-ce qu'ils gagnent? *How much do they earn?*
When **combien** is followed by a noun, you need **de/d'**.
Il nous reste combien de temps? *How much time have we got left?*
Vous avez combien d'enfants? *How many children do you have?*

C'est quel restaurant? *Which restaurant is it?*
Quelle langue est-ce que vous trouvez la plus facile? *Which language do you find easiest?*
Quelles activités sont prévues? *What/which activities are planned?*

There are several ways of asking *what?*
Qu'est-ce qui se passe? *What's happening?*
Qu'est-ce que vous voulez? *What do you want?*
Quoi?!? *What?!?*
C'est quoi, l'adresse mail? *What's the email address?*

sharing information

As you get to know people, you tend to share more information and go into more detail. Adjectives are very likely to feature, and there are things you need to know about how they work.

- They're listed in a dictionary with their masculine singular ending, but that ending has to change according to what you're talking about – masculine or feminine, singular or plural. This can affect the pronunciation.

- Adjectives ending in -e don't change for the feminine, and simply add -s for the plural. There is no change in pronunciation.

- Most other adjectives add -e when referring to a female, -s for more than one male or mixed company and -es for more than one female. If it's an adjective ending in a vowel, there's no change in pronunciation: **joli**, **jolie**, **jolis** and **jolies** *pretty* all sound the same, as do **têtu**, **têtue**, **têtus**, **têtues** *stubborn*.

- But adding -e or -es to an adjective ending in a consonant affects the way it's pronounced: the **t** is silent in **intéressant** and **intéressants** but sounded in **intéressante** and **intéressantes**.

- **Mauvais** *bad* sounds like *mo-vay*, but **mauvaise** is pronounced *mo-vez*. **Laid** *ugly* is pronounced *lay*, but **laide** is *led*; **fort** *strong* is pronounced *for*, whereas **forte** is more like the English word *fort*.

- Not all adjectives make their feminine with just an extra **-e**. Some are a bit different – but the change of ending in most of them is still predictable.

  australien australienne *Australian*
  mignon mignonne *attractive, pretty*
  gentil gentille *nice, kind*
  gros grosse *fat, big*
  actif active *active*
  franc franche *frank, outspoken*
  travailleur travailleuse *hard-working*
  heureux heureuse *happy*
  cher chère *dear*
  discret discrète *discreet*

Je suis ... *I'm ...* **Vous êtes ...?** *Are you ...?*

gallois(e) *Welsh*	**français(e)** *French*
anglais(e) *English*	**canadien(ne)** *Canadian*
irlandais(e) *Irish*	**suisse** *Swiss*
écossais(e) *Scottish*	**algérien(ne)** *Algerian*
américain(e) *American*	**marocain(e)** *Moroccan*
australien(ne) *Australian*	**sénégalais(e)** *Senegalese*
polonais(e) *Polish*	**congolais(e)** *Congolese*

Ma mère est écossaise. *My mother is Scottish.*
Sa grand-mère était algérienne. *His/her grandmother was Algerian.*
Mon grand-père était irlandais. *My grandfather was Irish.*
Notre belle-fille est polonaise. *Our daughter-in-law is Polish.*
Mon ex est sénégalais(e). *My ex is Senegalese.*
Mes beaux-parents sont français. *My in-laws are French.*

French is spoken by more than 270 million people, on all five continents. There are actually more French-speaking people in Africa than there are in France.

célibataire *single*, **en couple** *in a relationship*, **fiancé(e)** *engaged*, **marié(e)** *married*, **en union civile/pacsé(e)** *in a civil partnership*, **séparé(e)** *separated*, **divorcé(e)** *divorced*, **veuf** m/**veuve** f *widowed*, **hétéro** *straight*, **gay** *gay*, **lesbienne** *lesbian*, **bisexuel(le)** *bisexual*, **transgenre** *transgender*

J'ai .../Nous avons ... *I/we have ...*

un frère, une sœur *a/one brother, sister*
un fils/une fille *a son/a daughter*
trois enfants *three children*
deux filles et un fils *two daughters and a son*
deux filles adoptées *two adopted daughters*
trois enfants adultes *three grown-up children*
un petit-fils/une petite fille *a grandson/a granddaughter*
cinq petits-enfants *five grandchildren*

Nous sommes une famille d'accueil. *We're a foster family.*
Je n'ai pas/Nous n'avons pas d'enfants. *I/we don't have children.*
Je suis fils/fille unique. *I'm an only child.* (male/female speaking)

avoir *to have*

Avoir, one of the most common French verbs, translates *have, has* (*got*). It also has other uses where the English translation doesn't mention *have* at all.

j'ai	*I have (got)*	nous avons	*we have*
tu as	*you have*	vous avez	*you have*
il a	*he has, it has*	ils ont	*they have*
elle a	*she has, it has*	elles ont	*they have*
on a	*one has*		

Avoir is used in the widest sense of *to have* or *to own*:

J'ai **deux billets pour ce soir.** *I have two tickets for this evening.*
Tu as **les jumelles?** *Have you got the binoculars?*
Elle a **les yeux bleus.** *She has blue eyes.*
Le lait a **une date de péremption?** *Does the milk have a sell-by date?*
Ils ont **une grande maison avec un jardin.** *They have a large house with a garden.*
La maison n'a pas **de terrasse.** *The house doesn't have a terrace.*
Nous avons **deux chiens et un lapin.** *We have two dogs and a rabbit.*
Vous n'avez pas **d'animaux de compagnie?** *Haven't you got any pets?*

It's also used to talk about age, literally translating *to have ... years*:

Tu as **quel âge?**/Vous avez **quel âge?** *How old are you?*
J'ai **quinze ans.** *I'm 15.*
Ma mère a **soixante ans.** *My mother is 60.*
Les jumeaux ont **sept ans.** *The twins are seven.*

Il a **quel âge, le petit garçon?** *How old is the little boy?*
Il a **trois ans.** *He's three years old.*
Il a **l'air plus âgé.** *He looks older.*

Elle a **quel âge, ta grand-mère?** *How old is your grandmother?*
Elle a **quatre-vingt-douze ans.** *She's 92.*
Vraiment? Elle ne fait pas son âge. *Really? She doesn't look it.*
On ne lui donnerait pas son âge. *You wouldn't think she was that age.*

Avoir is used when talking about physical wellbeing.

J'ai ... *I have* ...
... **mal à la tête** ... *a headache.* ... **mal au ventre** ... *tummy ache.*
... **une douleur dans la poitrine.** ... *a pain in my chest.*
... **un mauvais coup de soleil.** ... *bad sunburn.*

Mon ami a ... *My friend has* ...
... **des maux d'estomac.** ... *an upset stomach.*
... **la diarrhée.** ... *diarrhoea.*
... **des vertiges.** ... *dizzy spells.*
... **la gueule de bois.** ... *a hangover.*
Il a mal au cœur. *He feels sick.*

Les enfants ont ... *The children have* ...
... **un rhume.** ... *a cold.*
... **le rhume des foins.** ... *hayfever.*
... **de la fièvre** ... *a temperature.*

---

word bank

Avoir features in dozens of everyday expressions, many of which don't use *have* in their English equivalent:

> **avoir faim/soif** *to be hungry/ thirsty*
> **avoir chaud/froid** *to be hot/cold*
> **avoir envie de** *to want*
> **avoir besoin de** *to need*
> **avoir le cafard** *to be down in the dumps, feel low*
> **avoir raison/tort** *to be right/wrong*
> **avoir peur** *to be afraid*
> **avoir de la chance** *to be lucky*
> **avoir horreur de** *to loathe, to hate*
> **avoir confiance en** *to trust*
> **avoir sommeil** *to be sleepy*

Nous avons une faim de loup. *We're famished.*
Vous avez trop froid? *Are you too cold?*
Elle a le cafard aujourd'hui. *She's down in the dumps today.*
Moi, je n'ai pas peur. *I'm not scared.*
Tu as vraiment de la chance. *You're so lucky.*
Vous avez confiance en lui/elle? *Do you trust him/her?*
J'ai sommeil; j'ai besoin de mon lit. *I'm sleepy; I need my bed.*

describing people

Il est comment, Nico? *What's Nico like?*
Elle est comment, Irène? *What's Irène like?*
Ils sont comment, ses parents? *What are his/her parents like?*
Nicolas est gentil et un peu timide. *Nicolas is kind and a bit shy.*
Irène est sympa. *Irene's nice.*
Ses parents sont sévères. *His/her parents are strict.*

> **Sympa** *nice* is a short form of **sympathique**. It can be used with both masculine and feminine nouns: **un copain sympa, une copine sympa.**

Il est comment physiquement? *What does he look like?*
Il est grand. Il mesure un mètre quatre-vingt-dix ... *He's tall. He's 1 m 90 ...*
  ... tandis qu'elle est petite. *... whereas she's short.*
Elle porte des lunettes. *She wears glasses.*
Il a les yeux bruns/bleus/gris. *He has brown/blue/grey eyes.*
Elle a les cheveux longs/courts/raides/frisés. *She has long/short/straight/ curly hair.*

You can bring your descriptions to life by slotting in:
très *very,* **pas très** *not very,* **vraiment** *really,* **assez** *quite,* **plutôt** *rather,* **un peu** *a bit,* **si** *so,* **trop** *too.*

Elle est très gentille. *She's very kind.*
Il n'est pas très bavard. *He's not very chatty.*
Les enfants sont assez paresseux. *The children are quite lazy.*
Ils sont vraiment enthousiastes. *They're really keen.*
Marie est un peu timide. *Marie's a bit shy.*
Tu es si curieux. *You're so nosy.*
Luc me semble plutôt égoïste. *Luc seems to me rather selfish.*
André est très intelligent mais trop impulsif. *André is very intelligent but too impulsive.*
Ma femme? ... Elle est super-patiente! *My wife? ... She's incredibly patient!*

> Or add some colour with these colloquial expressions:
> **Mon chef me tape sur les nerfs.** *My boss gets on my nerves.*
> **Elle est casse-pieds.** *She's a pain in the neck.* lit. *She breaks my feet.*

wordbank

beau/belle *beautiful, handsome*
blond *blonde*
brun *dark-haired*
chauve *bald*
costaud *sturdy, burly*
débraillé *scruffy*
dodu *plump*
élégant *elegant*

fort *strong*
grand *tall*
gros(se) *fat*
maigre *skinny*
mince *slim, thin*
musclé *muscular*
obèse *obese*
petit *short*

affectueux *affectionate*
agressif *aggressive*
anxieux *anxious*
artiste *artistic*
astucieux *canny, shrewd*
audacieux *bold, brazen*
aventureux *adventurous*
bête *dumb, stupid*
brave *clever, good*
décontracté *laid-back*
discret/discrète *tactful, diplomatic*
doué *talented, gifted*
égoïste *selfish*
fiable *reliable, trustworthy*
fidèle *faithful, loyal*
fou/folle *crazy*
généreux/euse *generous, kind-hearted*

impétueux *rash, impetuous*
impoli *rude*
impudent *cheeky*
insensible *insensitive*
irréfléchi *thoughtless*
irresponsable *irresponsible*
maladroit *clumsy*
méchant *nasty, mean*
naïf/naïve *naïve*
optimiste *optimistic*
pessimiste *pessimistic*
poli *polite*
prudent *cautious*
sensible *sensitive*
serviable *helpful*
assuré *confident*
travailleur/euse *hardworking*

Try describing a few people: family, friends or celebrities. Use some of these adjectives and/or look others up in a dictionary. Use extras such as très and assez, or add Il/elle ne fait pas son âge when saying how old people are.

Don't forget that when you're describing a female you'll need the feminine form of the adjective. If you need to, check with the guidelines on page 28. The feminine is included here only if it's irregular.

Then read your descriptions out loud.

talking about places

Vous habitez où? *Where do you live?*
C'est une grande ville? *Is it a big town/city?*
C'est à la campagne? *Is it in the countryside?*
C'est où exactement en Angleterre? *Whereabouts in England is it?*
La région, c'est comment? *What's the region like?*

Habiter and **vivre** both mean *to live*. You can use both to talk about where you live and who you live with, but only **vivre** in the wider sense of living, as opposed to dwelling/residing.
Tu habites où? Tu vis où? *Where do you live?*
Vous habitez où? Vous vivez où? *Where do you live?*
J'habite/Je vis à Brive. *I live in Brive.*
Nous habitons une ferme. *We live in a farmhouse.*
J'habite près de la gare. *I live near the station.*
J'habite/je vis seul. *I live alone.* **J'habite avec Max.** *I live with Max.*
Nous vivons ensemble. *We're living together.*
Je vis bien. *I live well.*
Vivre et laisser vivre. *Live and let live.*

You can say where you used to live simply by replacing **j'habite** with **j'habitais** and **je vis** with je **vivais**.

Vous logez où? *Where are you staying?*
Où est-ce que tu loges? *Where are you staying?*
Vous logez dans un hôtel/un appartement? *Are you (staying) in a hotel/ an apartment?*
Vous êtes dans quel hôtel? *Which hotel are you staying at?*
Où se trouve le camping? *Where's the campsite?*
C'est agréable? *Is it nice?*

Le village/la ville/l'hôtel est comment? *What's the village/town/hotel like?*
Il y a une piscine/un court de tennis? *Is there a pool/a tennis court?*
Est-ce qu'il y a un terrain de jeux pour les enfants? *Is there a play area for children?*
Qu'est-ce qu'il y a à faire ici? *What is there to do here?*
Il n'y a pas de piscine, il n'y a pas de restaurant. *There's no swimming pool, there are no restaurants.*

La région où on habite se trouve ... *The area we live in is ...*

    ... dans le nord-est de l'Angleterre. *... in the north east of England.*

    ... en Cornouailles/dans l'ouest du Yorkshire. *... in Cornwall/in West Yorkshire.*

C'est rural/urbain/montagneux. *It's rural/urban/mountainous.*

La ville où j'habite se trouve ... *The town where I live is ...*

    ... entre Cambridge et Londres. *... between Cambridge and London.*

C'est ... *It's...*

    ... grand/assez petit. *... big/quite small.*

    ... animé en été/tranquille en hiver. *... lively in summer/quiet in winter.*

    ... plein d'avenir. *... up and coming.*

    ... un trou perdu. *... a real backwater.*

C'est ... L'hôtel est ... *It is ... The hotel is ...*

    ... accueillant et bien équipé. *... welcoming and well-equipped.*

    ... très propre/plutôt délabré. *... spotless/somewhat run-down.*

    ... bien entretenu/assez mal tenu. *... well-kept/a bit neglected.*

Il a connu des jours meilleurs. *It's seen better days.*

Vaut le détour. *Worth visiting.*

Incontournable. *Unmissable.*

À éviter! Un endroit affreux. *Avoid! A dreadful place.*

Le camping/le village est ... *The campsite/village is ...*

    ... à cent mètres de la plage. *... 100 metres from the beach.*

    ... ensoleillé/à l'ombre. *... sunny/shaded.*

    ... sablonneux/boueux. *... sandy/muddy.*

Il y a beaucoup de choses à faire. *There's plenty to do.*

Il y a un terrain de golf tout près. *There's a golf course nearby.*

---

it is ...

Remember that in French everything has a gender so when you say *it* you need to think about whether *it* is masculine or feminine:

Il se trouve à 100 mètres d'ici. *It's 100 metres from here.* **(le camping)**

Elle se trouve dans le Kent. *It's in Kent.* **(la ville)**

To say *it is* + adjective when referring to things (but not people), you use **c'est**. The adjective that follows **c'est** is always masculine:

C'est joli. *It's pretty.* **(le camping/la ville)**

wordbank

> Use some of these adjectives to describe places, for example where you live, where someone you know lives, where you last went on holiday or even somewhere you saw in a film. Bring your descriptions to life with *très*, *un peu*, etc. and words like *mais* **but**, *aussi* **also**, *pourtant* **however**, *en plus* **what's more**.

petit *small*, **minuscule** *tiny*, **étroit** *narrow*
grand *big*, **énorme** *huge*, **spacieux** *spacious*, **luxueux** *luxurious*
imposant *imposing*

neuf/neuve *new*, **moderne** *modern*
vieux/vieille *old*, **ancien** *old/ancient*, **historique** *historic*
vétuste *dated*

urbain *urban*, **résidentiel(le)** *residential*, **central** *central*
animé *lively*, **bruyant** *noisy*, **bondé** *congested*, *busy*
commerçant *commercial*, **industriel(le)** *industrial*

isolé *remote*, **tranquille** *quiet*
clair *light*, *bright*, **ensoleillé** *sunny*, **ombragé** *shady*
accidenté *rugged*, *rough*, **boisé** *wooded*, **montagneux** *mountainous*
aride *dry*, *arid*, **boueux** *muddy*, **marécageux** *marshy*

agréable *pleasant*, **charmant** *charming*, **paradisiaque** *heavenly*
parfait *perfect*, **pittoresque** *picturesque*, **touristique** *touristy*
bourgeois *middle-class*

sale *dirty*, **délabré** *dilapidated*, **déprimant** *depressing*
mal entretenu *neglected*, **pollué** *polluted*

impeccable *immaculate*, **propre** *clean*, **superbe** *superb*
bien entretenu *well-kept*, **bien équipé** *well-equipped*

how to remember words

It's all very well having a bank of words to refer to — but how do you remember them?

The key to transferring a word to your long-term memory is to consciously *do something with it*. What you do depends on how you personally learn best. Try some of these suggestions and see which suit you.

Don't try and learn too many words at the same time. Aim for a group of seven or eight: it helps if there's some connection between them.

- Listen to the words online. If you enter *luxurious in French* into a search engine, one of the first results will be **luxueux**. Click on the speaker icon and listen to how it's said — as many times as you want. Try it with *spacious* and *marshy to* hear the same -**eux** ending.

- Say the words out loud — several times. Some people swear by doing this last thing at night, then again the next morning. Or try recording the words on your phone or tablet and leave a gap before giving the translation so that you can test yourself.

- Others remember the way words look on a page. If you have a visual memory, the unusual arrangement of the words opposite should help you. If so, use a similar technique when you make your own notes.

- Don't always think in individual words. Sometimes a pair or a string of words can be just as memorable, e.g. **plutôt délabré** or **la ville où j'habite se trouve ...**

- Write words down. It doesn't matter whether you write them on paper or key them in. Keep them in manageable groups rather than an endless list. Highlight words that you think will be the most useful (but don't discount others since you never know what someone is going to say to you).

- Learn tricky words first. You're going to remember words like **historique**, **résidentiel** or **région** anyway, so leave them until last.

- Use associations to help you remember words. For example, the French for *rugged* or *rough* is **accidenté**, so think of stumbling along a very rough track and having an accident.

- Use the words. Use the ones opposite as suggested, but don't stop at that. Whenever you're out and about, think of an adjective to describe the places you see. It could be factual: **étroit**, **bondé**, **vétuste**; or it could be subjective: **imposant**, **paradisiaque.**

talking the talk

Nico	C'est joli ici, non?
English woman	Oui, quelle belle vue!
Nico	Vous êtes ici en vacances ou pour le travail?
English woman	Je suis ici avec ma sœur.
Nico	Vous êtes d'où?
English woman	De Leeds. Nous sommes anglaises.
Nico	Hmmm... vous parlez bien français!
English woman	Merci. J'étudie le français.
Nico	Ah.
Nico	Sébastien, c'est mon grand frère. Il a vingt-neuf ans. Il est marié mais il est séparé de sa femme et ils ne vivent pas ensemble. Il a une petite fille, Lola, qui a juste un an. Elle vit avec sa mère et, Sébastien, il vit tout seul. Il a une petite maison à Bayonne, près de la gare. Il n'a pas de jardin, mais il a une belle terrasse. La ville est très agréable... c'est assez animé, surtout l'été. C'est parfait pour lui. Et toi, tu as des frères et sœurs, Sophie?
Sophie	Moi, non! Je suis fille unique. Mais j'ai un cousin et trois cousines. Une de mes cousines, Marion, habite tout près d'ici. Elle a un joli petit appartement moderne.
Nico	Elle est comment, ta cousine?
Sophie	Elle est très élégante, brune, mince, cheveux longs...
Nico	Et elle est sympa?
Sophie	Ben oui, un peu folle, mais très gentille!

verb practice 1

1   Fill the gaps with the correct forms of **être** *to be* (page 19) and say what the sentences mean.

   a   Je .... divorcée.

   b   Nous ne .... pas anglais.

   c   Christine .... très têtue.

   d   David et son frère .... jumeaux.

   e   Vous .... ici jusqu'à quand?

   f   L'hôtel .... propre et tranquille.

   g   Je ne .... pas très bavard.

   h   Monsieur Bassani n' .... pas marié.

   i   Vos enfants .... très sympas.

   j   Tu .... fiancée?

2   Now do the same using **avoir** *to have* (page 30).

   a   J' .... les yeux bleus mais mon père .... les yeux gris.

   b   Franck n'......... pas sommeil.

   c   Quel âge .... Camille?

   d   Ma femme et moi .... de la chance.

   e   Tu .... dix-neuf ou vingt ans?

   f   Vous .... trois enfants, c'est ça?

   g   Ils .... un petit appartement en ville.

   h   Vous n'........ pas soif?

3   How would you ask these questions in French?

   a   Is she Canadian or American?

   b   Are Martine and Mathilde happy?

   c   Does the hotel have a pool?

   d   Marc's gay, isn't he?

   e   Are you thirsty? [**tu** and **vous**]

   f   Is there a tennis court?

Have a go at writing about yourself. Include all the information you can but keep it structurally simple. Use je suis + nationality, your relationship status, what you look like; use j'ai and je n'ai pas de/d' with at least five nouns, e.g. siblings, children, pets, house; j'habite + where you live.

Now make a list of the questions you would need to ask to get this information from other people.

checkpoint 2

1   How do you tell people you're learning French?

2   *Isn't it, is she, aren't you, didn't we* at the end of a question can all be expressed by which words in French?

3   How would you ask how to say *farm* in French?

4   Name in French three recreational facilities you might expect to find in a holiday complex.

5   Rearrange these question words into the order *who, why, which, when, where, how, how many*: **où, pourquoi, quel, combien, qui, quand, comment**

6   How might you offer to lend someone a hand?

7   Give the French for: *I'm not thirsty. Are you cold? She's right. I've got a headache.*

8   Add the correct ending to these adjectives and translate the sentences: **Mon oncle est divorc... Mes amies sont gallois... Ma cousine est blond... Mon voisin est très travailleu... Ma copine est un peu paresseu...**

9   Work out the missing words in this sequence: **j'habite** *I live*, **je pense** *I think*, **j'aime** *I like*, **j'habitais** *I used to live*, ... *I used to think*, ... *I used to like*

10 Here are nine adjectives. Divide them into two groups of four according to meaning: **bavard, généreux, grand, gros, poli, fidèle, montagneux, mince, petit**. What does the one that's left over mean?

11 If you hear someone described as **méchante**, what sort of person would you expect her to be?

12 Rearrange **camping · où · le · trouve · se** to mean *Where is the campsite?*

13 Which of these means *I'm afraid*: **j'ai chaud, j'ai faim, j'ai peur, j'ai honte?**

14 What do you need to add to **Nous vivons** to say *We're living together?*

15 Sort these adjectives into pairs with opposite meanings: **énorme, tranquille, vieux, ensoleillé, propre, minuscule, animé, sale, neuf, ombragé**

trois
what you do in life

What do you do for a living? is one of the first questions that tends to be asked when people are getting to know each other.

It's tempting to suppose that all you need is the language to say what you do and to ask some questions. But when you ask the questions, you might be confronted with a wide variety of replies, so don't be too selective in the vocabulary you learn. If you're neither a pilot nor a postman, you're never going to want to say **Je suis pilote** or **Je suis facteur** ... but somebody might well say it to you and expect you to understand.

In the workplace, hierarchy is more in evidence in France than in English-speaking countries. Professional titles are more prevalent; introductions are likely to consist of a surname or a full name, together with the role in the company.

Being able to chat informally in French with your hosts, between meetings, over a meal or in the bar, is rated highly and puts everyone at ease. However, even if the culture seems to you to be casual, it's as well not to assume that immediate informality will break the ice quickly and forge strong relationships: uninvited use of **tu** and first names may instead take some people out of their comfort zone.

saying what you do

Qu'est-ce que vous faites dans la vie? *What do you do?*
Qu'est-ce que vous faites comme travail? *What sort of work do you do?*
These are considered rather personal questions in France, so you might want
to start with **Si ce n'est pas indiscret ...** *If you don't mind my asking ...*

Unlike English, you don't use **un/une** in the answer: **Je suis comptable** *I'm an*
accountant; **Ma femme est podologue** *My wife's a chiropodist*.

The French for *accountant, chiropodist* and many other occupations are the
same for men and women, but others have different masculine and feminine
endings, as seen below.

Don't confuse **chauffeur** *driver* with **chauffard**, which is the
word for a roadhog or reckless driver.

jobs you can guess

Many French occupations end in **-iste** for both masculine and feminine. Several, but not all, have an English equivalent ending in *-ist*: **biologiste** *biologist*, **dentiste** *dentist*, **économiste** *economist*, **graphiste** *graphic designer*, **journaliste** *journalist*, **orthophoniste** *speech therapist*, **styliste** *fashion designer*.

English professions ending in *-ologist* generally end in **–ologue**, e.g: **cardiologue, climatologue, criminologue, dermatologue, géologue, gynécologue, immunologue, neurologue, ornithologue, psychologue**.

not the 9 to 5

Je travaille ... *I work ...*

    ... à mon compte. *... freelance.*
    ... chez moi. *... from home.*
    ... à mi-temps/à plein temps. *... part time/full time.*
    Je ne travaille pas. *I don't work.*

Je suis ... *I am ...*

    ... photographe indépendant(e). *... a freelance photographer.*
    ... étudiant(e). *... a student.*
    ... stagiaire. *... a trainee/an intern.*
    ... au chômage. *... unemployed.*
    ... retraité(e). *... retired.*

Je prends ... *I'm taking ...*

    ... une année de césure. *... a gap year/a year out.*
    ... une année sabbatique. *... a sabbatical year.*

J'ai ma propre entreprise. *I have my own business.*
Je reste au foyer. *I'm a stay-at-home mum/dad.*
Je fais du travail bénévole. *I do charity work/I volunteer.*
J'aide ma fille. *I help my daughter.*
Je m'occupe de ... *I look after ...*

    ... mes petits-enfants. *... my grandchildren.*
    ... mes parents. *... my parents.*

In France, the minimum wage is known as **le Smic**. It stands for **Salaire minimum interprofessionnel de croissance.**

Make sure you can say what you do in French. If it's not listed here, then look it up. There are some excellent online dictionaries that let you hear how a word is pronounced.

how French verbs work

The -er ending of **travaill**er shows you it means *to work*. Grammatically, this form of the verb is called the infinitive.

To say that you or anyone else works, or is working, you replace -er with a different ending: **je travaill**e *I work, I'm working*, **tu travaill**es *you work*, **il travaill**e *he works*, **elle travaill**e *she works*, **ils travaill**ent *they work*. Despite the different spellings, all of these sound exactly the same.

The endings for **nous** and **vous** are different: **nous travaill**ons *we work*, **vous travaill**ez *you work*. Travaill**ez** sounds the same as **travaill**er.

Any regular verb ending in -er behaves in the same way.
rester *to stay* **Elle rest**e **au foyer.** *She's a stay-at-home mum.*
aider *to help* **Nous aid**ons **le chef.** *We're helping the chef.*
parler *to speak* **Vous parl**ez **anglais?** *Do you speak English?*
arriver *to arrive* **Ils arriv**ent **à quelle heure?** *What time are they arriving?*

Not all infinitives end in -er. There are two other groups, ending in -ir and -re. Regular verbs in these groups each have their own set of endings.

infinitive *to*	-er	-ir	-re
je/j' *I*	-e	-is	-s
tu *you*	-es	-is	-s
il/elle, on *he/she/it, one*	-e	-it	*nothing added*
nous *we*	-ons	-issons	-ons
vous *you*	-ez	-issez	-ez
ils/elles *they*	-ent	-issent	-ent

finir *to finish* **Ça fin**it **à huit heures.** *It finishes at eight o'clock.*
choisir *to choose* **Moi, je chois**is **celle-ci.** *I'm choosing this one.*
vieillir *to grow old* **Ils vieill**issent. *They're growing old.*

perdre *to lose* **Il perd toujours ses clés de maison.** *He's always losing his house keys.*
vendre *to sell* **Ils vend**ent **des huîtres?** *Do they sell oysters?*
attendre *to wait* **Qui est-ce que nous attend**ons? *Who are we waiting for?*
descendre *to go/come down* **Vous descend**ez **la rue Mouffetard.** *You go down Mouffetard Street.*

reflexive verbs

In a dictionary you'll find some verbs with se or s' in front of the infinitive. These are reflexive verbs; the English translation often includes or implies *oneself*.

Reflexive verbs use the same endings as non-reflexive verbs, and se changes depending on who or what the subject is to me, te, se, nous, vous or se:

se **laver**	*to wash (oneself)*
je me **lave**	*I wash (myself)*
tu te **laves**	*you wash (yourself)*
il/elle, on se **lave**	*he/she, one washes (him/herself, oneself)*
nous nous **lavons**	*we wash (ourselves)*
vous vous **lavez**	*you wash (yourself/selves)*
ils/elles se **lavent**	*they wash (themselves)*

Before a vowel you use m', t' and s'.

Je m'**appelle Claudine.** *My name's Claudine.* Lit. *I call myself Claudine.*
Il se **lève tôt.** *He gets up early.*
Nous nous **occupons des petits-enfants.** *We look after the grandchildren.*

In a negative sentence, me, te, se etc, stay with the verb and **ne ... pas** goes around them both:
Ils ne s'**amusent pas.** *They are not enjoying themselves.*
Tu ne te **couches pas?** *Aren't you going to bed?*

discussing work

Où est-ce que tu travailles/vous travaillez? *Where do you work?*
Je travaille *I work ...*

> à *in* **Londres** *London,* **Paris** *Paris,* **Bruxelles** *Brussels*

dans *in*

un atelier de réparation *a repair shop/garage*
une banque *a bank*
un bureau *an office*
un cabinet médical *a surgery*
un centre d'appels *a call centre*
un centre sportif *a sports centre*
une école *a school*
une ferme *a farm*

un hôpital *a hospital*
un magasin *a shop*
une jardinerie *a garden centre*
une salle de gym *a gym*
un supermarché *a supermarket*
une université *a university*
une usine *a factory*
une zone industrielle *an industrial estate*

dans

l'agriculture *agriculture*
la vente *sales/retail*
l'informatique *computing*
les relations publiques *PR*

dans le secteur ...

... de la santé *in the health sector*
... du tourisme *in tourism*
... public *in the public sector*
... privé *in the private sector*

Pour qui est-ce que tu travailles/vous travaillez? *Who do you work for?*
pour *for...*

une agence de presse *a news agency*
un avocat *a lawyer*
une banque internationale *an international bank*
l'OTAN *NATO*

une société de logiciels *a software company*
un vignoble *a vineyard*
Soco S.A. *Soco Ltd*
une organisation caritative *a charity*

C'est quoi, ton/votre domaine? *What's your field of expertise?*
Je travaille dans le service des ressources humaines. *I work in HR.*
Je suis responsable du système informatique. *I manage the IT system.*
Je m'occupe de l'entretien. *I work in maintenance.*
Je suis inspecteur/rice de la santé et de la sécurité. *I'm a Health and Safety inspector.*

C'est quoi, ton/votre rôle? *What's your role/position?*
Je suis ... *I'm ...*

> **... chef du marketing.** *... head of marketing.*
> **... coordinateur de projets.** *... a project co-ordinator.*
> **... le/la secrétaire du PDG.** *... the CEO's secretary.*
> **... directeur adjoint.** *... deputy director/ assistant manager.*
> **... chef de service, chef d'équipe, contremaître.** *... supervisor, head of department, foreman.*

Je m'occupe du site web de l'entreprise. *I look after the company website.*

Depuis quand est-ce que tu fais/vous faites ce métier? *How long have you been doing this work?*

While English uses ***have been*** *doing*, French uses a verb in the present tense + **depuis**.

Je fais ce métier depuis ... *I've been doing this work for ...*
Je suis douanier depuis ... *I've been a customs officer for ...*

> **... six mois.** *... six months.*
> **... dix ans.** *... ten years.*

Je travaille ici depuis ... *I've been working here since ...*

> **... l'année dernière.** *... last year.*
> **... le mois de septembre.** *.... September.*
> **... deux mille treize.** *... 2013.*
> **... aussi longtemps que je me souvienne.** *... as long as I can remember.*

---

working words
Un travail, un métier, un emploi and **un poste** all mean *a job.*
Informally, you'll also hear **un boulot** and **un job**.
Un homme/une bonne à tout faire is *a dogsbody.*
Bosser *to work (hard!)* is a slang word.
Il bosse dans une université. *He works in a university.*

---

*Choose a couple of the people you described in **Chapter 2** and add what they do to your descriptions, e.g. Je suis employée de bureau. Mon mari Martin est plombier et il a sa (his/her) propre entreprise. Ma mère est vendeuse, elle travaille à mi-temps. Aurélie ne travaille pas, elle reste au foyer.*

faire *to do, to make*

Not all verbs follow the regular patterns shown on page 44. **Faire** is one
of the irregular ones, the one-offs. Since it's one of the most used French
verbs, it's really worth making sure you know how it works.

je fais	*I make*	**nous** faisons	*we make*
tu fais	*you make*	**vous** faites	*you make*
il/elle fait	*he/she makes*	**ils/elles** font	*they make*

The basic translation of **faire** is *to do* or *to make*.
Qu'est-ce qu'on va faire? *What shall we do?*
Cela ne fait aucune différence. *It makes no difference.*
Je dois faire la cuisine. *I have to do the cooking.*
Il y a beaucoup de choses à faire. *There's a lot to do.*
Ça fait un drôle de bruit. *It's making a funny noise.*

However, **faire** is used in a wide range of contexts, many of which don't use
do or *make* in English.
It's often used in the context of work.
Qu'est-ce que vous faites comme travail? *What (work) do you do?*
J'aimerais faire architecte. *I'd like to be an architect.*
Est-ce que tu fais un apprentissage? *Are you doing an apprenticeship?*
De temps en temps je fais des heures supplémentaires. *I occasionally work
overtime.*
En ce moment le patron fait passer des entretiens. *The boss is interviewing
right now.*
Les syndicalistes font grève. *The trade-unionists are striking/on strike.*

It's used to talk about the weather, too.
    Il fait quel temps? *What's the weather like?*
    Il fait beau. *It's a nice day.*
    Il fait chaud. *It's hot.*
    Il fait froid. *It's cold.*

There's more on weather on pages 112–113.

Faire features in many everyday expressions, such as **faire la bise** or **faire un bisou** *to greet someone with a kiss on the cheek.*

Others include:

Je voudrais faire les magasins. *I'd like to go round the shops.*

Je fais du bricolage. *I do odd jobs. I potter around.*
Je fais des progrès. *I'm making progress.*

Tu fais ta valise? *Are you packing?*

Il fait soixante kilos. *He weighs 60 kilos.*
Il ne fait pas attention. *He doesn't pay attention.*
Elle fait de son mieux. *She is doing her best.*
Elle fait médecine cette année. *She's doing/studying medicine this year.*

Nous faisons du vélo/de la moto. *We cycle/ride motorbikes.*
Vous faites du foot/du basket? *Do you play football/basketball?*

Elles font la queue. *They're queuing.*
Ils me font peur. *They frighten me.*

... and there are literally dozens more, e.g.

> **faire mal** *to hurt*
> **faire la tête** *to sulk*
> **faire du lard** *to sit around doing nothing*
> **faire la grasse matinée** *to sleep in*
> **faire la sourde oreille** *to turn a deaf ear*
> **faire une promenade** *to go for a walk*
> **faire des économies** *to save up*
> **faire demi-tour** *to do a U-turn*
> **faire d'une pierre deux coups** *to kill two birds with one stone*
> **faire des bêtises** *to do stupid things*
> **faire l'enfant** *to behave like a child*
> **faire des châteaux en Espagne** *to build castles in the air* lit. *in Spain.*

 Try using some of these expressions in sentences talking about yourself or someone else.

talking the talk

Sophie	Ton frère Sébastien, qu'est-ce qu'il fait comme travail?
Nico	Sébastien? Il est photographe pour un magazine de mode.
Sophie	Waouh! Pas mal! Et ton père, il est professeur, non?
Nico	Ah non, mon père est à la retraite. Il était ingénieur.
Sophie	Ah. Et ta mère, qu'est-ce qu'elle fait?
Nico	Elle, elle travaille dans un hôpital. Elle est responsable du système informatique.
Sophie	Oh, intéressant! Moi aussi, j'aimerais faire un travail comme ça.
Nico	Et toi, ta mère travaille, Sophie?
Sophie	Oui, elle travaille dans le secteur du tourisme.
Nico	Elle travaille dans un hôtel?
Sophie	Non, elle travaille à l'office du tourisme. Elle s'occupe des relations publiques.
Nico	Bien, c'est intéressant comme travail.
Sophie	Oui, mais depuis six mois, elle travaille à mi-temps parce qu'elle s'occupe aussi du bébé de ma cousine.
Nico	Ahhh! S'occuper d'un bébé, ça, c'est du travail!!

verb practice 2

1   Add the correct present-tense endings to these regular -er verbs.

    a   **ajouter** *to add*: **Tu .... ton nom.** *You add your name.*

    b   **changer** *to change*: **Ils .... souvent d'avis.** *They often change their minds.*

    c   **trouver** *to find*: **Vous .... votre travail intéressant?** *Do you find your work interesting?*

    d   **durer** *to last*: **Elle .... un an.** *It lasts a year.*

    e   **poser** *to put*: **Nous .... beaucoup de questions.** *We ask a lot of questions.*

    f   **pleurer** *to cry*: **Je .... tout le temps.** *I'm always crying.*

    g   **parler** *to speak*: **Vous .... arabe?** *Do you speak Arabic?*

    h   **aimer** *to like*: **Il .... travailler en plein air.** *He likes working outdoors.*

    i   **détester** *to hate*: **Elles .... les bureaux sans cloisons.** *They hate open-plan offices.*

    j   **danser** *to dance*: **Tu .... le tango?** *Do you dance the tango?*

2   Fill the gaps with the correct present-tense form of a regular -ir or -re verb.

    a   **Je .... toujours le vin rouge.** *I always choose red wine.*

    b   **Ils .... à deux heures.** *They finish at two o'clock.*

    c   **Mon fils .... à tous ses examens.** *My son succeeds in all his exams.*

    d   **Tu ne .... pas.** *You're not getting old.*

    e   **Nous .... la voiture.** *We're selling the car.*

    f   **Vous .... tout de suite?** *Are you coming down right away?*

    g   **Elle se .... souvent.** *She often gets lost.*

    h   **J' .... jusqu'à six heures.** *I'll wait until six o'clock.*

3   Decide whether **me/m'**, **te/t'**, **se/s'**, **nous** or **vous** belongs in the gap.

    a   **Comment ... appelle le chien?** *What's the dog called?*

    b   **Mes parents ... occupent du restaurant.** *My parents look after the restaurant*

    c   **Nous ne ... levons pas tôt.** *We don't get up early.*

    d   **Vous ... douchez quand?** *When are you having a shower?*

    e   **Tu ... souviens?** *Do you remember?*

    f   **Je ... demande s'il pleut.** *I wonder if it's raining.*

    g   **Maintenant Laura ... couche.** *Laura's going to bed now.*

checkpoint 3

1   Match the people: **agriculteur, cuisinier, maître-nageur, médecin, professeur, vendeur** with their workplace: **école, ferme, hôpital, magasin, piscine**. What does the person left over do?

2   To say what your occupation is, do you normally use **un/une** after **je suis**?

3   What two words do you add to **je travaille ici ...... quinze ......** to say you've been working here for 15 years?

4   What do you think the French is for *archaeologist* and *meteorologist*? And what do you think a **rhumatologue**, an **opthalmologue** and a **radiologue** are?

5   Who are you most likely to come across if you're buying a house: **un agent immobilier, un agent de voyages** or **un agent de sécurité**?

6   What's the French for *It makes no difference?*

7   How would you tell a French person you are unemployed?

8   How would you say that your daughter is doing an apprenticeship?

9   Which is the odd one out? **un emploi, un poste, un travail, un employé, un job**

10 Where do people employed **dans le secteur de la santé** and in **un bureau** work?

11 How would you ask someone what their role is?

12 Without necessarily knowing what they mean, decide if these verbs relate to **tu, nous** or **vous: vends, aimez, choisissons, cherchez, finis, travaillons**

13 If the **chef du service** means *head of department*, what do you think a **chef d'usine** is?

14 Given that **je gagne** *I earn* comes from **gagner** *to earn*, what words are missing in this French translation? **.............. trois fois plus que lui** *We earn three times as much as him.*

15 Rearrange these words to form a sentence, then say what it means in English: **je site suis du responsable web**

quatre
the art of conversation

Once you're past the stage of exchanging basic information with someone, you tend to move on to more general conversation, which may well include comments, prompts, questions and exclamations.

The general principles — showing interest in the person you're talking to, knowing when to say something, how much or how little to say — are things we do in our first language without much conscious thought, but when you're speaking in a new language and concentrating on finding the right word at the right time, it helps to think about how to achieve them.

Even if you can't always say as much as you'd like, you can still contribute just by knowing how to keep a conversation going: there are a number of strategies you can use to show you're properly engaged. Gestures, eye contact, a smile, positive body language or a nod at the right time all show that you're actively listening and following what's being said — but they're not half as satisfying as coming up with a succinct comment or an exclamation.

For the strategies to work, it's important to concentrate your energies on listening to what's being said and to resist the temptation to half listen while you work out what you're going to say next. A conversation is unpredictable and, by the time you're ready with your perfect sentence, the thread might well have moved on.

following what's being said

When you're new to a language, it can seem as if it's spoken very rapidly. Nobody will mind if you ask for help now and again or find it necessary to slow the conversation down a little.

Excuse-moi ... *Excuse me ...* **tu**
Excusez-moi... *Excuse me ...* **vous**
Désolé(e) de vous interrompre mais ... *Sorry for interrupting you but ...*

Je ne comprends pas. *I don't understand.*
Je n'ai pas compris. *I didn't understand.*
Je ne sais pas si j'ai bien compris. *I don't know if I've understood properly.*
Je ne suis pas sûr(e) d'avoir bien compris. *I'm not sure I've understood.*

Qu'est-ce que ... veut dire? *What does ... mean?*
... veut dire ..., c'est bien ça? *... means ..., doesn't it?*

Qu'est-ce que tu as/vous avez dit? *What did you say?*

Est-ce que tu pourrais/vous pourriez ... *Could you ...*
Est-ce que tu peux/vous pouvez ... *Can you ...*
    ... répéter, s'il te/vous plaît? *... repeat that please?*
    ... parler plus lentement? *... speak more slowly?*
    ... me l'écrire? *write that down for me?*

You can show you're following by echoing what's been said before and offering a relevant comment or question.

Mon beau-frère travaille en Chine. *My brother-in-law works in China.*
En Chine? Vraiment? Où exactement? *In China? Really? Whereabouts exactly?*

 You know that **Je suis** means *I am*, but it has another meaning too: *I follow, I am following*, from the infinitive **suivre** *to follow*. So if you say **Je ne suis pas (ce que vous dites)**, it means *I'm not following (what you're saying)*.

making yourself understood

There will be times when you need to know if you're getting your message across.

Tu me comprends? Vous me comprenez? *Do you understand me?*
Tu suis? Vous suivez? *Are you following?*
Laissez-moi vous expliquer... *Let me explain, clarify ...*
Je ne sais pas si je m'explique bien. *I don't know if I'm explaining things very well.*

If you're stuck for a word, say so:
J'ai oublié le mot. *I've forgotten the word.*
Je ne trouve pas le mot qu'il faut. *I can't find the right word.*
Je l'ai sur le bout de la langue. *It's on the tip of my tongue.*
Comment est-ce qu'on dit cela en français? *How do you say that in French?*
Comment ça s'appelle? *What's this/that called?*

French has some handy words for when you're stuck for the right word: **le machin, le truc** and **le bidule** all mean *thingy, whatsit,* while **le type** and **le mec** are used for *guy, bloke.*

Monsieur Machin is how you say *Mr What's-his-name* if you have forgotten someone's name — not, of course, to be used in someone's hearing!

Comment ça s'appelle? is useful only when you can point to what you're talking about. If not, paraphrasing can be effective.

C'est le contraire de ... *It's the opposite of ...*
Ce n'est pas ... *It's not ...*
C'est une sorte de ... *It's a sort of ...*
C'est un peu comme ... *It's a bit like ...*
Ça ressemble à ... *It looks like ...*
On s'en sert pour ... *It's used to ... / for ...*

If all else fails, you can resort to gestures and mime.
C'était grand comme ça. *It was this big.*
Il avait la tête comme ça. *His face was like this.*

educated guesswork

When you don't know a word in French, it can be worth guessing as French and English have a lot of vocabulary in common. Some words are written identically, and some are very similar.

It's really useful to know that almost all words ending in -tion have direct equivalents in French, e.g. **imagination**, **conversation**, **attention**, etc. Just be aware that the -tion is pronounced differently in French (**see-on**). This also applies to -tion- in the middle of words such as **nationalité** and **international**.

There are many other word endings that have parallels in the two languages:

🇬🇧	🇫🇷	
-our, -or	-eur	couleur, odeur, docteur
-ncy	-nce	agence, enfance, urgence
-ary	-aire	imaginaire, ordinaire, solitaire
-ive	-if	agressif, impulsif, exclusif, répulsif
-ous	-eux	anxieux, dangereux, désastreux

Hundreds are easily recognisable with minor adjustments to vowel sounds.
e.g. **adulte, allergique, central, dentiste**
    économie, géographie, million, musique
    possible, science, tourisme, université

Others are easy to guess when you know the key sound differences to listen out for. In French, many final consonants aren't pronounced, so words like **élégant**, **important** and **port** sound quite different from English.

faux amis *false friends*
Although most of the time words that look the same do mean the same, there are unfortunately a few that don't, for example:
Un bras is not an undergarment, but *an arm.*
You might think **blessé** means *blessed*, but it actually means *wounded.*
La monnaie is *loose change*, not money in general (which is **l'argent**).
Don't think that **la déception** necessarily has anything to do with being deceived. It simply means *disappointment.*
Une journée is not *a journey*, it's *a day*, as in **Bonne journée!** *Have a nice day!*
And although the meaning of **un coin** might seem obvious, it actually means *a corner.*

prompting

Simple prompts are very effective at moving a conversation along:

Et puis? *And then?*
Et après? *And afterwards?*
En ce qui concerne Manon ... *About Manon ...*
Quant à la réunion ... *Talking of the meeting ...*

tu **Dis-moi tout.** *Tell me all about it.*
Raconte ce qui s'est passé après. *Tell me what happened after.*
Explique-moi comment tu t'es retrouvé là-bas. *Explain to me how you ended up there.*
Parle-moi un peu de ... *Tell me a bit about ...*

vous **Dites-le moi.** *Tell me.*
Expliquez-moi pourquoi. *Explain to me why.*
Parlez-moi un peu de ... *Tell me a little about ...*
Parlez-nous un peu de l'accident de voiture. *Tell us about the car accident.*

Often, a question word on its own will promote further conversation:

Où? *Where?*
Quand? *When?*
Qui? *Who?*
Avec qui? *Who with?*
Comment? *How?*
Combien? *How much? How many?*
À quelle heure? *At what time?*
Lequel?/Laquelle? *Which one?*
Lesquels?/Lesquelles? *Which ones?*

Words like **après** and **puis** also come in handy when you're describing a sequence of events:

D'abord, on a visité le musée. *First of all, we visited the museum.*
Puis on a fait un peu de shopping. *Then we did a bit of shopping.*
Ensuite, on a retrouvé les autres. *Then we met up with the others.*
Et après, on a mangé dans un restaurant marocain. *Afterwards we ate in a Moroccan restaurant.*

showing empathy

A well-chosen interjection shows that you're listening and understanding the mood of the conversation.

To endorse what's being said, you can say:
Tout à fait! *Absolutely! Too right!*
C'est tout à fait ça! C'est bien ça! *That's just it!*
C'est juste. *That's right.*
Exact! Exactement! Précisément! *Exactly! Spot on!*
Heureusement! *Fortunately!*
Bien dit! *Well said! Hear, hear!*

Je suis d'accord means *I agree*. Adding **tout à fait** strengthens it: **Je suis tout à fait d'accord** *I quite/completely agree.*

I don't agree is **je ne suis pas d'accord.** You can add **vraiment**: **Je ne suis pas vraiment d'accord** *I don't really agree* – and you can be more emphatic by changing the order to **Je ne suis vraiment pas d'accord** *I really don't agree.*

Like English, French has expressions that can equally well convey interest, admiration, incredulity, indignation, amusement, concern, fascination or horror, depending on the tone of your voice and the expression on your face.

> **Vraiment?** *Really?*
> **Sérieusement?** *Seriously?*
> **Waouh!** *Wow!*
> **Ouf!** *Phew!*
> **Mon Dieu!** *OMG! Goodness me! Good grief!*
> **Allez!** *You don't say! Oh, come on!*
> **Pas possible!** *No!*
> **Tiens donc! Incroyable!** *Fancy that! Well I never!*
> **Tu plaisantes! Vous plaisantez!** *You're joking!*
> **Sans blague!** *Wow! No joking!*
> **Oh là là!** *For goodness' sake!*

unexpected meanings

You might hear comments that completely baffle you, since some expressions are far removed from their literal meaning.

Une barbe is *a beard* but if you say **Quelle barbe!** it means *What a drag! What a nuisance!*

Le nickel is the metal *nickel*, but **C'est nickel!** translates *Job well done! Perfect!!*

Une barre is *a rod* (usually made of metal) but **Point barre!** means *Period! That's all there is to it!*

Un bordel is the word for a brothel, but if someone says **Quel bordel!** it means *What a mess! What a shambles!* Use this sparingly, in informal conversation only, as it's stronger than the English.

Un bouquet is *a bunch of flowers*, but **C'est le bouquet!** means *That takes the biscuit!*, *That's the last straw!*

Une andouille is a type of sausage, but **Quelle andouille!** translates *What a fool! What a prat!*

La gueule is the mouth of an animal, but if you have **une gueule de bois** it means you have a hangover.

Le poil means *hair* or *fur*, but if you are **à poil**, you are *stark naked* (in nothing but your body hair). Don't confuse that with **au poil**, though, which means *great, perfect*.

Canadian French
In French-speaking parts of Canada, particularly the province of Quebec, you might hear some colourful words and expressions not in common usage in France. Spot the English influence in French Canadian words like:

starter *to start*
ronner/runner *to run*
se parker *to park*
badtripper *to panic*
un troub' (from trouble) *a problem*

commenting

A simple comment is often all that's needed to keep the conversation flowing.

Quel/quelle + a noun, is the equivalent of *What a ...* or sometimes *How ...*

Quelle bêtise! *How stupid!*
Quelle cata(strophe)! *What a disaster!*
Quelle chance! *What (a stroke of) luck!*
Quelle coïncidence! *What a coincidence!*
Quel coup de génie! *What a stroke of genius!*
Quelle déception! *What a disappointment!*
Quel dommage! *What a pity!*
Quelle folie! *What a crazy thing to do!*
Quelle frousse! *How scary!*
Quelle générosité! *What generosity! How generous!*
Quelle horreur! *How dreadful!*
Quelle journée! *What a day!*
Quel plaisir! *What a pleasure!*
Quel soulagement! *What a relief!*
Quelle bonne nouvelle! *What good news!*

You can use **quel/quelle** + a noun to comment on a person as well as a situation:
Quel hypocrite! *What a hypocrite!*
Quel rabat-joie! *What a killjoy/spoilsport!*
Quelle fille sympa! *What a nice girl!*
Quel type extraordinaire! *What an amazing guy!*

The combination noun + adjective can also deliver a pithy comment, with or without **quell(le)** or **c'est**.
Bonne idée! *Good idea!*
Un vrai cauchemar! *A real nightmare!*
Quelle belle surprise! *What a lovely surprise!*
C'est bien dommage! *That really is a shame!*
Un coup dur, non? *A body blow, isn't it?*
C'est un problème grave. *It's a major problem.*

wordbank

Sometimes a well-chosen adjective is all you need, on its own, with **(Que) c'est ...** *How ...*, *That's so ...*, or with a word like **très** or **vraiment**.

Impeccable! *Perfect!* **Extraordinaire!** *Extraordinary! Amazing!*
Que c'est bête! *How stupid!* **C'est génial!** *That's so brilliant!*
Très drôle! *Very funny!* **Si bizarre.** *So odd.* **Vraiment triste.** *Really sad.*

admiration, appreciation
commode *convenient*
exceptionnel *exceptional*
exquis *exquisite*
facile *easy*
impressionnant *impressive*
merveilleux *wonderful*
passionnant *thrilling*
satisfaisant *satisfying*

concern, empathy
courageux *brave*
décevant *disappointing*
difficile *difficult*
ennuyeux *boring, tedious*
honnête *honest*
sincère *sincere, honest*
sensible *sensitive*
sociable *friendly, sociable*

horror, sympathy
catastrophique *catastrophic*
dégoûtant *disgusting*
désagréable *unpleasant*
grave *serious*
horrible *horrendous, horrible*

malheureux *unfortunate*
méchant *nasty, naughty*
stressant *stressful*
terrible *terrible*
tragique *tragic*

astonishment, amusement
absurde *absurd*
amusant *amusing*
curieux *curious, odd*
étrange *strange*
imprévu *unexpected*
incroyable *incredible*
insolite *unusual*
ridicule *ridiculous*

general
approprié *appropriate*
efficace *effective*
évident *obvious*
logique *logical*
original *original, distinctive*
pratique *handy, practical*
raisonnable *sensible*
utile *useful*

Find six of these words that are new to you and that you wouldn't have been able to guess. Think of situations where you might use them and say them out loud, on their own and with *très*, *vraiment* or *Que c'est ...* If you need a reminder of how some adjectives change in the feminine, go to page 177.

adding structure and fluency

Real conversations tend to include words like *well, besides, anyway, let's see, frankly, however, in fact*. Some of them add structure to what you say, others add emphasis, while some simply bring a natural feel to a conversation. They also give you time to think.

Euh ben … Alors … Eh bien … *Well then … So … Right then …*
et *and*, **aussi** *also*
en plus *what's more*, **d'ailleurs** *furthermore*
mais *but*, **pourtant** *however*, **plutôt** *instead, rather*
toutefois, cependant *still, and yet*
ainsi, alors, donc *so, therefore*
de toute façon *anyway*
manifestement *clearly*, **évidemment** *obviously*
en fait *actually*
en réalité *in fact, indeed*
dans l'ensemble *on the whole*
à vrai dire *to be honest*, **franchement** *frankly*
en effet, effectivement *as a matter of fact, indeed*
bref *to cut a long story short*
par exemple *for example*
c'est-à-dire *that is, in other words*
on verra *we'll see*

C'est une bonne idée … en effet, c'est génial! *It's a good idea, terrific in fact!*
Qu'est-ce que tu en penses? Qu'est-ce que vous en pensez? *What do you reckon?*
Eh bien, on verra. *Well, let's see.*
Et pourtant, je n'étais pas au courant. *And yet I didn't know.*

For a more formal discussion:
premièrement *firstly*
deuxièmement *secondly*
d'un côté *on the one hand*; **d'un autre côté/en revanche** *on the other hand*
pour faire court *to cut a long story short*
en résumé, pour conclure *in short, in conclusion*
finalement, en conclusion *finally, to conclude*

talking the talk

Sophie	Alors, ça va, Nico?
Nico	Euh ben, oui, ça va.
Sophie	Et ton frère, Sébastien?
Nico	Ben en fait, Sébastien, il a eu un accident de voiture.
Sophie	Vraiment? Il va bien?
Nico	Oui oui, mais sa voiture est irréparable.
Sophie	C'est dommage, mais heureusement qu'il va bien.
Nico	Tout à fait. Mais tu sais qu'il vient d'avoir une bonne nouvelle, là, récemment — il a gagné au loto!
Sophie	Il a gagné au Loto? Sans blague? Ben, c'est incroyable, ça! Quelle chance!
Nico	Eh oui!
Sophie	Alors, dis-moi tout. Il a gagné combien? Il peut acheter une voiture neuve!

gagner = *to win, to earn*
une voiture neuve = *a brand new car*

1   What's the French for *I didn't understand*?

2   If you're getting blank looks, how can you check whether you're making sense?

3   If someone says **Quelle chance!**, has something good or bad happened?

4   How would you say *What a good idea!*?

5   How do you ask how to say *crisis* in French?

6   What do you add to **difficile** to say *too difficult*?

7   Which of these is the odd one out? **merveilleux, génial, passionnant, ennuyeux, fantastique, satisfaisant**

8   What's the difference between **d'abord** and **pour conclure**?

9   Class the following as positive or negative: **quelle déception, quel soulagement, quel dommage, quel plaisir, quelle bêtise**

10 How do you ask somebody if they would mind writing it down for you?

11 Which of these are *not* used to say *Well*? **alors, eh bien, bref, ben, mais**

12 How would you ask someone you don't know well to speak more slowly?

13 What's *for example* in French?

14 Apart from talking about a sausage, when might you say **Quelle andouille!**?

15 **insolite, désagréable, horrible, stressant, dégoûtant, étrange** Which of these could describe **un cauchemar**?

16 Does **de toute façon** or **c'est-à-dire** mean *in other words*?

17 How would you ask a close friend to repeat a question?

18 Fill the gap: **.......** , **c'est trop cher.** *To be honest, it's too expensive.*

19 Which indicates a feeling of relief: **allez, ouf** or **waouh**?

20 How do you say something's on the tip of your tongue?

cinq
been there, done that

Conversations can be unpredictable: there will be times when a conversation is confined to the here-and-now, but very often it will weave comfortably between the present, future and past as you talk about what's going on, what your plans are, where you've been and what you've been doing and seeing.

Knowing how to talk about what's been happening brings a whole new dimension to your French. It's more straightforward than it is in English. Using *to play* as an example, English has *I played* and *I have played* — whereas French conveys both of them with **j'ai joué**, the perfect tense of **jouer** *to play*.

It's easy to practise talking about the past in French: every so often you can say to yourself what you've been doing, preferably out loud; every day spend a few minutes writing a journal. You'll be using the same structures over and over, and your vocabulary will expand exponentially as you look up any new words you need.

saying what you have done

To talk about what you did or have done, you use the perfect tense, which is in two parts, just like *have + played* in English.

1   **avoir** *to have*

j'ai	nous avons
tu as	vous avez
il/elle/on a	ils/elles ont

2   plus the past participle. In English, this often ends in *-ed*, e.g. *worked, watched, sneezed*; in French, the ending depends on the infinitive:

-er → -é	**travaill**er *to work*	**travaill**é *worked*
-ir → -i	**fourn**ir *to provide*	**fourn**i *provided*
-re → -u	**vend**re *to sell*	**vend**u *sold*

J'ai mangé les chocolats. *I have eaten the chocolates. I ate the chocolates.*
J'ai travaillé jusqu'à onze heures. *I worked until 11 o'clock.*
Quelqu'un a laissé un message. *Someone (has) left a message.*
Nous avons recherché son nom sur internet. *We (have) looked up his name on the internet.*
J'ai fini la tarte aux amandes. *I (have) finished the almond tart.*
Votre fils a beaucoup grandi. *Your son has grown much taller.*
Il a perdu son sac. *He (has) lost his bag.*

Questions and negatives in French have no equivalent of *did*.
Qu'est-ce que vous avez choisi? *What have you chosen? What did you choose?*
Vous avez vendu votre vieille voiture? *Have you sold your old car? Did you sell your old car?*
Tu as commencé à quelle heure? *What time did you start?*
Tu as mangé où? *Where did you eat?*
Qui a laissé le message? *Who left the message?*
Est-ce que Lucas a payé les glaces? *Has Lucas paid for the ice creams? Did Lucas pay for the ice creams?*

Je n'ai pas terminé le sudoku. *I haven't finished the sudoku.*
Hier je n'ai pas terminé le sudoku. *I didn't finish the sudoku yesterday.*
Ils n'ont rien acheté. *They haven't bought/didn't buy anything.*

past participles

The past participles of all -**er** verbs end in -**é** but this isn't the case for -**ir** and -**re** verbs. Just as English has unpredictable past participles such as *eat → eaten, catch → caught, freeze → frozen*, so too does French. These are described as irregular.

avoir *to have* → eu
dire *to say* → dit
faire *to do, to make* → fait
voir *to see* → vu
devoir *to have to* → dû
pouvoir *to be able* → pu
savoir *to know* → su
tenir *to hold/keep* → tenu
venir *to come* → venu
vouloir *to want* → voulu
devenir *to become* → devenu

mettre *to put* → mis
prendre *to take* → pris
rire *to laugh* → ri
suffire *to be enough* → suffi
suivre *to follow* → suivi
craindre *to fear* → craint
joindre *to attach* → joint
peindre *to paint* → peint
ouvrir *to open* → ouvert
offrir *to offer* → offert
découvrir *to discover* → découvert

Qu'est-ce que tu as fait hier? *What did you do yesterday?*
Rien. J'ai eu une de mes migraines. *Nothing. I had one of my migraines.*
J'ai voulu sortir mais je n'ai pas pu parce que j'ai dû travailler. *I wanted to go out but I couldn't as I had to work.*
Quand je l'ai vu, j'ai su qui il était. *When I saw him, I knew who he was.*
Hier soir j'ai tellement ri au théâtre. *I laughed so much at the theatre yesterday evening.*

Il a tenu sa promesse et il est devenu végétarien. *He has kept his promise and has become vegetarian.*
Il a suivi les conseils du docteur mais ça n'a pas suffi. *He (has) followed the doctor's advice but it wasn't enough.*
Il m'a offert des fleurs. *He gave me some flowers.*

Ma femme a découvert ce magasin quand il a ouvert l'an dernier. *My wife discovered this shop when it opened last year.*

Nous avons repeint toute la maison. *We (have) repainted the whole house.*

Vous n'avez pas joint le document à votre mail. *You didn't attach/haven't attached the document to your email.*

saying where you have been

All French verbs have two parts for the perfect tense but a small group use être for the first part:

je suis	nous sommes
tu es	vous êtes
il/elle/on est	ils/elles sont

Most verbs relating to movement and existence belong in this group. The following are among the most common:

aller *to go*
apparaître *to appear*
arriver *to arrive*
décéder *to die*
descendre *to go down*
devenir *to become*
entrer *to enter*
intervenir *to intervene, to take part*
monter *to go up*

mourir *to die*
naître *to be born*
partir *to leave*
passer *to come by, go through*
rentrer *to come back*
rester *to stay*
retourner *to return*
sortir *to go out*
tomber *to fall*
(re)venir *to come (back)*

The past participle of verbs taking **être** changes in the same way as adjectives do.
Léa, tu es déjà allée en Bretagne? *Léa, have you ever been to Brittany?*
Pourquoi Sarah est-elle sortie? *Why did Sarah go out?*
Mes parents sont restés à la maison. *My parents (have) stayed at home.*
Moi, je suis né à Paris mais ma femme est née en Corse. Ses sœurs sont nées en Corse aussi. *I was born in Paris but my wife was born in Corsica. Her sisters were born in Corsica too.*

In a conversation, different endings aren't an issue since **allé, allée, allés** and **allées**, for example, all sound the same, as do **venu, venue, venus** and **venues**, and the others. **Mort**, the past participle of **mourir**, is an exception as it ends in a consonant: the t is silent in **mort** and **morts** but sounded in **morte** and **mortes**.

Try saying these two sentences out loud:
Il est mort la semaine dernière. *He died last week.*
Madame André est morte il y a six mois. *Mrs André died six months ago.*

Reflexive verbs such as **s'amuser** *to enjoy oneself*, **se réveiller** *to wake up* **s'ennuyer** *to get bored* (page 45) all use **être** in the perfect tense. They behave just like any other **être** verb, but with the addition of **me, te, se, nous, vous, se.**

À quelle heure est-ce que tu t'es couchée? *What time did you (f) go to bed?*
Tu t'es réveillé tôt ce matin? *Did you (m) wake up early this morning?*
Tu t'es bien amusée hier soir, Annie? *Did you have fun last night, Annie?*
Non, je me suis ennuyée alors je suis rentrée. *No, I (f) got bored so I came home.*
Le bébé s'est endormi dans la voiture. *The baby fell/has fallen asleep in the car.*
Ils ne se sont jamais habitués à la chaleur. *They never got used to the heat.*
Vous vous êtes bien amusées? *Have you (f) all enjoyed yourselves?*
Oui, nous nous sommes régalées! *Yes, we (f) enjoyed absolutely every minute of it!* (**se régaler** lit. *to relish*)

alternative meanings

Don't be surprised if you come across some of the verbs from the **être** list used with **avoir** instead. This is because they have alternative meanings.

With **avoir**:
descendre can mean *to take (something) down*
Il a descendu les valises du grenier. *He took the suitcases down from the attic.*

passer can mean *to spend (time)*
Nous avons passé un weekend à Paris. *We spent a weekend in Paris.*

rentrer can mean *to bring (something) in*
Elle a rentré les poubelles. *She has brought in the bins.*

retourner can mean *to turn over*
J'ai retourné la crêpe. *I flipped the pancake over.*

sortir can mean *to take (something) out*
J'ai sorti le chien tout à l'heure. *I took the dog out a little while ago.*

conversation starters

Questions about what someone's been doing are a good way of starting a conversation or moving it along.

Vous avez vu ce film? *Have you seen this film?*
Vous avez goûté de ce petit beaujolais nouveau? *Have you tried some of this nice little Beaujolais Nouveau?*
Tu as visité les catacombes hier? *Did you visit the catacombs yesterday?*
Qu'est-ce que tu as fait de beau ce matin? *What interesting things have you been up to this morning?*

Déjà *ever* or **jamais** *never* can be easily slotted in:
Vous êtes déjà allé à Notre-Dame? *Have you ever been to Notre-Dame?*
Vous avez déjà mangé des galettes de sarrasin? *Have you ever tasted buckwheat pancakes?*
Vous avez déjà fait de la planche à voile? *Have you ever done windsurfing?*

Vous n'êtes jamais monté à l'Arc de Triomphe?! *You've never been up the Arc de Triomphe?!*
Tu n'as jamais entendu parler de la brasserie Chartier? *You've never heard about the Chartier brasserie?*
Personnellement, je n'ai jamais mangé de bouillabaisse, et toi?
Personally, I've never tried bouillabaisse. What about you?
Vous avez trouvé le chemin facilement? *Did you find your way here easily?*
Est-ce que vous êtes passés par le centre-ville? *Did you go through the town centre?*

You could find out more about the people you're talking to:
Vous êtes né(e) où? *Where were you born?*
Vous avez grandi ici en Normandie? *Did you grow up/Were you brought up here in Normandy?*
Vous avez toujours vécu en Bretagne? *Have you always lived in Brittany?*
Où est-ce que vous vous êtes rencontrés? *Where did you meet?*
Quand est-ce que vous vous êtes mariés? *When did you get married?*

 Choose five occasions from the list opposite and say out loud what you did at that time. Now jot the sentences down — keeping a journal in French is no more than doing this on a regular basis. Hier matin, je me suis levé(e) à sept heures. Hier après-midi, j'ai lavé la voiture. **Yesterday morning, I got up at seven. Yesterday afternoon, I washed the car.**

wordbank

hier *yesterday*
hier matin/après-midi/soir *yesterday morning/afternoon/evening*
avant-hier *the day before yesterday*
l'autre jour *the other day*

le jour d'avant/la veille *the day before*
le jour avant la fête/la veille de la fête *the day before the party*
la semaine d'avant/la semaine précédente *the week before*
le mois d'avant/le mois précédent *the month before*
l'année d'avant/l'année précédente *the year before*
deux ans avant *two years before*

lundi/dimanche dernier *last Monday/Sunday*
la semaine dernière *last week*
le mois dernier *last month*
en janvier dernier *last January*
l'an dernier/l'année dernière *last year*

le jour d'après/le lendemain *the day after*
le surlendemain *two days later/after*
la semaine d'après/la semaine suivante *the week after/following*
l'année d'après/l'année suivante *the year after*

il y a **une demi-heure** *half an hour ago*
il y a deux jours *two days ago*
il y a quinze jours/deux semaines *a fortnight ago*
il y a (environ) un mois *(about) a month ago*
il y a deux/trois/dix ans *two/three/ten years ago*

> **Tout à l'heure** means *a short while ago* when you're talking about the past, but when you're talking about the present or the future, it means *shortly*.
>
> **Je te l'ai déjà dit tout à l'heure!** *I already told you so earlier!*
> **Dépeche-toi, on va partir tout à l'heure.** *Hurry up! We're going to leave shortly.*

coping in a crisis

In an emergency situation, you need to know how to get help.

Au secours! *Help!* **C'est une urgence!** *It's an emergency!*
Vous pouvez m'aider? *Can you help me?*
J'ai besoin d'aide. *I need help.*

To say what's going on now, you use the present tense:
Il y a un incendie. *There's a fire.*
Ça sent le gaz. *There's a smell of gas.*
Je ne peux pas respirer. *I can't breathe.*
Il saigne. *He's bleeding.*
C'est une crise d'asthme. *It's an asthma attack.*

... but to explain what's already happened, you need the perfect tense.

Je suis tombé(e) de l'échelle. *I fell/I've fallen off the ladder.*
Elle a trébuché sur le trottoir. *She (has) tripped on the pavement.*
Il a perdu connaissance. *He (has) lost consciousness.*
Elle s'est évanouie. *She (has) fainted.*
Elle a été violée. *She's been raped.*

Il y a eu un vol/un cambriolage. *There's been a theft/a burglary.*
Il y a eu un accident de la route. *There's been a road accident.*
La voiture a dérapé ... *The car skidded ...*
... et a percuté un lampadaire. *... and crashed into a lamp post.*

On m'a agressé(e). *I've been attacked/mugged.*
On m'a volé mon sac. *My bag has been snatched.*
Ils m'ont volé mon portefeuille. *They stole my wallet.*
J'ai perdu mon porte-monnaie. *I've lost my purse.*

In France, the emergency number is **112**, and they'll direct you to the appropriate services. Alternatively, you can dial:

15: **SAMU Service d'Aide Médicale Urgente** medical emergencies
17: **Police**
18: **Sapeurs-pompiers** firefighters, who are also paramedics
197: **Alerte attentat** terror attack hotline

saying something had taken place

In French, just as in English, the only difference between saying something *has* happened (perfect tense) and *had* happened (pluperfect tense) is the tense of *have*. To talk about what *had* happened in French, you use the imperfect of **avoir** or **être** (pages 78–80); everything else is the same.

J'avais oublié de faire le plein. *I had forgotten to fill up with petrol.*
J'avais déjà demandé pourquoi. *I had already asked why.*
Il n'avait pas bien dormi. *He hadn't slept well.*
Si seulement nous avions su! *If only we had known!*
Vous aviez lu le livre avant de voir le film? *Had you read the book before seeing the film?*
La veille ils avaient travaillé tard. *They had worked late the day before.*
Ils en avaient déjà mangé la moitié. *They had already eaten half of it.*

J'étais tombé deux mois avant. *I had fallen two months earlier.*
Si j'étais arrivé plus tôt ... *If I had arrived earlier ...*
Tu étais déjà parti? *Had you already left?*
Elle était partie à la pêche avec Julien. *She had gone fishing with Julien.*
Nous étions arrivés en avance. *We had arrived early.*
Vous étiez partis en même temps? *Had you left at the same time?*
Ils étaient descendus à toute vitesse. *They had come down in a hurry.*

À quelle heure est-ce que vous vous étiez réveillé? *What time had you woken up?*
Elle s'était endormie. *She had fallen asleep.*
Est-ce qu'ils s'étaient bien amusés? *Had they enjoyed themselves?*

You can say that something had *just* taken place with the imperfect of **venir (juste) de** + the infinitive:
Nous venions de finir de manger quand il est arrivé. *We had just finished eating when he arrived.*
Il venait de se lever quand tu l'as appelé. *He had just got up when you called him.*
Je venais juste de rentrer chez moi quand il a commencé à pleuvoir. *I had just got home when it started raining.*

talking the talk

Sophie	Qu'est-ce que tu as fait hier soir, Nico?
Nico	Hier soir? Ben, rien de spécial.
Sophie	Tu n'es pas sorti?
Nico	Ben ... non. Je voulais sortir mais je n'ai pas pu, finalement.
Sophie	Ah bon, pourquoi?
Nico	J'ai eu une migraine abominable.
Sophie	Oh non, mon pauvre! C'est horrible, les migraines. Ça va mieux maintenant?
Nico	Oui, oui, aujourd'hui, ça va.
Nico	Et toi, Sophie? Tu es sortie?
Sophie	Oui, je suis allée au cinéma avec un de mes collègues.
Nico	Qu'est-ce que vous avez vu comme film?
Sophie	On a vu un film d'amour un peu bête ... mais on s'est bien amusés!
Nico	Un film d'amour ... eh! C'est romantique! Et après ça?
Sophie	Eh bien, après, euh... on est allés prendre un café ... dans le bar, tu sais, près de la gare.
Nico	Soirée sympa, alors!
Sophie	Ben ... oui et non! Parce que, malheureusement, la soirée a mal fini.
Nico	Ah bon, pourquoi? Qu'est-ce qui s'est passé?
Sophie	Ben, au bar, on m'a volé mon sac ... je l'avais mis sous la table, et puis ...
Nico	Oh non! Tu as appelé la police?

verb practice 3

1   Write these verbs in the perfect tense: all the past participles are regular.

   a   **parler** *to talk* **tu**
   b   **sortir** *to go out* **vous** (m plural)
   c   **perdre** *to lose* **il**
   d   **tomber** *to fall* **je**
   e   **choisir** *to choose* **ils**
   f   **attendre** *to wait* **nous**
   g   **vendre** *to sell* **elles**
   h   **envoyer** *to send* **on**
   i   **rentrer** *to come back* **elle**

2   Now change them to the pluperfect and say what they mean.

3   Although many **-re** verbs have irregular past participles, there are clusters that form their past participle in the same way. See if you can work these out:

- **mettre** *to put* **mis: admettre** *to admit* ....; **commettre** *to commit* ....; **permettre** *to allow* .... **promettre** *to promise* ....
- **prendre** *to take* **pris: comprendre** *to understand* ....; **apprendre** *to learn* ....; **surprendre** *to surprise* ....
- **écrire** *to write* **écrit: décrire** *to describe* ....; **prescrire** *to prescribe* ....; **dire** *to say* ....; **prédire** *to predict* ....
- **rire** *to laugh* **ri: sourire** *to smile* ....; **suffire** *to be sufficient* ....
- **conduire** *to drive* **conduit: réduire** *to reduce* ....; **séduire** *to seduce* ....; **traduire** *to translate* ....; **cuire** *to cook* ....; **construire** *to build* ....; **détruire** *to destroy* ....
- **connaître** *to know* **connu: méconnaître** *to be unaware of* ....; **reconnaitre** *to recognise* ....
- **peindre** *to paint* **peint: atteindre** *to reach* ....; **éteindre** *to switch off* ....; **joindre** *to join* ....; **se plaindre** *to complain* ....

4   Use these jottings as the basis of a journal entry for yesterday.

worked till 12, went to town after lunch, saw Martin, did the shopping (les courses), spent (dépenser) too much!, sent an email to William & left a message for mum (à maman), Pauline arrived at 6

Add that Pauline had just left when your father phoned.

1   What are the past participles of **rêver** *to dream*, **maigrir** *to lose weight* and **répondre** *to answer*, all of them regular?

2   Would you use **J'ai retourné** or **Je suis retourné** here? .... **dans la ville où je suis né.**

3   .... **nous avons visité l'île.** What needs inserting for the sentence to say *We visited the island the day before yesterday*?

4   How would you tell someone you've lost your purse?

5   In the perfect tense, which of these verbs use **avoir** and which **être**: **naître** *to be born, to* **vivre** *to live*, **rester** *to stay*, **mourir** *to die*, **manger** *to eat*, **monter** *to go up*, **courir** *to run*?

6   How would you tell someone you (plus friends) went on a cruise last year and stayed five days at sea? (**faire une croisière** *to go on a cruise*; **en mer** *at sea*)

7   How would you say you've just called the police?

8   Using **vous**, how would you ask your friend's mother where she went yesterday?

9   Given that **satisfaire** *to satisfy* and **stupéfaire** *to amaze* both behave like **faire** *to do*, what are their past participles? How would you say *he satisfied* and *he amazed*?

10 What are the two meanings of **tout à l'heure**?

11 **bu, dû, eu, lu, pu, su, vu** are the irregular past participles of which verbs?

12 What word needs adding to **Vous êtes allée en Corse?** for it to mean *Have you ever been to Corsica?*

13 If you hear **Comment est-ce que vous vous êtes rencontrés?** when you're with your partner or friend, what information are you being asked for?

14 What's the difference between **nous avons prévu** and **nous avions prévu**, and between **je suis sorti** and **j'étais sorti**?

15 Complete the sentence to mean *He arrived a week ago*: **Il est arrivé .... une semaine.**

16 Change the following from the perfect to the pluperfect? **j'ai dormi; ils sont partis; vous vous êtes ennuyés?; nous n'avons pas mangé**

six
how things were

Saying what you used to do and describing how things were bring yet another dimension to a conversation. French has a set of verb endings for this, called the imperfect tense. They're not difficult to recognise when you hear them because all the endings except for **nous** and **vous** sound the same: much like -**ais** in **Calais**.

These are the endings you use to talk about what was happening, what used to happen, what happened often/regularly or carried on over a period of time. English uses *I was playing, I used to play, I would (often) play, I played (regularly)*, while **je jouais** covers them all in French.

Words such as *often, regularly, usually* are characteristic of the imperfect, but French doesn't always include them because using the imperfect tense is in itself enough to convey a sense of continuity.

You use the imperfect of **être** when you're describing: **J'étais tellement en colère** *I was so angry*, **C'était incroyable** *It was incredible*. If you're keeping a journal, try to include at least one description every day.

talking about what you used to do

Tu allais où en vacances quand tu étais petit? *Where did you go on holiday when you were little?*

Allais and quand tu étais petit show that the question isn't referring to a specific event, and so you need the imperfect to answer it.

Imperfect endings fit onto the **nous** form of the present tense minus **-ons**:

nous travaill~~ons~~	**je travaillais** / *I was working*
nous finiss~~ons~~	**je finissais** / *would finish*
nous pren~~ons~~	**je prenais** / *used to take*
	nous travaillions *we were working*
	nous finissions *we would finish*
	nous prenions *we used to take*

J'allais **souvent en Bretagne.** *I often used to go to Brittany.*
Je jouais **sur la plage des heures entières.** *I played on the beach for hours on end.*
Nous descendions **au même hôtel tous les ans.** *We would stay in the same hotel every year.*
Nous achetions **notre fromage au marché.** *We (always) used to buy our cheese in the market.*
Nous photographiions **les enfants presque tous les jours.** *We took photos of the kids almost every day.*

It might look odd, but the **nous** and **vous** endings for verbs ending in **-ier**, such as **photographier** and **étudier**, are actually written with **ii**: **Nous étudiions le français à l'école.** *We used to study French at school.*

The endings for *you:*	tu	travaillais	finissais	prenais
	vous	travailliez	finissiez	preniez

Toi, tu habitais où à ce moment-là? *Where were you living at that time?*
Tu travaillais pour la SNCF, c'est bien ça? *You used to work for the French railways, didn't you?*
Est-ce que vous fréquentiez souvent ce bar? *Did you (use to) go to this bar often?*

Pourquoi est-ce que vous choisissiez toujours ce restaurant? *Why did you always choose this restaurant?*

Est-ce que vous preniez le bus ou le métro? *Did you take the bus or the underground?*

-**ait** is the ending for *he/she/one* and -**aient** for *they*:

| il/elle/on | travaillait | finissait | prenait |
| ils/elles | travaillaient | finissaient | prenaient |

Éric travaillait avec moi. *Éric used to work with me.*

On recevait un bonus en fin d'année. *We used to get a bonus at the end of the year.*

Isabelle venait chez nous tous les samedis. *Isabelle came to our house every Saturday.*

Bébé, elle souffrait de coliques. *When she was a baby, she suffered from colic.*

Ça fonctionne aujourd'hui mais ça ne fonctionnait pas hier. *It's working today but it wasn't working yesterday.*

Mes grands-parents vivaient très simplement. *My grandparents lived a very simple life.*

Pourquoi est-ce qu'elles dépensaient autant? *Why were they spending so much?*

Ils passaient souvent leurs vacances à l'étranger. *They often used to spend their holidays abroad.*

The endings -ais, -ait and -aient are all pronounced in exactly the same way. They sound more or less like the *e* in *bed*.

The imperfect used with **depuis** is the way to say how long something *had been* going on.

Ils habitaient là depuis longtemps? *Had they been living there long?*

Il fumait depuis dix ans. *He had been smoking for 10 years.*

Elle travaillait dans cette boîte depuis vingt-cinq ans quand elle a été licenciée. *She had been working for that company for 25 years when she was made redundant.*

Je la connaissais depuis l'école primaire. *I had known her since primary school.*

saying how things were

To say where something was or describe how it used to be, you use the imperfect of **être** *to be* — the only verb that's irregular in the imperfect.

j'étais	*I was*	nous étions	*we were*
tu étais	*you were*	vous étiez	*you were*
il/elle/on était	*he/she/it, one was*	ils/elles étaient	*they were*

Hier j'étais à Nice. *I was in Nice yesterday.*
Le soir j'étais fatigué. *I was tired in the evening.*
Comment était le voyage? *What was the journey like?*
Le film était passionnant. *The film was captivating.*
C'était très sympa. *It was very nice.*
Quand elle était petite, Christine était assez maladroite. *When she was little, Christine used to be quite clumsy.*
Quand nous étions étudiants, nous partagions un appartement. *When we were students, we used to share a flat.*
Il y a vingt ans, ces bâtiments étaient luxueux. *Twenty years ago these buildings were luxurious.*

English doesn't often use *was*, *were* or *used to* with feelings or with verbs unrelated to physical activity, such as **aimer** *to like*, **vouloir** *to want*, **avoir** *to have* — but you still need the imperfect in French.

Je me sentais bien. *I felt well.*
Quand j'étais jeune je préférais le vin blanc. *I preferred white wine when I was young.*
Je voulais venir mais je ne pouvais pas me libérer. *I wanted to come but I couldn't get away.*
Mon frère détestait les études mais il voulait un diplôme. *My brother hated studying but he wanted a degree.*
Nous pensions être amoureux. *We thought we were in love.*
Vous croyiez en Dieu? *Did you believe in God?*
Vous aimiez l'endroit où vous êtes né? *Did you like the place where you were born?*
Ils n'osaient rien dire. *They didn't dare say anything.*
À cette époque-là, ils avaient trois chevaux. *At that time they had three horses.*

word bank

quand j'étais petit(e) *as a child, when I was little*
quand j'étais jeune *when I was young*
quand nous étions enfants *when we were children*

toujours *always*
souvent *often*
d'habitude, habituellement, normalement, généralement *usually*
régulièrement *regularly*
pendant un moment *for a while*
quelquefois, parfois *sometimes*
tant de fois *so many times*
plusieurs fois *several times*
de nombreuses fois *many times*
rarement *rarely*
jamais *never*

tous les jours, chaque jour *every day*
toutes les semaines, chaque semaine *every week*
tous les ans, chaque année *every year*
de temps en temps *now and then*
une fois de temps en temps, de temps à autre *once in a while*

il y a longtemps *a long time ago*
à cette époque-là, à ce moment-là *at that time*
dans les années quatre-vingt-dix *in the 1990s*
dans les années deux mille *in the noughties*
dans les années deux mille dix *in the 2010s*
au Moyen Âge *in the Middle Ages*
dans un passé lointain *in the dim and distant past*
il était une fois *once upon a time*

 Choose four of these expressions and use them in a sentence with a verb in the imperfect tense. Either recycle some of the verbs from the examples or use different verbs – all except être are regular in the imperfect.

reminiscing

When people are getting to know each other, there's usually a mutual interest in finding out about background.

Since you are born only the once, you need the perfect tense:

Vous êtes né où? *Where were you born?*
Je suis né en Suisse. *I was born in Switzerland.*

From then on, you use the imperfect.
Tu habitais où? Vous habitiez où? *Where did you use to live?*
Nous habitions un village près du lac de Neuchâtel. *We lived in a village near Lake Neuchâtel.*
C'était un coin plutôt tranquille. *It was rather a quiet area.*
Chaque hiver, il neigeait ... *Every winter it snowed ...*
... mais en été, il faisait chaud. *... but in summer it was hot.*

Nous avions un chalet. Il n'était pas grand: en fait, il était tout petit.
We had a chalet. It wasn't big: in fact it was really small.

Mon père travaillait à son compte; il voyageait régulièrement.
My father worked freelance; he used to travel regularly.

De temps en temps, mes grands-parents venaient chez nous.
Now and then, my grandparents would come to our house.
Ça n'arrivait pas souvent parce qu'en ce temps-là ils tenaient un hôtel.
It didn't happen often because they were hoteliers at that time.

Ma sœur et moi, nous allions tous les jours à l'école du village.
My sister and I went to the village school every day.

J'adorais cette école! *I loved that school!*
La maîtresse s'appelait Madame Leroy. *The teacher was called Mrs Leroy.*
Elle portait des lunettes très épaisses. *She wore very thick glasses.*
Elle nous racontait des contes de fées. *She would tell us fairy tales.*

Peau d'Âne *Donkey Skin* is a classic French **conte de fées**. It starts with *Once upon a time* and it's all about a princess, the daughter of an important king (**un roi**). It starts ...

> **Il était une fois** un roi si grand, si aimé de ses peuples, si respecté de tous ses voisins et de tous ses alliés, qu'on pouvait dire qu'il était le plus heureux de tous les monarques.

See how much of this you understand (the English is on page 199).

chatting about the past

You'll find that you often need the imperfect and the perfect tenses in the same sentence.

This could be when you want to describe the circumstances in which something took place.

J'avais vingt ans quand j'ai rencontré **Marion.** *I was 20 when I met Marion.*
Il faisait nuit quand ils sont arrivés. *It was dark when they arrived.*
Le restaurant était **bondé quand** nous y sommes allés. *The restaurant was packed when we went there.*

Or it could be to explain what someone was doing when something happened:

Je prenais un selfie quand je suis tombé! *I was taking a selfie when I fell over!*
Elle attendait son ami quand la bombe a explosé. *She was waiting for her friend when the bomb exploded.*
Ils regardaient un film et n'ont pas entendu **le téléphone.** *They were watching a film and didn't hear the phone.*

If you want to convey being right in the middle of doing something when something else happened, you can use the imperfect of **être en train de** + the infinitive.

J'étais en train de sauvegarder le document quand l'ordinateur s'est arrêté tout seul. *I was just saving the file when the computer crashed.*
Qu'est-ce que tu étais en train de **faire quand** je suis arrivé? *What were you doing when I arrived?*
Nous étions en train de préparer le dessert quand le mixeur est tombé en panne. *We were right in the middle of making the dessert when the food processor broke down.*

Now that you know how to manipulate verbs to say what you're doing, what you were doing and what you did, you can come up with some interesting and varied French.

Start by saying where you are and what you're doing today. Then say what you did yesterday: include a couple of descriptions and say how you were feeling. After that, have a go at putting together a few sentences about when you were little: where you lived and went to school, what your parents did, where you went on holiday.

talking the talk

Nico   Tu aimais l'école quand tu étais petite?

Sophie   Ah oui! J'adorais l'école primaire. J'habitais dans un petit village et l'école n'était pas très grande et donc il n'y avait pas beaucoup d'élèves. C'était sympa, je connaissais tout le monde. Et toi?

Nico   Ah moi, je détestais l'école!

Sophie   C'est vrai?

Nico   Absolument! Je ne voulais jamais y aller. À midi, je rentrais manger à la maison, et quelquefois, je ne retournais pas en classe l'après-midi.

Sophie   Oh là là!

Sophie   Tu habitais en Afrique quand tu étais petit, non?

Nico   Oui. Mon père était ingénieur et on voyageait beaucoup à cause de son travail. Nous avons passé cinq ans au Sénégal.

Sophie   Intéressant! Ça t'a plu?

Nico   Oui, assez. Nous avions un grand appartement à Dakar — la capitale. J'avais beaucoup de copains là-bas.

Sophie   Et quand est-ce que vous êtes revenus en France alors?

Nico   Oh, il y a longtemps! Je suis revenu quand j'avais dix ans.

Sophie   Ah oui, en effet!

verb practice 4

1   Write these verbs in the imperfect tense.

   a   **vouloir** *to want* **tu** ....

   b   **avoir** *to have* **nous** ....

   c   **connaître** *to know* **elle** ....

   d   **regarder** *to watch* **on** ....

   e   **prendre** *to take* **je** ....

   f   **aller** *to go* **ils** ....

   g   **être** *to be* **il** ....

   h   **faire** *to do* **vous** ....

2   Change the present tense verbs to the imperfect.

   a   **Habituellement, il prend le train de 11h15**.

   b   **Je vais faire du yoga une fois par semaine.**

   c   **Je me lève tôt quand il fait beau.**

   d   **Ma fille a souvent mal à la gorge.**

   e   **Vous préférez le vin rouge?**

   f   **Thierry vérifie ses mails toutes les dix minutes!**

   g   **Nous allons aux sports d'hiver tous les ans, en février.**

   h   **De temps en temps ils jouent au tennis ensemble.**

   i   **À quelle heure vous dînez en général?**

   j   **Lucie et Anne habitent un pavillon dans la banlieue de Lille.**

3   Fill the gaps with the French for the words in brackets, then translate
   the sentences. Some of them are in the perfect tense – if you need
   to refresh your memory, have a look at Chapter 5.

   a   .... **avec Lucas;** .... **au centre-ville quand je** .... **sur le
      trottoir.**

      (*I was; we were; fell*)

   b   .... **en 1984; enfant,** .... **à Grasse, en Provence, où ses
      parents** .... **une parfumerie.**

      (*she was born; she lived; had*)

   c   .... **à l'endroit où ta mère** .... **ton père quand il** ....
      encore au Sénégal?

      (*did you go; met; worked*)

check point 6

1   What's the French for *every now and then*? And what two ways can you think of to say *usually* in French.

2   Do you use the perfect, the pluperfect or the imperfect to talk about i) what you had done, ii) what you used to do when you were growing up?

3   Which is the only irregular verb in the imperfect?

4   What's missing from **Nous .... à la plage avec des amis** for it to mean *We were at the beach with friends*?

5   What would you need to change in **Nous travaillons tous les jours** to say *We used to work every day*; and in **On prend beaucoup de photos** to say *We used to take a lot of photographs*?

6   How do you tell someone that you met Amélie when you were twelve?

7   Rearrange the words to form a sentence: **était Julie suis en lire quand je arrivé train de**

8   Which word is needed here to mean *I'd known them for years*? **Je les connaissais .... des années.**

9   Fill the gap so that **À l'école, elle .... toujours de bonnes notes en français** means *At school she always had good marks in French*.

10   What's the French for *when I was little* and *when I was a student*?

11   Place **allait** and **est allé** in the correct place in the sentence: **Ce matin, il .... visiter l'église où, enfant, il .... avec sa grand-mère.**

12   What key word is missing in this sentence talking about what someone was doing when something else happened? **Elle l'attendait depuis une heure .... il est enfin arrivé.**

13   **Il y a** means *there is/are* in the present. So how would you say *There were lots of people in the cinema*?

14   How would you convey being right in the middle of doing something?

15   Which tense will you need to translate this sentence? *As a child, Claire wanted to become an astronaut.* Fill in the verb. **Enfant, Claire .... (vouloir) devenir astronaute.**

16   Which tense will you need to translate this sentence? *At 18, Claire stopped her studies and went abroad.* Fill in the verbs. **À dix-huit ans, Claire .... (arrêter) ses études et .... (partir) à l'étranger.**

17   What's the French for *I used to enjoy working freelance*?

18   Given that the imperfect of **c'est** is **c'était**, what's the imperfect of **ce sont**? How would you say *They were my friends from Paris*.

sept
lifestyle choices

Knowing how to say what you like and enjoy – or don't – comes in useful in all sorts of situations, whether you're referring to food or the weather, discussing work, sport, people, music, places, your interests or your pet hates.

Aimer means *to love*. It is most intense in simple sentiments such as **Je t'aime** *I love you*, **Pierre aime ses enfants** *Pierre loves his children*. Additional words dilute the intensity, and edge **aimer** closer to *like* than *love*: **Je t'aime bien** *I like you a lot*, **Nous aimons beaucoup danser** *We really like dancing*.

You'll also hear **Ça te plaît?** for *Do you like it?*, literally *Does it please you?* It's the same verb as in **s'il vous plaît**, literally *if it pleases you*.

Don't forget that *like* in English has other, quite separate meanings. *I like coffee* and *I'd like a coffee* mean quite different things and in French they're **J'aime bien le café** and **Je voudrais un café**.

To look like is **ressembler à**:
Qu'est-ce qu'elle ressemble à sa mère! Elle est le portrait craché de Nathalie! *She looks so like her mother. She's the spitting image of Nathalie!*

Comme can translate into English as *like*: **comme neuf** *like new*, **comme ça** *like this, like that*.
boire comme un trou *to drink like a fish* lit. *like a hole*
chanter comme une casserole *to sing terribly* lit. *like a saucepan*

saying what you do and don't like

J'aime bien la Provence. *I like Provence.*
Tu aimes bien tes collègues? *Do you like your colleagues?*
Ma fille aime bien les films d'action. *My daughter likes action films.*
On aime bien le football. *We like football.*

Je n'aime pas cette couleur. *I don't like this colour.*
Vous n'aimez pas les grandes villes? *Don't you like cities/big towns?*
Mes parents n'aiment pas les tatouages. *My parents don't like tattoos.*

While English uses a verb ending in *-ing* after *like*, French uses an infinitive:
J'aime bien chanter. *I enjoy singing.*
Je n'aime pas perdre mon temps. *I don't like wasting my time.*

If someone asks if you like their new jacket or if you like oysters, you don't repeat *new jacket* or *oysters* in your answer: you use *it* or *them* instead. In French, you can either include these or not.
Tu aimes ma nouvelle veste? *Do you like my new jacket?*
Oui, j'aime bien. *Yes, I like it.*
Vous aimez les huîtres? *Do you like oysters?*
Oui, j'aime ça. *Yes, I like it/them.*
Euh non, je n'aime pas vraiment ça. *Er no, I don't really like it/them.*

It works differently when you're talking about liking people: you insert **l'** *him/her* or **les** *them* before **aimer**.
Tu aimes le batteur/la chanteuse? *Do you like the drummer/the singer?*
Oui, je l'aime beaucoup. *Yes, I like him/her a lot.*
Est-ce que vous aimez les voisins? *Do you like the neighbours?*
Oui, je les aime bien. *Yes, I like them.*
Non, je ne l'/les aime pas trop. *No I don't much like him/her/them.*

(See pages 180–181 for more on pronouns.)

For a change, you can use the verb **plaire** to say what you like or don't like.
Ça te/vous plaît? *Do you like it?*
Oui, ça me plaît beaucoup. *Yes, I like it very much.*
Non, ça ne me plaît pas. *No, I don't like it.*

saying what you liked

There are two ways of translating *I liked* in French: **j'aimais** and **j'ai aimé**, depending on the circumstances.

J'aimais, the imperfect, is used in the sense of *I used to like*, even when English might sometimes also use *I liked*:

> **J'aimais les dessins animés.** *I used to like cartoon films.*
> **Quand j'étais petit, j'aimais bien la lecture.** *When I was little, I liked/ used to like reading.*
> **Tu n'aimais pas l'école?** *Didn't you like/use to like school?*

J'ai aimé *I liked, I enjoyed* is the perfect tense, used to talk about a one-off situation:

> **J'ai bien aimé le spectacle hier soir.** *I liked the show last night.*
> **Nous avons bien aimé le repas.** *We enjoyed the meal.*
> **Vous n'avez pas aimé le dessert?** *Didn't you enjoy the dessert?*

You can add **toujours** to say *have always liked*:

> **J'ai toujours aimé le sport.** *I've always liked sport.*
> **Nous avons toujours aimé Montmartre.** *We've always liked Montmartre.*

You can use **plaire** in the past too. You change **plaît** to **plaisait** for the imperfect, and to **a plu** for the perfect.

> **Ça te plaisait?** *Did you use to like it?*
> **Avant, ça me plaisait.** *Before, I used to like it.*
> **Le film, ça t'a plu?** *Did you like the film?*
> **Oui, ça m'a beaucoup plu.** *Yes, I liked it a lot.*

Did you know that **oui** isn't the only French word for *yes*?
If someone asks you a question phrased in a negative way and you want to contradict them with a positive answer, *yes* is **si**.
Le film, ça ne t'a pas plu? *Didn't you like the film?*
Si, ça m'a beaucoup plu. *Yes, I liked it a lot.*
Tu n'aimes pas mon copain? *Don't you like my friend?*
Si, je l'aime bien. *Yes, I do like him.*

adding nuance

Adorer *to love* and **détester** *to hate* are useful words for expressing extremes:
J'adore ta coiffure. *I love your hairstyle.*
Je déteste les gens égoïstes. *I hate selfish people.*

Slotting words like **beaucoup** *a lot, very much* or **assez** *quite* into a sentence adds nuance or depth to what you're saying. It's simple to do: these are adverbs – unlike adjectives there's nothing about them to change. They work in any context and are especially useful when you're talking about what you like, since *I like/I don't like* alone can sound rather stark.

J'aime beaucoup habiter ici. *I like living here very much.*
J'aime énormément travailler avec les enfants. *I absolutely love working with children.*
Nous aimons assez ce climat. *We quite like this climate.*
Vous aimez vraiment ça? *Do you really like it?*
J'aime trop le chocolat. *I like chocolate too much.*
Ils aiment tellement le nouveau système. *They like the new system so much.*
Il aime sa moto à la folie. *He's crazy about his motorbike.*
Ça me plaît assez. *I quite like it.*

You add emphasis to the things you don't like with words like **pas trop** *not much* or **pas du tout** *not at all*:
Je n'aime pas du tout l'impolitesse. *I can't stand rudeness.*
Nous n'aimons pas trop jouer aux cartes. *We don't much like playing cards.*

There are other negative expressions you can use too:
J'aimais la musique rock mais je n'aime plus ça. *I used to like rock music but I don't like it any more.*
Elle n'aime plus sortir? *Doesn't she like to go out any more?*

Tu n'aimes personne ici? *Don't you like anybody here?*
Personne n'aimait ce restaurant. *Nobody liked that restaurant.*

Je n'ai jamais aimé la natation. *I've never liked swimming.*
Nous n'avons jamais aimé cet aéroport. *We've never liked this airport.*
Nadine n'a jamais aimé les hôpitaux. *Nadine has never liked hospitals.*

saying what interests you

... **m'intéresse/m'intéressent** mean ... *interest(s) me*, although in English you're more likely to say *I'm interested in* ...
L'histoire m'intéresse. *I'm interested in history.*
Votre argument m'intéresse **beaucoup.** *Your point interests me greatly.*
Ses théories m'intéressent. *I'm interested in his/her theories.*

For things that don't interest you, you put **ne** before **m'intéresse/ m'intéressent** and **pas** afterwards:
Le patinage ne m'intéresse **pas.** *Skating doesn't appeal to me.*
Les mots croisés ne m'intéressent **pas.** *Crosswords don't interest me.*

m' is replaced by **t', l', nous, vous** or **les** to say what other people are interested in:
La pêche t'intéresse? *Are you keen on fishing?* lit. *Does fishing interest you?*
Les courses automobiles l'intéressent? *Is he/she interested in motor racing?*
Le bricolage ne nous **intéresse pas beaucoup.** *We're not very interested in DIY.*
Ces peintures vous **intéressent?** *Are you interested in these pictures?*
La mode ne les **intéresse pas.** *They're not interested in fashion.*

There are two ways of talking about what interested you in the past.

... **m'intéressait/m'intéressaient** (imperfect)
Au collège, le dessin m'intéressait. *At school I was interested in art.*
Quand j'étais jeune, les bandes dessinées m'intéressaient. *When I was young, I used to be interested in comic books.*

... **m'a intéressé(e)/m'ont intéressé(e)** (perfect)
Le football m'a toujours **intéressé(e).** *I've always been interested in football.*
Ses idées m'ont toujours **intéressé(e).** *I've always been interested in his/her ideas.*
Les paris en ligne ne m'ont jamais **intéressé(e).** *Online gambling has never interested me.*
For more on the agreement of the past participle **intéressé**, see page 185.

More often than not, **bande dessinée** *comic strip, cartoon* is shortened to **BD** or **bédé: Moi, j'adore les bédés Astérix.** *I just love the Asterix cartoons.*

wordbank

le sport *sport*

l'alpinisme, l'escalade *mountaineering, climbing*
les arts martiaux *martial arts*
la course, le jogging *running*
l'équitation *horse riding*
le foot(ball) à sept *seven-a-side football*
la natation *swimming*
le parachutisme *parachuting*
le parapente *paragliding*
le patinage *skating*
la randonnée *walking, hiking*
le saut à l'élastique *bungee jumping*
le ski *skiing*
la spéléologie *potholing*
la voile *sailing*

A number of sports use the English terms, e.g. **le badminton, le golf, le rugby, le squash, le tennis.**

en plein air *in the great outdoors*

l'activité physique *exercise*
l'air pur *fresh air*
une baisse de tension artérielle *drop in blood pressure*
le bien-être *sense of well-being*
la forme *fitness*
une réduction du stress *reduction of stress levels*
les abeilles *bees*
la boue *mud*
les crottes de chiens *dog poo*
les fourmis f pl *ants*
les guêpes f pl *wasps*
les mouches f pl *flies*
les orties f pl *nettles*
les moustiques f pl *mosquitoes*
les tiques f pl *ticks*

You put **le, la, l'** or **les** before a noun when saying what you like/are interested in, even when it isn't needed in English:
J'aime le yoga. *I like yoga.*
Elle n'aimait pas les araignées. *She didn't like spiders.*
L'activité physique ne m'intéresse pas. *I don't like exercise.*

les arts *the arts*

> **la musique classique/pop** *classical/pop music*
> **la musique symphonique/de chorale/de chambre** *symphonic/ choral/chamber music*
> **l'opéra** *opera*
> **la musique alternative** *alternative music*
> **la musique contemporaine** *modern music*

Most modern music adapts the English words, e.g. **le rock, le hard-rock, le jazz, le punk, le blues, le hip-hop, le rap, la techno, le heavy metal.**

> **un acteur/une actrice** *actor/actress*
> **l'acteur principal/l'actrice principale** *leading actor/actress, star*
> **l'art abstrait/conceptuel** *abstract/conceptual art*
> **le cinéma** *cinema*
> **le concert** *concert, gig*
> **la danse moderne/de salon** *modern/ballroom dance*
> **la distribution** cast
> **l'exposition** *exhibition*
> **la galerie d'art** *(art) gallery*
> **le musée** *museum*
> **le spectacle** *show/performance*
> **le spectacle en direct** *live performance*
> **le théâtre** *theatre*

Sometimes French uses a singular word where English uses the plural, and vice versa.
Vous avez des renseignements? *Do you have any information?*
L'athlétisme m'intéresse. *I'm interested in athletics.*
J'aime bien les pâtes. *I like pasta.*
J'aime bien les cheveux roux. *I like red hair.*
Vous n'aimez pas mes conseils? *Don't you like my advice?*
Je n'aime pas du tout son pantalon. *I don't like his trousers at all.*

 Use the words on this page, the previous page and the next to practise talking about what you like or don't like, what does and doesn't interest you. If your interests or pet hates aren't included, look them up in a dictionary and make a note of them. There are tips on using a dictionary on page 99.

Remember that where English uses a verb ending in -ing after like, *French uses an infinitive or a noun:* J'aime nager/la natation *I like swimming,* Il aime lire/la lecture *He likes reading.*

wordbank

les tâches ménagères *household jobs*
faire du jardinage *to garden*
tondre la pelouse *to cut the grass*, **couper la haie** *to cut the hedge*
faire du bricolage *to do DIY*
repeindre *to decorate*, **tapisser** *to wallpaper*, **peindre** *to paint*

faire les courses *to do the food shopping*
faire la cuisine *to cook*
donner à manger *to feed*
... au bébé *the baby*, **... au chien** *the dog*, **... au hamster** *the hamster*
s'occuper *to look after*
... du lapin *the rabbit*, **... du poney** *the pony*, **... du cheval** *the horse*
promener le chien *to walk the dog*
ranger *to tidy up, to clear up*

épousseter *to dust*, **passer l'aspirateur** *to vacuum*
nettoyer *to clean*
    le four *the oven*, **les fenêtres** *the windows*
    la salle de bains *the bathroom*
laver *to wash*
    la vaisselle *the dishes*, **le sol** *the floor*, **la voiture** *the car*
faire le lit *to make the bed*
faire la lessive *to do the washing*
étendre le linge *to hang out the washing*
repasser *to iron*
faire de la couture *to sew*
charger/vider *to load/unload*
    la machine à laver *the washing machine*
    le lave-vaisselle *the dishwasher*
    le sèche-linge *the dryer*
vider/sortir les poubelles *empty/put out the rubbish*

S'occuper du lapin means *to look after the rabbit* but **poser un lapin à quelqu'un** doesn't have the literal meaning *to put a rabbit on someone*. It means *not to turn up for a meeting, to stand someone up*.
Lisa m'a posé un lapin hier soir. Lisa stood me up yesterday evening.

using *on*

On is an essential little word you need in a natural-sounding French conversation. Literally it means *one* (**On doit être patient.** *One must be patient*), but it is very flexible. As *one* is a bit old-fashioned and stilted in modern everyday conversation in English, **on** is usually translated as *you*, *we*, *they* or *people*. In spoken language, it very often replaces **nous** when you're referring to *we*.

On is very easy to use: it takes the same form of the verb that follows **il** and **elle** (third person singular), even when it refers to lots of people. You can use it with a verb in any tense.

On y va! *Let's go!*
On sort demain? *Shall we go out tomorrow?*
Est-ce qu'on peut visiter le musée en fauteuil roulant? *Can you/we go round the museum in a wheelchair?*
Généralement en France, on mange du pain avec le repas. *In France, people generally eat bread with a meal.*
Au Maroc, on boit du thé à la menthe. *In Morocco, they drink mint tea.*
Dans les années soixante, on n'avait pas de portables. *In the sixties, we/ people didn't have mobile phones.*

You might want to use **on** when describing your likes and dislikes or your daily routine.
Pendant la semaine, on se lève à six heures. *During the week, we get up at six o'clock.*
Le weekend, on aime bien faire la grasse matinée. *We like to have a lie-in at the weekend.*
On ne mange pas beaucoup le matin. *We don't eat a lot in the mornings.*
On ne fume plus. *We don't smoke any more.*

On can often be used where English uses a passive verb:
Ici on parle français. *French is spoken here.*
On n'a rien trouvé. *Nothing was found.*
On a déjà nettoyé la chambre. *The room has already been cleaned.*

On can also be used where in English we would say *someone*:
On sonne. *Someone's ringing the bell.*
On m'a volé mon sac. *Someone stole my bag.*

expressing a preference

Je préfère **les épinards.** *I prefer spinach.*
Je préfère mon vieux portable. *I like my old phone better.*
Je préfère ne pas savoir. *I prefer not to know.*
Je préfère celui-ci à celui-là. *I prefer this one to that one.*
On préfère y aller à pied. *We prefer to walk there.*
Nous préférons l'autre; il y a plus d'ombre. *We like the other one better; there's more shade.*

Je préférerais **avoir plus d'options.** *I would prefer to have more options.*
Je préférerais ne pas y aller tout seul. *I'd rather not go on my own.*
On préférerait y aller en voiture: c'est plus rapide. *We'd rather go by car: it's quicker.*

Better is **meilleur** when it's an adjective, i.e. when it means *more good*. It goes in front of the noun, and it changes to match that noun, adding **-e** for a feminine word, **-s** for masculine plural and **-es** for feminine plural:
Ce gâteau est meilleur: il est moins lourd. *This cake is better: it's less heavy.*
J'ai une meilleure idée. *I've got a better idea.*
Notre université est parmi les meilleures du monde. *Our university is among the best in the world.*

Better is **mieux** when it's an adverb, i.e. when it means *more well*. It usually goes after the verb and never changes.
Je vais mieux aujourd'hui. *I feel better today.*
Les enfants vont mieux aussi. *The children are better too.*
Je conduis mieux quand j'écoute de la musique. *I drive better when I listen to music.*
Laquelle marche mieux? *Which one works better/best?*

The word for *favourite* is **préféré**. Like the majority of adjectives, it comes after the noun it describes.
Vivaldi est mon compositeur préféré. *Vivaldi's my favourite composer.*
Londres est ma ville préférée. *London is my favourite city.*
Devinez quels sont mes sites web préférés. *Guess which my favourite (web) sites are.*
Voici mes recettes préférées. *Here are my favourite recipes.*

talking the talk

Nico	Dis donc, Sophie, tu n'aimes pas le sport, toi?
Sophie	Si, moi, j'aime bien. Je fais même beaucoup de sport. Je fais un peu d'équitation mais surtout de la natation. En fait, mon sport préféré, c'est la voile. J'adore ça! Et toi, tu es sportif?
Nico	Euh ben … oui, assez, hein, oui. L'activité physique, c'est super important pour le bien-être, hein! Moi, je fais de l'escalade; ça me plaît bien et j'ai les qualités qu'il faut: je suis déterminé et je sais coopérer avec les autres. C'est important, ça, la coopération, quand on fait de l'escalade.
Sophie	De l'escalade, tu es sérieux? Mais c'est hyper dangereux, ça, non?
Nico	Nooooon! C'est génial! Mais, à vrai dire, je pense que mon activité préférée, c'est la randonnée.
Sophie	Vraiment? Tu aimes les activités de plein air, alors!
Nico	Exact. Pas toi? Les beaux paysages, l'air pur…
Sophie	Mmm. Les mouches, les abeilles, les guêpes, les moustiques …
Nico	Oh là là … je vois, tu n'aimes pas les insectes! Je comprends maintenant pourquoi tu préfères les sports nautiques!

checkpoint 7

1 Which is the odd one out and why? **abeille, ortie, mouche, moustique, guêpe**

2 How would you say in French: *We really like the room?*

3 If **Est-ce que les jeux vidéo l'intéressent?** means *Is he interested in computer games?*, what's the French for *Are they interested in computer games?*

4 How do you tell somebody in French that you don't like cheese?

5 If someone tells you **Vous chantez comme une casserole**, is it a compliment?

6 What is the opposite of **j'adore** *I love*?

7 Would you use **j'aimais** or **j'ai aimé** while commenting on a wine you've recently tasted?

8 How do you spell the French word for *favourite* when used to talk about French wines, a region, a museum, music, films, photos?

9 Which expresses a stronger dislike: **Je n'aime pas trop** or **Je n'aime pas du tout**?

10 Which version of **préférer** follows **tu**: préfère, préfères, préférez? And which follows **vous**?

11 Can you give two different ways to say *I like jazz*, using **aimer** and **plaire**?

12 Give two different words/phrases that could go after **je n'aime pas** to say that you really don't like something.

13 What's the word that needs to be added to **J'ai .... aimé la peinture** for it to mean *I've always liked painting*?

14 Which of these means that the speaker would like some water? **J'aime bien l'eau. J'aimais l'eau. Je voudrais de l'eau.**

15 Is **meilleur** or **mieux** the word missing from **Ce plat est ....?** *This dish is better.*

16 These words are used with **J'aime** in a **sondage** *survey*. Put them in order, starting with the least favourable: **beaucoup, assez, énormément**

17 How would you tell someone that you don't much enjoy vacuuming, that you prefer gardening?

how to
use a dictionary

A dictionary is an essential tool for language learning, allowing you to personalise structures and talk about exactly what you choose.
There are a number of dictionaries on the internet and available as apps. Some of them are much better presented, more detailed and more user-friendly than others, and it's a case of trying a few and seeing which suits you.
In print, dictionaries come in all sizes from tiny pocket versions to huge tomes. It's not necessarily a case of the bigger the better: a very large dictionary can be so densely packed with information that it becomes overwhelming.

grammatical terms and abbreviations

As with most tools, there's a skill to using a dictionary effectively. And, because of fundamental differences between the languages, using a French > English dictionary raises different issues from using the English > French version.

For both, you need to understand basic terms such as adjective, adverb, noun, verb (page 172), because each dictionary entry is defined by its grammatical category. This is abbreviated, and the abbreviations are very similar in both languages, with *noun* a notable exception: its translation is **nom** or **substantif** and dictionaries abbreviate it to **n.** or **subst.**

art. **article** *article*	*adj.* **adjectif** *adjective*
adv. **adverbe** *adverb*	*fam.* **familier** *familiar/colloquial*
f./fém. **féminin** *feminine*	*inv.* **invariable** *invariable*
irrég **irrégulier** *irregular*	*m./masc.* **masculin** *masculine*
n. **nom** *noun*	*pl./plur.* **pluriel** *plural*
pers. **personne** *person*	*prép.* **préposition** *preposition*
pron. **pronom** *pronoun*	*ptp.* **participe passé** *past participle*
s./sing. **singulier** *singular*	*subst.* **substantif** *noun*
v. **verbe** *verb*	

v.i./v.tr. **verbe intransitif/transitif** *intransitive/transitive verb*
v.pr. **verbe pronominal** *reflexive verb*
vulg. **vulgaire** *vulgar*

Most dictionaries include a comprehensive list of the abbreviations used.

français → anglais

Some words belong in more than one grammatical category, and a few nouns look identical but have a different gender and meaning.

---

finale I *nm (mus)* finale. **II** *nf (sport)* final. **III** *adj* final
livre I *nm* book; **II** *nf* **1** pound, half a kilo **2** *(monnaie)* pound
personnel I *nm* personnel, staff. **II** *adj* personal: **fortune ~le** private fortune
premier, -ière I *adj* **1** first **au ~ étage** on the first floor; **2** top **de ~ ière qualité** top quality; **II** *nm* first (one) **parler le ~** to speak first; **III** *nf* **1** *(gén)* first **une ~ mondiale** a world first **2** *(théât)* first night **3** *(aut)* first gear, *(transp)* **en ~** in first class, *(scol)* year 12

Many online dictionaries allow you to search for a word exactly as you come across it. But a traditional French > English dictionary lists nouns in the singular, adjectives with the masculine singular ending and verbs in the infinitive. This means that a word you're looking for may not appear exactly as you came across it. For example:

- **Épinards** is the plural of **épinard** *spinach*, which is what you'll find listed. Irregular plurals such as **gâteau/gâteaux** *cake*, **journal/journaux** *newspaper*, **œil/yeux** *eye/eyes* tend to be flagged up.

- Nouns are usually listed in their masculine form, so to find the meaning of **serveuse**, you will need to work out the masculine form of that noun, which is **serveur**. Under **serveur**, you will see **serveur, -euse** *waiter, waitress*.

- To find the meaning of **sortons**, you need to work out that **-ons** is the verb ending for **nous** and that the infinitive is **sortir** *to go/take out*.

- If ever you struggle with a verb, think of irregulars. For example, **vais** *I go* bears little resemblance to **aller** *to go*. However, a good dictionary will include common irregularities.

English → French

Many English words belong in a single grammatical category, e.g. *terrain* is always a noun, *write* can only be a verb, *genuine* can only be an adjective. But there are also many that belong in two or more categories, e.g. *sock* can be something you wear on your foot (noun) or *to hit somebody* (verb); *snipe* can be a bird (noun), *to shoot* or *to jeer* (verbs); *back* can be the rear part (noun), *to support* (verb) or the opposite of *front* (adjective). You need to be sure to locate the part of speech and the meaning you want.

---

content I *n* **1** contenu *m*; **2 book** ~**s** table des matières *m*. **II** *adj* content, satisfait.

lock I *n* **1** serrure *f*: **combination** ~ serrure à combinaison; **2** (*hair*) boucle *f*; **3** (*wrestling*) clé *f* de bras; **4** (*rugby*) deuxième ligne *f*; **5** (*canal*) écluse *f*. **II** *v* fermer à clé, verrouiller.

pitch I *n* **1** (*music*) ton *m*; **2** (*sales*) argument de vente *m*; **3** (*sports*) terrain *m*; **4** bitume, goudron, asphalte *m*; **5** ~ **and putt** minigolf *m*. **II** *adj* ~ **black** nuit noire f. **III** *v* **1** throw lancer; **2** (*tent*) planter.

table I *n* **1** (*furniture*) table *f*; **bedside** ~ table de chevet *f*; **dressing** ~ coiffeuse *f*; **2** (*chart*) tableau *m*; **3** (*chem*) **periodic** ~ tableau périodique *m*. **4** (*math*) ~**s** tables de multiplication *f pl*; **5** (sport) ~ **tennis** ping-pong *m*. **II** *adj* de table. **III** *v* ~ **a motion** soumettre une proposition.

Spelling is, of course, critical. While *hangar* and *hanger* might sound the same in English, they have no connection whatsoever in French: *a hangar* is **un hangar** while *a hanger* is **un porte-manteau** or **un cintre**.

Armed with a dictionary, it can be easy to get carried away and start translating word for word from English. One of the many reasons why this is a recipe for disaster lies in English phrasal verbs, which are made up of two parts: a verb followed by a preposition or adverb, e.g.

ask in, ask out, ask around
break down, break in, break out, break up
get away, get by, get in, get off, get on, get over
give away, give back, give in, give up
hang on, hang out, hang up
throw away, throw up

Each has a specific meaning and so has to be treated as an individual item, not as two words. More often than not, the French equivalent is a single word.

look v 1 regarder; 2 ~ **at** regarder, analyser; 3 ~ **after** s'occuper de; 4 ~ **into** rechercher, étudier; 5 ~ **for** chercher; 6 ~ **out** faire attention; 7 ~ **over** (*inspect*) inspecter, (*overlook*) oublier, négliger; 8 ~ **up** (*seek info*) chercher.

put v 1 mettre; 2 ~ **away** ranger; 3 ~ **down** (*disparage*) dénigrer, (*kill*) euthanasier; 4 ~ **off** (*deter*) dissuader, décourager; (*postpone*) reporter; 5 ~ **out** (*fire*) éteindre, (*inconvenience*) déranger; 6 ~ **up** (*accommodate*) héberger; (*raise*) augmenter; 7 ~ **up with** supporter, tolérer.

take v 1 prendre; 2 ~ **after** ressembler à; 3 ~ **apart** démonter; 4 ~ **away**, (*math*) soustraire, (*food*) à emporter; 5 ~ **off** enlever; (*imitate*) imiter; (*aero*) décoller; 5 ~ **out** extraire, retirer, inviter à sortir.

If ever you're not sure which option to use, look it up in the other half of the dictionary to see if it gives the translation you're looking for.

Above all, never attempt a literal translation of idiomatic phrases such as *the elephant in the room, the dog's dinner, I could eat a horse, to go cold turkey, he's my rock, to spit with rain* or *to spit feathers*, which don't have the idiomatic meaning in French.

French has many interesting idioms of its own:
le coup de foudre *love at first sight* (lit. *a lightning strike*)
faire la grasse matinée *to have a lie in* (lit. *to do a fat morning*)
coûter les yeux de la tête *to cost an arm and a leg* (lit. *to cost the eyes in your head*)

1 Which of these fit into more than one grammatical category (i.e. verb and adjective, verb and noun)?
clear, drive, duck, jam, moral, online, permit, port, present, press, rock, sand, sardine, square, squash, state

2 Work out what you'd need to look up to find the English meaning of these words, then look them up in a dictionary.

nouns: **animaux, travaux, coraux**
adjectives: **familiaux, blanche, joyeuse, belles**
verbs: **perdez, comprennent**

(See page 199 for answers.)

huit
making plans

The word **une fête**, originally *a feast day*, is now used for any celebration, festival, saint's day or party. **Un jour de fête** is *a day of celebration*, and **les fêtes** are celebrated in style, with family, food and drink playing a central role. If you're invited along, it's worth making sure you know how to accept or to decline graciously. It's also pretty crucial to be able to talk about the date and the time.

The French embrace their celebrations with enthusiasm, starting twelve days after Christmas with **l'Épiphanie**, also known as **la fête des Rois**. In February, pancakes are made for **la Chandeleur** *Candlemas* and **Mardi gras** *Shrove Tuesday*, and lovers dine out on the 14th for **la Saint-Valentin**. After **Pâques** *Easter* comes **la fête du travail** *Labour Day* on May 1st — this is also called **la fête du muguet** *Lily of the Valley Day* and lily of the valley is given for luck. People take to the streets again on **le quatorze juillet** *the 14th of July* for **la fête nationale** *Bastille Day*. It starts with a military parade in Paris and ends with street parties and fireworks all over France. The next big family gathering revolves around **le réveillon de Noël** *Christmas Eve* and **le jour de Noël** *Christmas Day*. **Le réveillon de la Saint-Sylvestre** *New Year's Eve* is usually celebrated with friends.

When a public holiday falls on a Tuesday or a Thursday, many people make a long weekend of it by taking the Monday or Friday off as well. This is called *making the bridge*: **faire le pont**.

when?

lundi *Monday*
mardi *Tuesday*
mercredi *Wednesday*
jeudi *Thursday*
vendredi *Friday*
samedi *Saturday*
dimanche *Sunday*

Je ne peux pas venir jeudi: le jeudi/tous les jeudis j'aide Céline au magasin.
I can't come on Thursday: I help Céline in the shop on Thursdays/ every Thursday.
À dimanche. *See you on Sunday.*
C'est fermé le dimanche. *It's closed on Sundays.*

janvier *January*	**juillet** *July*
février *February*	**août** *August*
mars *March*	**septembre** *September*
avril *April*	**octobre** *October*
mai *May*	**novembre** *November*
juin *June*	**décembre** *December*

En août/tous les mois d'août je vais au pays de Galles. *I go to Wales in August/every August.*
Je suis né(e), il est né/elle est née *I was born, he/she was born*
    ... en janvier *in January.*
    ... le premier juin *on the first of June.*
    ... le douze octobre *on October the 12th.*
    ... en mille neuf cent quatre-vingt-treize *in 1993.*
    ... en deux mille quinze *in 2015.*

There are several ways of arranging to meet someone.
Ça vous va, le quinze? *How about the 15th?*
Lundi, ça vous convient? *Does Monday suit you?*
Retrouvons-nous samedi. *Let's get together on Saturday.*
On se retrouve mardi/le vingt-deux? *Shall we meet on Tuesday/on the 22nd?*

 In French, days of the week and months do not start with a capital letter. They are all masculine.

what time?

The general word for time, as in *There's not enough time*, is **le temps**, but *time* as in *time of day* is **l'heure**.

Quand? À quelle heure?	*When? At what time?*
à midi/à minuit	*at midday/at midnight*
à une heure	*at one o'clock*
à deux heures, à trois heures	*at two o'clock, at three o'clock, etc.*
à six heures et demie	*at half past six*
à neuf heures trente	*at 09.30*
à quatre heures quarante	*at 04.40*
à vingt-trois heures	*at 23.00, at 11 p.m.*
à trois heures de l'après-midi	*at three (o'clock) in the afternoon*

> Although you can miss out *o'clock* in English, in French you always have to include **heure**, except with **midi** and **minuit**.

avant minuit	*before midnight*
avant onze heures	*before 11 o'clock*
de neuf heures à treize heures	*from 09.00 to 13.00*
jusqu'à midi	*until midday*
jusqu'à dix heures du soir	*until ten o'clock in the evening*
après deux heures du matin	*after two o'clock in the morning*

You confirm a time in much the same way as the date:

Huit heures trente, ça vous va? *How about 8.30?*
Six heures trente, ça vous convient? *Does 6.30 suit you?*
Rendez-vous à sept heures devant le cinéma. *See you at seven o'clock in front of the cinema.*
C'est un peu tôt/un peu tard, non? *That's a bit early/a bit late, isn't it?*
J'y serai à dix heures précises. *I'll be there at exactly ten o'clock.*

> Listen out for other expressions relating to time:
>
> **à l'heure** *on time*
> **à cinq heures pile** *at five on the dot*
> **à l'aube** *at the crack of dawn*
> **au petit matin** *in the small hours*
> **aux heures de pointe** *at rush hour*

suggesting things to do

The simplest way of suggesting doing something is to use **on: On va à la plage?** *Shall we go to the beach? Are we going to the beach?*

Another option is to use **si on** + the imperfect (page 78). **Si on allait** literally means *if one went.*

Si on allait à Quiberon? *How about going to Quiberon?*
Si on faisait un piquenique? *Shall we have a picnic?*
Si on allait prendre un verre au bar ? *Let's have a drink in the bar.*

Si can be used with **tu** and **vous** as well.

Si tu venais déjeuner à la maison demain? *How about you come to us for lunch tomorrow?*
Samedi, nous allons à la montagne. Et si vous veniez aussi? *On Saturday we're going to the mountains. Would you care to come too?*

Alternatively, you might use **pourquoi ne pas?** *why not?* with an **infinitive.**
Pourquoi ne pas faire une partie de tennis demain? *Why don't we have a game of tennis tomorrow?*
Pourquoi ne pas aller à la fête du vin dimanche? *Why don't we go to the wine festival on Sunday?*
Pourquoi ne pas prendre le petit déjeuner chez nous? *Why not have breakfast at our place?*

Other phrases used with an infinitive include:
Ça te dit de faire un peu de voile sur le lac? *Would you like to do a bit of sailing on the lake?*
Ça vous dit d'aller marcher le long de la rivière? *How would you like to walk along the river?*
Tu voudrais faire une promenade? *Would you like to go for a walk?*
Vous voudriez venir nous retrouver au bar? *Would you like to join us in the bar?*
On pourrait aller au ciné? *How about going to the cinema?*
On pourrait peut-être se retrouver au resto? *How about meeting up at the restaurant?*

A suggestion can also take the form of an invitation:
Vous êtes tous invités chez nous vendredi: ma mère fête ses soixante ans. *You're all invited to ours on Friday: my mother is celebrating her 60th birthday.*

wordbank

Structures like **pourquoi ne pas** and **ça vous dit de** are easy to use — you can follow them with any phrase starting with an infinitive, such as:

aller en ville *go into town*

se promener dans la vieille ville *wander round the old town*

voir l'amphithéâtre *see the amphitheatre*

visiter la cathédrale *visit the cathedral*

faire les magasins *visit the shops, go window shopping*

aller à l'opéra/au concert *go to the opera/to a concert*

manger des crêpes *eat pancakes*

passer chez Simon *drop in on Simon*

louer un vélo *rent a bike*

prendre le train pour aller à ... *take the train to go to ...*

explorer les environs *explore the surrounding area*

aller à la fête de la truffe/de la fraise *go to the truffle/strawberry fair*

faire un tour au marché fermier *wander round the farmers' market*

flâner dans les vignobles *stroll round the vineyards*

déguster les vins/les produits locaux *taste local wines/products*

faire du cheval; il y a un centre équestre pas loin *go riding; there are stables nearby*

monter sur les collines/les falaises *climb the hills/the cliffs*

faire de l'escalade en montagne/de l'alpinisme *go mountain climbing*

faire une promenade en raquettes *go snowshoeing*

aller se promener le long de la plage *go for a walk along the beach*

jouer aux boules/à la pétanque *have a game of boules/petanque*

aller nager *go swimming*

faire une promenade en bateau *go on a boat trip*

aller pêcher en haute mer *go deep-sea fishing*

essayer le ski nautique *have a go at waterskiing*

prendre une leçon à l'école de plongée *have a lesson at the diving school*

traverser l'île à pied *walk across the island*

> *Practise using a few of these with, for example, vous voudriez. Out loud, of course. Then practise the imperfect by using some others with Si on ... e.g. Si on traversait l'île à pied? How about walking across the island?*

accepting and declining graciously

Merci de m'avoir invité(e)/de nous avoir invité(e)s. *Thank you for inviting me/us.*

Je vous remercie pour l'invitation. *Thank you for the invitation.*

Je suis très touché(e) par votre invitation. *I'm very touched by your invitation.*

C'est très gentil(le) de ta/votre part. *It's very kind of you.*

yes please

Oui, bien sûr! *Yes, of course!*

Bien volontiers. *I'd love to./We'd love to.*

D'accord! *OK/Yes please!*

Certainement. *Certainly.*

Super! Génial! *Brilliant! Fantastic!*

Je serais ravi(e) *Gladly.*

Avec grand plaisir. *With great pleasure.*

Quelle bonne/super idée! *What a good/fantastic idea!*

J'y serai! *I'll be there!*

Comptez sur moi! *Count on me!*

J'ai hâte! *I can't wait!*

Il me tarde déjà. *I look forward to it.*

no thank you

Malheureusement ... *Unfortunately ...*

Je regrette mais ... *I'm sorry but ...*

C'est impossible. *It's impossible.*

Je ne pourrai pas. *I won't be able to.*

Je ne peux pas/Nous ne pouvons pas ... *I/we can't ...*

Je ne pense pas pouvoir... *I don't think I can ...*

Je ne suis pas sûr(e) de pouvoir *I'm not sure if I can*

  ... à cause du travail. *... for work reasons.*

  ... parce que je ne suis pas libre. *... because I'm not free.*

  ... je suis déjà invité(e) ce jour-là. *... I already have an invitation for that day.*

Quel dommage! *What a shame!*

C'est vraiment dommage mais ... *It's a real shame but ...*

J'aimerais bien mais ... *I wish I could but ...*

Merci quand même. *Thank you anyway.*

There may be times when you want to be more expressive:

Je crains de ne pas pouvoir. *I'm afraid I can't.*
Je suis navré(e) de devoir refuser. *I'm really sorry I have to decline.*
J'espère pouvoir venir mais ... *I hope to be there but ...*
Je suis désolé(e) mais ... *I'm sorry but ...*
Je suis navré(e) mais ... *I'm really sorry but ...*
Je vais faire de mon mieux mais *I'll do my best but*
       ... je serai en déplacement. *... I'll be out of town.*
       ... on a déjà quelque chose de prévu. *... we've already got something on.*
Je vais voir ce que je peux faire *I'll see what I can do*
       ... on se sait jamais! *... you never know!*

But there may also be times when you want to make it clear that you're not keen.

Peut-être un autre jour. *Maybe another day.*
Une autre fois. *Another time.*
Ça m'est égal. *I don't mind.*
Ça ne me dit pas grand-chose. *It doesn't really appeal to me.*
Ça ne me dit rien. *It doesn't appeal to me at all.*
Non, merci. *No, thank you.*

And if **non merci** doesn't get through, you could try:
Ne compte pas dessus. *Don't count on it.*
Ne te fais pas pas trop d'illusions. *Dream on.*
Ce n'est pas demain la veille. *That'll be the day. Don't hold your breath.*
lit. *Tomorrow is not the day before*, i.e. *It's impossible.*

talking about the future

French verbs have endings for talking about the future. Unlike present and imperfect endings, these are simply tacked on to the infinitive (although infinitives ending in **-re** drop the **-e** first).

je	-ai	**nous**	-ons
tu	-as	**vous**	-ez
il/elle/on	-a	**ils/elles**	-ont

arriver *to arrive*	**j'arriverai** *I will arrive*
sortir *to go out*	**elle sortira** *she will go out*
répondre *to reply*	**nous répondrons** *we will reply*

Vous resterez bien manger ce soir? *You'll stay for dinner with us tonight, won't you?*
Je sortirai le chien plus tard. *I'll take the dog out for a walk later.*
Elle nous attendra. *She will wait for us.*

Être *to be* is irregular – **je serai** *I will be* – as are certain other verbs. The 'r' sound before the endings helps makes them recognisable as being the future.

aller *to go* → j'irai	**savoir** *to know* → je saurai
avoir *to have* → j'aurai	**tenir** *to hold* → je tiendrai
devoir *to have to* → je devrai	**venir** *to come* → je viendrai
faire *to do* → je ferai	**voir** *to see* → je verrai
pouvoir *to be able to* → je pourrai	

En septembre, mon fils ira à la fac. *In September my son will go to uni.*
Il y aura une réunion demain. *There will be a meeting tomorrow.*
Vous viendrez bien au marché avec moi? *You'll be coming to the market with me, won't you?*
Mes amis ne pourront pas m'héberger cette fois-ci. *My friends won't be able to put me up this time.*

Although English uses the present after *when*, French uses the future:
Quand vous arriverez, il sera trop tard. *When you <u>get</u> there, it will be too late.*
Quand il aura son bac, il fera des études de médecine. *When he <u>has</u> his baccalaureate (A levels), he'll study medicine.*
Tu m'aideras à plier les draps quand tu pourras? *Will you help me fold the sheets when you <u>can</u>?*

saying what you're going to do

In French, just as in English, you say you're **going to** do something when talking about the near future. You use the present tense of **aller** *to go* + the infinitive.

je	vais	chanter	*I'm going to sing*
tu	vas	partir	*you're going to leave*
il/elle, on	va	boire	*he/she's, one's going to drink*
nous	allons	essayer	*we're going to try*
vous	allez	répondre	*you're going to answer*
ils/elles	vont	choisir	*they're going to choose*

Je vais faire de mon mieux. *I'm going to do my best.*
Tu penses qu'il va pleuvoir? *Do you think it's going to rain?*
À tous les coups, ils vont perdre! *They're going to lose for certain!*
Vous allez revenir bientôt? *Are you going to come back soon?*
Quand est-ce que tu vas me donner ta réponse? *When are you going to give me your answer?*
Elle ne va pas mettre une robe blanche pour son mariage? *Isn't she going to wear a white dress for her wedding?*

To say that something is *not* going to happen, *never* going to happen or *not* going to happen *again*, you wrap **ne ... pas, ne ... jamais** or **ne ... plus** around **aller**:
Je ne vais pas sortir ce soir. *I'm not going to go out tonight.*
Ils ne vont jamais me croire! *They're never going to believe me!*
Je ne vais plus acheter de chaussures sur Internet. *I'm not going to buy shoes on the internet again.*

There are some imaginative ways of emphasising that something's just about to happen. They're all followed by an infinitive:
Il est sur le point de perdre son permis de conduire. *He's on the verge of losing his driving licence.*
J'étais à deux doigts de raccrocher. *I was this close to hanging up.*
lit: *to be two fingers away from*
Nous étions à un cheveu de rater notre train! *We were a whisker away from missing our train!*

Using **être sur le point de** negatively means there's no way you'll do something again: **Je ne suis pas sur le point de le revoir, celui-là!** *I'm not about to see him again for sure!*

weather permitting

Outdoor activities such as sailing, flying, mountaineering, skiing – and even organising a barbecue – require thinking ahead and understanding **la météo/le bulletin météo/les prévisions météorologiques** *the weather forecast.*

Il va faire quel temps demain? *What's the weather going to be like tomorrow?*
Comment sera la météo les jours prochains? *What's the weather forecast for the next few days?*
On prévoit du soleil pour dimanche. *The forecast is for sun on Sunday.*

Dès demain, il y aura une canicule. *As from tomorrow, there's going to be a heatwave.*
On s'attend à des vents forts. *Strong winds are forecast.*
Pourquoi ne pas faire un barbecue s'il fait beau? *Why don't we have a barbecue if it's fine?*
Même s'il n'y a pas beaucoup de vent, je voudrais faire de la planche à voile. *Even if there isn't much wind, I'd like to go windsurfing.*
S'il y a assez de neige, on peut aller faire du snowboard. *If there's enough snow, we can go snowboarding.*
Si la météo est favorable, on ira faire une randonnée en montagne. *If the forecast is good, we'll go hiking in the mountains.*

The image of a frog on a ladder in a jar is often linked to the weather forecast in France. This dates back to the research of a zoologist in the 19th century who noted that when the weather was about to turn dry, the frogs would climb up the ladder. Now, when a weather forecaster gets it wrong, people say **Sa grenouille est malade** *His frog is sick.*

The weather is often the subject of conversation:
Qu'est-ce qu'il fait beau! *What lovely weather!*
Qu'est-ce qu'il fait froid! *It's so cold!*
Qu'est-ce qu'il fait lourd aujourd'hui! *Really muggy today, isn't it!*
Quel mauvais temps, hein! *Miserable weather, isn't it?*
Quel vent! Une véritable tempête! *So windy, a real gale!*
Ce petit crachin m'énerve. *This drizzle is getting on my nerves.*
Je déteste quand il pleut comme ça. *I hate it when it rains like this.*
Je ne supporte pas ce brouillard. *I can't stand this fog.*

the weather now

Quel temps fait-il? *What's the weather like?*
Il fait, il y a and c'est are all used in phrases to describe the weather.
Il fait beau/mauvais aujourd'hui. *It's a lovely/horrible day today.*
Il fait quarante degrés à l'ombre. *It's 40 degrees in the shade.*
Il fait trop chaud, c'est la canicule. *It's too hot, it's a heat wave.*
Il fait froid, un froid de canard. *It's cold, freezing cold.* lit. *duck cold.*
Il fait un temps de chien. *It's miserable.* lit. *dog's weather.*
Il fait un peu frais. *It's a bit chilly.*
Il fait doux. *It's mild.*

Il y a un petit vent frais. *There's a bit of a breeze.*
Il y a un vent à décorner les bœufs. *It's blowing a gale.* lit. *There's a wind that removes the horns from the cows.*
Il n'y a pas mal de soleil. *It's quite sunny.*
Il n'y a pas beaucoup de neige. *There's not much snow.*

C'est très humide/orageux. *It's very humid/stormy.*
C'est très brumeux par endroits. *It's very foggy in places.*
Il neige en montagne. *It's snowing in the mountains.*
Il gèle pendant la nuit. *It drops below zero at night.* lit. *It freezes at night.*

... and what it was like

Il faisait quel temps? Il a fait quel temps? *What was the weather like?*
The reply can use the imperfect tense (page 78) or the perfect (page 66), depending on whether you're describing ongoing or one-off weather.
Hier il pleuvait. *It was raining yesterday.*
Il a plu pendant la nuit. *It (has) rained during the night.*
Il neigeait quand nous sommes arrivés. *It was snowing when we arrived.*
Il a neigé pendant trois jours. *It (has) snowed for three days.*

French also uses both tenses for expressions with **il fait** and **il y a**, even though English tends to use only *was*:
il fait chaud *it's hot*; **il faisait chaud, il a fait chaud** *it was hot*
il y a du vent *it's windy*; **il y avait du vent, il y a eu du vent** *it was windy*

Expressions with **c'est** (e.g. **C'est un peu nuageux.** *It's a bit cloudy.*) tend to use only the imperfect in the past:
C'était un peu nuageux. *It was a bit cloudy.*

saying what you would do

Just as there are future verb endings to convey *will/shall do*, there are conditional endings that convey *would do*. *Would* is very often shortened to *'d* in English, e.g. *I'd like, we'd see, he'd prefer.*

These conditional endings fit onto the infinitive, just as future endings do:

je	-ais	nous	-ions
tu	-ais	vous	-iez
il/elle/on	-ait	ils/elles	-aient

All of them, except for the **nous** and **vous** endings, sound the same.

arriver *to arrive*   **j'arriverais** *I would arrive*
sortir *to go out*   **je sortirais** *I would go out*
répondre *to reply*   **je répondrais** *I would reply*

Je n'oserais jamais! *I would never dare!*
Je mangerais bien un croissant mais je suis au régime. *I'd eat a croissant but I'm on a diet.*
Tu aimerais voir une pièce de Molière? *Would you like to see a play by Molière?*

Irregular verbs in the future are the same as irregular verbs in the conditional – the only difference being the endings, e.g:
être *to be* **je serai** *I will be,* **je serais** *I would be,* etc.
avoir *to have* **j'aurai** *I will have,* **j'aurais** *I would have,* etc. (page 110).

Je vous serais très reconnaissant(e). *I would be very grateful.*
Ce serait trop cher. *It would be too expensive.*
J'irais bien faire les soldes cette année. *I wouldn't mind going to the sales this year.*
Il ferait bien de se faire couper les cheveux! *He'd do well to have a hair cut!*

A verb coming after the conditional + *if* is in the *imperfect*.
Je voyagerais plus si j'avais l'argent. *I would travel more if I had the money.*
On reviendrait plus souvent si c'était moins cher. *We'd come more often if it were cheaper.*

The conditional has nothing whatsoever to do with the other English meaning of *would* that refers to the past and means *used to,* as in *She would sit and stare for hours.*

offering good wishes

Special occasions call for good wishes, and **meilleurs vœux** *best wishes* is an all-purpose way of offering them. In addition, every celebration and milestone has a tailor-made greeting:

Bon/Joyeux anniversaire. *Happy Birthday.*
Bonne année et bonne santé. *Wishing you a happy and healthy new year.*
Bonne fête. *Happy name day. Happy saint's day.*
Bonne fête des Mères/Pères. *Happy Mother's/Father's Day.*
Joyeux Noël. *Happy Christmas.*
Joyeuses Pâques. *Happy Easter.*

Merci, à toi/vous de même. *Thank you and the same to you too.*

The custom of offering good wishes isn't confined to big occasions:
Bonne journée. *Have a good day.*
Bonne soirée. *Enjoy your evening.*
Bon weekend. *Have a good weekend.*
Bon séjour. *Have a pleasant stay.*
Bonnes vacances. *Enjoy your holiday. Have a good holiday.*

Amuse-toi bien./Amusez-vous bien. *Have a good time. Enjoy yourself/ yourselves.*
À la tienne! À la vôtre! *Cheers!* (when toasting)
À ta santé! À votre santé! *To your health!* (when toasting)

Bonne chance. *Good luck.*
Bon courage. *Good luck* (for a difficult task ahead).
Bon rétablissement. *Get well soon.*

You can be more formal by starting with **Je te/vous souhaite** *I wish you*:
Je te souhaite plein de bonnes choses. *I wish you all the best.*
Je vous souhaite bon voyage. *I wish you a safe journey.*

Don't be surprised if you hear people say **Merde!** *Sh*t!* in a friendly and encouraging way – they are not being rude but wishing you good luck!

This dates back to 19th-century theatres, when piles of horse manure outside meant lots of spectators, hence a sign that the show was doing well. You cannot mention **chance** *luck* in a theatre: **Ça porte malheur!** *It's bad luck!*

talking the talk

Nico	On se retrouve mardi soir?
Sophie	Mardi soir?
Nico	Ben oui, je sais que ce n'est pas la Chandeleur mais si on allait manger des crêpes? Il y a une nouvelle crêperie, rue Saint-Jean.
Sophie	Bien volontiers. J'adore les crêpes!
Nico	Rendez-vous là-bas alors, à neuf heures, ça te va?
Sophie	Neuf heures, c'est un peu tard, non? Je mange plus tôt, moi!
Nico	À quelle heure alors? Huit heures, ça te convient mieux?
Sophie	Oui, d'accord, huit heures, c'est parfait! Alors, à mardi soir!
Nico	D'accord. Ciao!
Sophie	Quelle bonne idée de venir ici! J'ai trouvé les crêpes super bonnes.
Nico	Moi aussi!
Sophie	Qu'est-ce qu'il a fait beau aujourd'hui! Quel temps il va faire samedi?
Nico	On prévoit du soleil ... à partir de demain, ce sera même la canicule, il paraît!
Sophie	J'ai une idée ... Pourquoi ne pas faire un barbecue chez moi, samedi, s'il fait beau?

verb practice 5

1   Write the future forms of these verbs and say what they mean.
    a   **commencer** .... (tu)
    b   **aller** .... (ils)
    c   **prendre** .... (vous)
    d   **finir** .... (ça)
    e   **mettre** .... (nous)
    f   **tenir** .... (on)
    g   **devoir** .... (je)
    h   **faire** .... (il)
    i   **pouvoir** .... (nous)
    j   **venir** .... (elle)
    k   **être** .... (je)
    l   **avoir** .... (tu)

2   Now change them all to the conditional and say what they mean.

3   Identify these as present, perfect, imperfect, future or conditional
    and say what they mean. If you need to refresh your memory of the
    tenses, see pages 182–187.
    a   **ça dépendra**   b   **je me suis préparé**
    c   **il a téléphoné**   d   **ils étudieraient**
    e   **nous déciderons**   f   **elle va revenir**
    g   **ils préféraient**   h   **vous intervenez**
    i   **ils sont allés**   j   **je mangeais**

4   Choose the correct options to make these sentences correct.
    a   S'il **pleut/pleuvra** demain, je visiterai les musées.
    b   Si **j'avais/j'aurais** de l'argent, je t'inviterais!
    c   Je passerai la voir si vous me **donnerez/donnez** son adresse.
    d   Si j'avais le temps, **j'irais/j'irai** plus souvent à la salle de gym.
    e   On aimerait bien venir plus souvent si on **pouvait/pourrait**.
    f   Si je peux, je vous **aiderai/aidais** à nettoyer le jardin.

1   Which are the two days on either side of **vendredi**, and the three months before **août**?

2   What's the difference in meaning between **Je viendrai à seize heures** and **je viendrais à seize heures**?

3   What do you add to **joyeux** or **bon** on someone's birthday, at Christmas, to wish them to get well, on a journey and at the weekend?

4   Compose a text to your friends inviting them to come and celebrate Christmas Eve at your place, using *Would you like to* ...

5   Which of these are you unlikely to use when accepting an invitation? **Je serais ravi, avec plaisir, malheureusement, volontiers**

6   What phrase can you use to confirm a meeting (time or place)? And what can you add to **à sept heures** to emphasise punctuality?

7   In reply to good wishes, how do you say *The same to you*?

8   What is the difference between **Lundi je vais au marché** and **Le lundi je vais au marché**?

9   **Je visiterai les musées pendant mon séjour à Paris.** Which word has to change for this to say *I would visit the museums*?

10 Which phrase will you use when you're politely declining an invitation: **Ça ne me dit rien, Comptez sur moi!, Ne compte pas dessus, C'est vraiment dommage**

11 **Si tu .... moins occupé** *busy*, **on irait faire un tour au village.** Is the missing word **étais** or **serais**? What does the sentence mean?

12 How do **Il fait froid** and **C'est pluvieux** change when referring to last week?

13 Complete the answer to the question: **C'est quand la fête du muguet? La fête du muguet, c'est** ....

14 Talking to a couple, and therefore using **vous**, how would you say *I'd wait for you if I could*?

15 What does **aux heures de pointe** mean?

16 How do you wish someone luck for an exam? And for a difficult task ahead?

17 **Ça vous dit de faire de la voile à dix heures le trente mai?** Reply saying *Sorry, I can't*. Then suggest midday on the following day, starting with *How about us going* ...

neuf
needs must

Words like *want, must, may, can, could, should, ought* crop up all the time in conversation. These are not words you can easily look up in a dictionary: in French they're expressed via three key verbs **vouloir** *to want,* **devoir** *to have to* and **pouvoir** *to be able to.*

You're likely to have already come across them, probably associated with practical situations such as:
Je voudrais réserver une chambre. *I'd like to book a room.*
Est-ce que je dois changer de train? *Do I have to change trains?*
Je peux payer ici? *Can I pay here?*

Too often they stay associated in the mind with these situations and their potential usefulness in general conversation gets overlooked – when in reality these verbs are truly indispensable. They take your French to a new level, letting you voice your wildest dreams and your most mundane obligations.

Vouloir, devoir and **pouvoir** are easy to use and they all work in the same way, with the verb following them in the infinitive. When you add information, it goes after the two verbs: **Je voudrais rencontrer votre fils** *I'd like to meet your son* ... unless it's a pronoun, in which case it gets sandwiched between the two: **Je voudrais le rencontrer** *I'd like to meet him.*

want

Vouloir is the verb you use to say what you want to do. It's also how you find out what other people want and is the basis of invitations.
It's irregular in the present tense:

je veux, tu veux, il veut, nous voulons, vous voulez, ils veulent

Je veux **prendre une photo de groupe.** *I want to take a group photo.*
Je veux **te montrer quelque chose.** *I want to show you something.*
Je ne veux pas **vous déranger mais ...** *I don't want to bother you but ...*
Nous voulons **savoir comment ça marche.** *We want to know how it works.*
Nous voulons **vous remercier.** *We want to thank you.*
Son père? Elle ne veut pas **le contacter.** *Her father? She doesn't want to get in touch with him.*
Je ne sais pas ce que les autres veulent **faire.** *I don't know what the others want to do.*
Tu veux **acheter du vin?** *Do you want to buy some wine?*
Tu ne veux pas **venir avec nous?** *Don't you want to come with us?*
Vous voulez **aller en ville?** *Do you want to go to town?*
Vous voulez **vous reposer?** *Do you want to rest?*

I want can sound rather blunt or demanding, so **je voudrais** *I'd like*, which is the conditional, can be used instead, often with **bien**. To talk about other people, it's just a matter of substituting **-ais** with the relevant ending (page 114).

Je voudrais **bien voir le port.** *I'd really like to see the harbour.*
Je voudrais **proposer un toast.** *I'd like to propose a toast.*
Je voudrais bien **sortir avec lui.** *I'd love to go out with him.*
Nous voudrions **mieux vous connaître.** *We'd like to get to know you better.*
Elle voudrait **en savoir plus.** *She would like to find out more.*
Ils voudraient **vous aider.** *They would like to help you.*

Tu voudrais **goûter aux huîtres?** *Would you like to try some oysters?*
Tu voudrais **aller nager?** *Would you like to go for a swim?*
Vous voudriez **aller au match?** *Would you like to go to the match?*
Ils voudraient **nous rejoindre?** *Would they like to meet up with us?*

When talking about the past, English generally uses *wanted*, while French uses both the imperfect **je voulais** (which is regular) and the perfect **j'ai voulu**.

The imperfect is probably the tense you'll use more often. It's about wanting to do something for an indeterminate period of time.
Quand j'étais petit, je voulais être professeur. *When I was little, I wanted to become a teacher.*
Je ne voulais pas faire de yoga, mais maintenant, j'adore ça! *I didn't use to want to do yoga but now I love it!*
Comme nous ne voulions plus rester à Londres, nous avons déménagé en Cornouailles. *As we didn't want to stay in London any longer, we (have) moved to Cornwall.*

The perfect tense expresses a one-off desire or urge that took place at a specific moment in time; the outcome is usually known.
Ce matin, à neuf heures, j'ai voulu lui téléphoner mais il n'était pas là. *This morning, at nine, I wanted to phone him, but he wasn't there.*
J'ai tout de suite voulu vérifier. *I wanted to check straightaway (and I did).*
On n'a pas voulu vous réveiller. *We didn't want to wake you up (and we didn't).*
Nous avons toujours voulu voyager. *We've always wanted to travel.*

Vouloir isn't the only means of saying what you want to do in French.

Souhaiter *to wish, to desire* is often used in formal circumstances:
Nous souhaitons faire une réclamation. *We wish to make a claim.*

Avoir envie de means *to fancy*.
J'ai envie de tout changer dans ma vie. *I really fancy a change of lifestyle.*
Je n'ai pas vraiment envie de travailler. *I don't really feel like working.*

Aimer and **plaire** in the conditional are often used, with **bien** added for emphasis.
J'aimerais bien visiter Toulouse. *I'd love to visit Toulouse.*
Ça me plairait bien de les revoir. *I'd just love to see them again.*
Ça te plairait d'aller en Australie? *Would you like to go to Australia?*

must, have to, need to

It sounds surprising, but *must, have to, ought, should, need to, had to, be supposed to, be obliged to, be required to, be meant to* can all be conveyed by the various tenses of **devoir**, with some overlap between them.
It's irregular in most tenses, particularly the present:

je dois, tu dois, il doit, nous devons, vous devez, ils doivent

Je dois vous féliciter. *I must congratulate you.*
Je dois admettre que je suis soulagé! *I have to admit I'm relieved!*
Il doit se lever tôt demain matin. *He needs to get up early tomorrow morning.*
On doit absolument partir. *We really do have to leave.*
Nous devons confirmer la date. *We need to confirm the date.*
Nous devons bientôt reprendre contact. *We must catch up soon.*
Tu ne dois pas oublier tes médicaments. *You mustn't forget your pills.*
Vous devez vraiment partir tout de suite? *Do you really have to leave straightaway?*

Another common way of talking about obligation or necessity in French is **il faut**. As with **devoir**, it has many translations in English.
Il faut partir maintenant. *We have to leave now.*
Il faut vraiment se lever tôt demain matin? *Do we really have to get up early tomorrow?*
Il faut bien lire le mode d'emploi. *You must read the instructions carefully.*
Il ne faut pas s'inquiéter. *You mustn't worry.*
Qu'est-ce qu'il faut faire? *What needs to be done?*

Using the conditional of **devoir** changes the meaning to *should* or *ought to*. *I ought to* is **je devr**ais.
Je devrais vérifier. *I ought to check.*
Je ne sais pas ce que je devrais faire. *I don't know what I should do.*
Tu devrais laisser un message à Camille. *You ought to leave a message for Camille.*
Nous devrions nous dépêcher. *We ought to hurry.*
Vous ne devriez pas hésiter. *You shouldn't hesitate.*
Ils devraient aller à l'enterrement. *They ought to go to the funeral.*

When talking about the past, French uses the imperfect **je devais** (regular) and the perfect **j'ai dû**. The rationale is similar to **vouloir**, with the imperfect used most of the time but the perfect needed for a one-off event.

The imperfect conveys *had to* and phrases such as *was supposed to, were meant to* and *should have*.

Je devais toujours marchander, même pour une babiole. *I always had to haggle, even for a little souvenir.*

Nous devions les attendre tous les matins. *We had to wait for them every morning.*

L'année dernière on devait partir en vacances mais ... *We were meant to be going/we should have gone on holiday last year but ...*

Tu devais m'appeler hier. *You were supposed to call me yesterday.*

Vous deviez souvent aller en Guadeloupe? *Did you have to go to Guadeloupe often?*

Vous ne deviez pas partir aujourd'hui? *Weren't you meant to leave today?*

The perfect tense translates *had to, have had to, was obliged to.*

Toutes mes excuses, hier soir j'ai dû partir très vite. *My apologies, I had to leave very quickly last night.*

Après la crevaison, on a dû faire le reste du chemin à pied. *After the puncture, we had to/were obliged to walk the rest of the way.*

Qu'est-ce que tu as dû faire? *What did you have to do?*

Tu as dû tout recommencer? *Have you had to/Did you have to start all over again?*

The conditional of **avoir** + **dû** means *should have, ought to have.*

J'aurais dû acheter des boissons. *I should have bought some drinks.*

Nous n'aurions pas dû demander. *We ought not to have asked.*

Tu aurais dû laisser un message. *You ought to have left a message.*

On aurait dû s'y attendre. *We should have suspected.*

As well as all the possible meanings of **devoir** relating to obligation and necessity, when it's used with a noun, it can also mean *to owe*.
Je te dois une bière. *I owe you a beer.*
Elle me doit une explication. *She owes me an explanation.*

wish lists

What you want to do and what you have to do are often very different things. **Vouloir** is the verb for wishes and dreams, whether it be the decisive **je veux** *I want to* or the more aspirational **je voudrais** *I'd like to*.

There may be things that you want to do in the short to medium term.

changer de profession change jobs
perdre dix kilos lose 10 kilos
retrouver/garder la forme get/keep fit
courir un demi-marathon run a half-marathon
obtenir le permis de conduire get a driving licence
visiter Berlin visit Berlin
aller aux États-Unis go to the States

*List five things you want to do in the next 12 months. If they involve going to places, **to** is* en *with continents, feminine countries, most regions and islands:* en Australie, en Europe, en France, en Irlande, en Bourgogne, en Normandie, en Corse, en Crète

... but à *with masculine countries, cities, towns and anything smaller:* au Canada, aux États-Unis, à Bordeaux, à Londres

Think long term. Are any of the following on your *bucket list* **liste de choses à faire avant de mourir,** literally *list of things to do before you die*?

nager avec les dauphins swim with dolphins
visiter Angkor Wat au Cambodge visit Angkor Wat in Cambodia
contourner le cap Horn à la voile sail round Cape Horn
voir le soleil de minuit en Antarctique see the midnight sun in Antarctica
regarder le soleil se lever à l'équateur watch the sun rise at the equator
faire un safari dans le Masaï Mara go on safari in the Masai Mara
faire l'ascension du mont Kilimandjaro climb Mount Kilimanjaro
faire une randonnée à cheval en Mongolie go pony trekking in Mongolia
faire de la plongée sur la Grande Barrière de Corail dive in the Great Barrier Reef

Create your bucket list in French, looking up any words you need, and say out loud what's on it.

... and to-do lists

Now for the things that you need to do. First, the ones that have to be done as soon as possible: for these you can use **je dois** or **j'ai (vraiment) besoin de** *I (really) need to* (page 31).

retrouver mes baskets find my trainers
acheter du lait buy some milk
faire le plein fill the car up
recharger mon portable charge my mobile
retirer de l'argent au distributeur get some money from the cash machine
contacter Luc get in touch with Luc
payer les factures pay the bills
envoyer une carte d'anniversaire à **Maman** send Mum a birthday card
téléphoner à **Thomas** phone Thomas
dire à **Olivier qu'il y a entraînement demain** tell Olivier there's practice tomorrow

In French you send to someone, phone to someone and tell to someone.

For things that aren't urgent but that you probably ought to be getting on with, you can use the conditional **je devrais** or **j'aurais besoin de**.

faire un peu plus d'exercice do a bit more exercise
ranger le grenier tidy the attic
finir le module/projet finish the module/project
dégivrer le congélateur defrost the freezer
prendre rendez-vous chez le dentiste make a dental appointment
mettre ma tablette à jour update my tablet
nettoyer l'intérieur de la voiture clean the inside of the car
renouveler le contrat/l'assurance renew the contract/insurance
aller voir mes grands-parents visit my grandparents

Now compile your to-do lists in French. As well as writing lists, most of us conduct a running commentary in our heads, reminding ourselves of what we need to do, who we need to get in touch with, what we might like to do at the weekend and so on. If you regularly use French for this inner monologue, you'll find that it becomes a habit, one which results in a step-change in your progress. Try simple comments and questions: how interesting; when's Will's birthday? What a good idea!, etc. It goes without saying that, whenever you're on your own, you do this out loud.

can, could

You use **pouvoir** to say what you can do. It also translates *may* in a question. Like **vouloir** and **devoir**, it's irregular in the present tense.

je peux, tu peux, il peut, nous pouvons, vous pouvez, ils peuvent

Je peux voir? *Can/May I see?*
Tu peux m'aider à mettre les photos en ligne? *Can you help me put the photos online?*
Quand on veut, on peut. *When you want to, you can. Where there's a will, there's a way.*
Tout peut changer. *Everything can change.*
On peut se garer ici? *Can we park here?*
Est-ce que ton ami peut m'aider à allumer le barbecue? *Can your friend help me start the barbecue?*
Tout le monde ne peut pas être riche et célèbre! *Not everyone can be rich and famous!*
Nous pouvons vous emmener quelque part? *May we offer you a lift?*
Je n'en peux plus! *I can't take it any more!*

More formally, **puis-je?** can be used instead of **je peux?**
Puis-je proposer un toast? *May I propose a toast?*
Puis-je faire une suggestion? *May I make a suggestion?*

In shops and services, you'll often hear:
Puis-je vous aider? *May I help you?*

Using the conditional of **pouvoir** changes the meaning to *could, would be able to* or *might. I would be able to* is **je pourrais**. If you're talking about someone other than **je** or **tu** the -ais ending changes (page 114).

Tu pourrais me donner un coup de main? *Could you give me a hand?*
Nous pourrions peut-être vous accompagner? *Might we perhaps come with you?*
Tu pourrais peut-être passer la voir? *Perhaps you could drop in on her?*
Vous pourriez inviter les voisins. *You could/might invite the neighbours.*
Je ne pourrais jamais faire ça. *I could never do that.*

Could is a word to look out for because not only does it mean *would be able to* (**je pourrais**), but it also means ***was able to/used to be** able to,* which is translated by the imperfect in French: **je pouvais, tu pouvais,** etc.

Je pouvais voir la mer depuis la terrasse. *I could see the sea from the terrace.*
Nous ne pouvions pas en demander plus. *We couldn't ask for/expect more.*
Enfant, tu pouvais jouer aux jeux vidéo quand tu voulais? *As a child, could you play videogames when you wanted?*
Avant, on pouvait circuler facilement dans la ville. *Before, we used to be able to get around easily in town.*
Est-ce que vous pouviez bien voir la scène? *Were you able to see everything on stage?*

J'ai pu, the perfect tense, is also translated *could* or *was able to* in English.

J'ai enfin pu lui parler ce matin. *At long last I could/was able to talk to him this morning.*
Je n'ai pas pu m'empêcher de lui dire ce que je pensais. *I couldn't help telling him what I thought.*
Nous n'avons pas pu rentrer, la porte était fermée à clé. *We couldn't get in, the door was locked.*

Look out for the following, where *can/could* are not translated by **pouvoir**:
When *can* means *know how to*, **savoir** is used (see next page):
Ils savent nager? *Can they swim?*
Elle ne savait ni lire ni écrire. *She couldn't read or write.*

When *can* means *manage to*, **arriver** à is often used.
Je n'arrive pas à dormir. *I can't sleep.*
Tu arrives à lire ce qui est écrit? *Can you read what's written?*
On n'arrive pas à y croire ! *We can't believe it!*

knowing someone or something

Savoir and **connaître** both mean *to know* but they're not interchangeable.
Savoir: to know how to do something or to know a fact; **connaître**: to know or get to know a person, to be familiar with a place or a concept.

In the present, they're both quite straightforward, although they're irregular.

je sais, tu sais, il sait, nous savons, vous savez, ils savent

je connais, tu connais, il connaît, nous connaissons, vous connaissez, ils connaissent

Il sait faire la cuisine? *Does he know how to cook? Can he cook?*
Je sais qu'ils habitent par ici. Je le sais. *I know that they live round here. I know (it).*
Comment tu le sais? *How do you know (it)?*
Elle ne connaît pas mes collègues. *She doesn't know my colleagues.*
À propos, je connais bien Paris. *By the way, I know Paris well.*
Nous connaissons ce poème par cœur. *We know that poem by heart.*

And, as you might expect, the imperfect translates *knew* or *used to know*.
Je savais où en trouver. *I knew where to find some.*
Je connaissais tous les raccourcis. *I used to know all the shortcuts.*
Elle connaissait toutes ses chansons. *She knew all his songs.*
Vous le saviez déjà? *Did you already know?*

... but in the perfect, **savoir** can also mean *learnt* or *found out*, while **connaître** can also mean *met*:
J'ai su la vérité hier. *I learnt/found out the truth yesterday.*
Comment est-ce que vous avez su où me trouver? *How did you know where to find me?*
On a toujours su pourquoi. *We've always known why.*

Où est-ce que tu as connu la femme de tes rêves? *Where did you meet the woman of your dreams?*
J'ai connu Stéphane il y a trois ans. *I met Stéphane three years ago.*
Je ne connaissais pas cette association: je l'ai connue par Internet. *I didn't know this association: I got to know it via the internet.*

le vouloir, le devoir, le pouvoir

As well as being verbs, the words **vouloir, devoir** and **pouvoir** can be nouns.

Le bon vouloir means *goodwill*:
On dépend de son bon vouloir. *We depend on his/her goodwill.*
But if you hear of someone doing something **selon son bon vouloir**, it means they're doing it on their own terms, at their own discretion.
Tu peux continuer selon ton bon vouloir. *You can carry on as you see fit.*

Le devoir means *duty*:
Fais ton devoir. *Do your duty. Do what you have to do.*
The plural les devoirs is a word school children dread:
Tu as fait tes devoirs? *Have you done your homework?*

The French learn early about **les droits et les devoirs du citoyen** *the rights and duties of a citizen*, through citizenship lessons at school: **l'enseignement moral et civique**. They can refresh their memory with quizzes on the French government website.
Why don't you have a go?
Go to: http://www.vie-publique.fr/ and look for quizzes.

Le pouvoir means *power, capacity*.
Le sport a le pouvoir de changer le monde. *Sport has the power to change the world.*
Les médias exercent un pouvoir immense. *The media exert immense power.*
Cet homme-là semble assoiffé de pouvoir. *That man seems thirsty for power.*
Ma mère doit avoir des pouvoirs surnaturels! *My mother must have supernatural powers!*
On dit que l'avocat et la noix de coco ont des super pouvoirs. *They say that avocado and coconut have superpowers.*
La plupart des enfants ont un grand pouvoir d'adaptation. *Most children have a great capacity to adapt.*
On a parlé à un représentant des pouvoirs publics. *We talked to a government representative.*

talking the talk

Nico	Allô.
Sophie	Allô, Nico. C'est Sophie.
Nico	Salut!
Sophie	Écoute … Je veux te remercier pour hier soir. C'était très sympa.
Nico	Je t'en prie. C'est vrai, c'était sympa … Et au fait, pour le barbecue dimanche, tu veux un peu d'aide? Je peux te donner un coup de main si tu veux.
Sophie	Oh merci! Oui, il y a beaucoup de choses à faire! Je dois faire une liste. Tu pourrais peut-être organiser la musique?
Nico	Bien sûr! Pas de problème! Mais le plus important, c'est le repas, non? Tu sais faire la cuisine, j'espère?
Sophie	Je sais faire un barbecue, oui…plus ou moins.
Nico	Je peux t'aider. Nous pouvons le faire ensemble, si tu veux!
Sophie	D'accord, je veux bien. À propos … tu as pu inviter ton frère? Il peut venir?
Nico	Sébastien? Oui, il doit organiser un baby-sitter, mais il veut bien venir.
Sophie	Super!
Sophie	Catastrophe!
Nico	Quoi? Ça ne va pas?
Sophie	J'ai voulu acheter les boissons pour le barbecue mais je n'ai pas pu!
Nico	Pourquoi, je ne comprends pas …
Sophie	Je n'avais pas ma carte de crédit avec moi, je ne la trouve plus. J'ai dû la laisser chez un copain … enfin, j'espère!
Nico	Ne panique pas, je peux les acheter, les boissons, ce n'est pas un problème! Tu pourras me rembourser plus tard.
Sophie	Super, merci beaucoup. Si tu savais comme je suis soulagée …

verb practice 6

1 Sort these into three groups under the headings **vouloir**, **pouvoir**, **devoir**:

   ought, could, was supposed to, wanted to, may, must, should have, would like to, can, had to, used to have to, used to be able to.

   For the following activities you need to be familiar with the various endings of **vouloir, pouvoir** and **devoir**.

2 Fill the gaps as quickly as you can with the present tense of **devoir, pouvoir** and **vouloir**. Time yourself – then do this again in a couple of hours' time, again in a day, and again in two days. Come back to it yet again after a week.

a	devoir	il	vous ....
b	vouloir	nous	tu ....
c	devoir	elles	je ....
d	pouvoir	ils	je ....
e	vouloir	on	vous ....
f	pouvoir	tu	nous ....
g	devoir	tu	vous ....
h	pouvoir	vous	on ....
i	vouloir	je	ils ....

3 Have a go at putting **devoir, pouvoir** and **vouloir** in the imperfect and conditional tenses.

   Then try using a few in sentences and say them out loud. The vocabulary in this and previous chapters might come in useful, but you might also like to personalise what you say by looking up some new words.

1 What's the difference between **Vous devez changer de train** and **Vous pouvez changer de train**?

2 Arrange these phrases into two groups of four — one group being what you want or would like to do, and one what you have to/must do: **j'aimerais, nous devrions, nous voulons, je dois, j'ai besoin de, j'ai envie de, je pourrais, il faut, je voudrais**
What does the one left over mean?

3 How would you explain that Julien has to leave and that he wants to take a group photo?

4 How will you apologise if you have to leave a party very early: **Désolé, je dois partir très tôt** or **Désolé, j'ai dû partir très tôt**?

5 How would you say to someone that you don't wish to bother them but can you ask them a question?

6 Adapt **Nous voulons visiter Paris** to ask a couple of friends if they'd like to visit Bordeaux?

7 What is the difference between **J'aime faire du sport, J'aimerais faire du sport** and **Je devrais faire du sport**?

8 What's the French for *I would like to learn, I ought to learn, I must learn, I want to learn, I need to learn, I fancy learning*?

9 Ask someone what needs to be done.

10 Fill in this sentence to say you were not able to come to the cinema last night and that you should have let them know: **Désolé, je n'** .... **pas** .... **venir au cinéma hier soir et j'** .... **vous prévenir.**

11 Ask a friend they fancy going to the wine festival.

12 Say I owe you a nice meal. (use **tu**)

13 If **ils n'ont pas pu voyager** means *they couldn't travel*, how will you say *they didn't want to travel*.

14 Choose the verb to say that you can't dive (because you never learnt):
Je ne peux pas/Je ne sais/Je n'arrive pas à... faire de la plongée.

15 You've just been given a gift, say *You shouldn't have*. (use **vous**)

dix
sharing opinions

Whether you're chatting to a neighbour or someone you've met on holiday, socialising with French-speaking business contacts, taking part in a cultural exchange or meeting your son's new French mother-in-law, it's very satisfying to be able to exchange views on anything and everything.

Regardless of whether the subject under discussion is a mutual acquaintance, a local **brasserie**, the state of the beach, international sport or major issues such as climate change or migration, the basic language structures you need are the same. It helps to be able to air your views without sounding blunt or over-assertive, and, of course, to invite other people's views.

As a foreign visitor, you might well be asked questions that will range from **Que pensez-vous de la situation politique dans votre pays?** *What do you think of the political situation in your country?* to **Tu supportes quelle équipe?** *Which team do you support?*

A point of view becomes much more convincing when it's supported. There are words that make an opinion sound persuasive and self-evident, such as **vraiment** *really* and **évidemment** *obviously*, but what usually clinches an argument is a solid rationale and/or an impressive statistic or two.

asking someone's opinion

When you're listening to someone and they look at you and say **Tu ne trouves pas?** or **Vous ne trouvez pas?**, they're asking for your opinion on the matter.

Il est génial, tu ne trouves pas? Quelle voix! *He's amazing, don't you think (lit. don't you find)? What a voice!*

C'est compliqué, vous ne trouvez pas? *It's complicated, don't you think?*

Ils ont bien joué hier, vous ne trouvez pas? *They played well yesterday, don't you think?*

There are other ways of asking what someone thinks.

Qu'est-ce que tu en dis/vous en dites? *What do you think about it? What's your view on this?*

Qu'est-ce que tu dis de ce site? *What do you think of this site?*

Je voudrais connaître votre opinion sur cette question. *I'd like to know your take on this issue.*

And there are phrases that you can easily insert at the beginning or the end of any question.

À ton avis, cette couleur me va ou pas? *Does this colour suit me, do you think/in your opinion?*

Vous allez pouvoir arriver à l'heure à votre avis? *Will you be able to get there on time, do you think?*

C'est possible, d'après toi/vous? *Is it possible, in your opinion?*

Qui va gagner la coupe selon toi/vous? *Who's going to win the cup, in your view (lit. according to you)?*

Or you can use **penser** *to think* and **croire** *to believe/to think.*

Tu trouves que c'est assez épicé? Qu'est-ce que tu en penses? *Do you think it's spicy enough? What do you reckon?*

C'est inadmissible. Qu'est-ce que vous en pensez? *It's intolerable. What do you think/What's your view on this?*

Vous pensez que c'est une bonne idée? *Do you think it's a good idea?*

Tu crois que c'est prêt? *Do you think it's ready?*

Vous croyez que c'est la meilleure solution? *Do you believe it's the best solution?*

Tu crois/Vous croyez vraiment? *Do you really think so?*

saying what you think

The most straightforward way of offering your opinion is to include **à mon avis**, **selon moi** or **d'après moi** within what you're saying.

À mon avis, ils sont tous fous! *In my opinion, they're all mad!*
À mon humble avis, vous devriez refuser son offre. *In my humble opinion, you should refuse his offer.*
C'est très grave à mon avis. *It's very serious, in my view.*
D'après moi, c'était le meilleur match de la saison. *I reckon it was the best match of the season.*

In English, when you are making a point about what **you** think, you stress the word *I*. In French, you say **Moi, je ...**
Moi, je ne suis pas du tout d'accord. *I don't agree at all.*
Moi, je suis absolument contre la vivisection. *I am completely against vivisection.*
Moi, je suis persuadé(e) qu'il va venir ce soir. *I'm convinced he'll come tonight.*
Moi, je suis convaincu(e) qu'il existe des univers parallèles. *I'm convinced that parallel universes exist.*

Another way of introducing your views is to start with **pour ma part**, **personnellement** or **en ce qui me concerne**.
Pour ma part, je crois qu'il mérite plus que quatre étoiles. *Personally, I think it deserves more than four stars.*
Personnellement, je crois que Paul a tort. *Personally, I believe that Paul's wrong.*
En ce qui me concerne, ça ne fait aucun doute dans mon esprit. *As far as I'm concerned, there's no doubt in my mind.*

Croire à means *to believe in*. The à changes to **au/aux** when it's combined with **le/les**.
Je crois sincèrement à la liberté d'expression. *I believe wholeheartedly in free speech.*
Je crois profondément au karma. *I believe strongly in karma.*
Je crois aux extraterrestres. *I believe in aliens.*
Je ne crois pas aux fantômes. *I don't believe in ghosts.*

the subjunctive

When views are being aired, don't be surprised if you hear unexpected verb forms – these will be subjunctive endings. The subjunctive exists in English too: *If I were in charge ..., She's insisting you be there*, but it's no longer heard widely. French uses its subjunctive more routinely, in defined circumstances.

If you forget to use the subjunctive, don't worry: you will still be understood. In any case, the difference in sound is marginal for many verbs.

recognising the subjunctive

The present subjunctive is very simple to form, as for all regular verbs and a large number of irregular verbs it has the same set of endings and is based on the **ils/elles** part of the present tense:

parler = ils/elles **parlent**   **perdre** = ils/elles **perdent**
finir = ils/elles **finissent**   **sortir** = ils/elles **sortent**

The subjunctive endings that replace -ent are:
je parl**e**, tu parl**es**, il parl**e**, nous parl**ions**, vous parl**iez**, ils parl**ent**
je perd**e**, tu perd**es**, il perd**e**, nous perd**ions**, vous perd**iez**, ils perd**ent**
je sort**e**, tu sort**es**, il sort**e**, nous sort**ions**, vous sort**iez**, ils sort**ent**
je finiss**e**, tu finiss**es**, il finiss**e**, nous finiss**ions**, vous finiss**iez**, ils finiss**ent**

Not many verbs are irregular in the subjunctive, but these are worth recognising as they are very commonly used:

aller *to go*	j'aille	**faire** *to do/make*	je fasse
avoir *to have*	j'aie	**pouvoir** *to be able to*	je puisse
devoir *to have to*	je doive	**savoir** *to know*	je sache
être *to be*	je sois	**vouloir** *to want*	je veuille

using the subjunctive

You don't need the subjunctive after **je pense que** *I think that* or **je crois que** *I believe that* – but you *do* need it after **je ne pense pas que** *I don't think that*, **je ne crois pas que** *I don't believe that*, and similar phrases.
Je ne pense pas que ce soit la solution idéale. *I don't think it's the ideal solution.*
Je ne crois pas que ce soit vrai. *I don't believe it's true.*
Je ne suis pas convaincu(e) qu'elle veuille venir. *I'm not convinced she wants to come.*

que

The subjunctive is usually introduced by **que,** which means *that.* Even though *that* is often left out in English, **que** is always needed in French.

The types of verbs and expressions that are followed by que + subjunctive are those that involve personal attitudes, sentiments, tastes, opinions, needs and desires. For example:

Je voudrais que **tu** viennes **avec moi.** *I'd like you to come with me.*
Il préfère que **j'y** aille **sans lui.** *He prefers me to go without him.*
Êtes-vous déçu que **l'équipe ne** soit **pas qualifiée?** *Are you disappointed the team didn't qualify?*
Je doute que **ce** soit **un vin de qualité à ce prix-là.** *I doubt that it is a good wine at that price.*
Je crains qu'il **ne** sache **pas quoi faire.** *I fear he doesn't know what to do.*
Il faut qu'on écrive **une carte postale.** *We have to write a postcard.*
Il est possible qu'il **ne** soit **pas d'accord.** *It's possible that he doesn't/won't agree.*

The perfect subjunctive uses the subjunctive of **avoir** or **être** + a past participle.
Je ne crois pas qu'il soit parti **aujourd'hui.** *I don't believe he left today.*
Je suis désolé que tu n'aies **pas pu venir.** *I'm sorry you couldn't come.*
J'ai peur que **nous** ayons raté **le dernier métro.** *I'm afraid we might have missed the last tube.*

Surprisingly, **imaginer**, **supposer** and **espérer** *to hope* are *not* followed by the subjunctive: **Je suppose que tu viens avec nous.** *I suppose you're coming with us.*

The subjunctive *is* used after words like **bien que** *although*, **pourvu que** *provided that*, **à moins que** *unless*:
J'aime bien cet opéra bien qu'il soit **un peu long.** *I like that opera although it is a bit long.*
Je viendrai à moins que je sois **encore malade**. *I'll come unless I'm still ill.*

... and also often with superlatives:
C'est le restaurant le plus chic que je connaisse. *It's the poshest restaurant I know.*
C'est le meilleur cidre que j'aie **jamais** bu! *It's the best cider I've ever drunk!*

agreeing and disagreeing

How you agree and disagree with someone has all to do with the context of the discussion. There's a world of difference between a dialogue on quality issues in the boardroom, an exchange of views on immigration at a reception, friendly banter about football in the bar, and discussing a meal.

agreeing

Bien dit! Bravo! *Well said! Hear, hear!*
En effet! Tout à fait! *Indeed!*
C'est bien vrai! *It's true/So true!*
Précisément! C'est tout à fait ça! *Precisely! Exactly right!*
Tu as/vous avez raison. *You're right.*
Je suis de ton/votre avis. *I agree with you.*
Nous sommes entièrement d'accord. *We're completely agreed.*
Sans aucun doute. *Undoubtedly.*
Sans l'ombre d'un doute. *Without a shadow of a doubt.*
Tu as vu juste! *You've got it/Spot on!*

disagreeing

J'en doute! *I doubt it.*
Non, je suis désolé(e) mais je ne partage pas ton/votre avis. *No, I'm sorry but I don't share your opinion.*
Il y a un malentendu, je pense. *It's a misunderstanding, I think.*
C'est une question d'opinion. *It's a matter of opinion.*
Ce n'est pas du tout ça! *Nothing of the sort!*
Absolument pas! *Absolutely not!*
Mais bon sang! Tu plaisantes ou quoi? *For pity's sake! Are you kidding or what?*
Rien que des bêtises! *Utter twaddle!*

Alternatively, you can use moi aussi, pas moi, moi si or moi non plus.

affirmative sentence	**Je vais prendre le poisson. Et toi?** *I'll have the fish. What about you?*
you agree	**Moi aussi.** *Me too. So will I.*
you disagree	**Pas moi.** *I won't. Not me.*
negative sentence	**Je n'aime pas ce vin. Et vous?** *I don't like this wine. What about you?*
you agree	**Moi non plus.** *Neither do I.*
you disagree	**Moi si.** *I do.*

making a case

Phrases such as **par exemple** *for example*, **tout d'abord** *first of all*, **en conclusion** *to conclude* help to structure a discussion.

You'll also need words like **parce que, car** *because*; **vu que** *given that, in view of the fact that*; **puisque, comme** *since, as*; **du moment où/que** *as long as*.

Ce n'est pas juste parce qu'ils paient des impôts. *It's not fair because they pay taxes.*

Je ne m'engage pas car la question est trop complexe. *I'm keeping quiet because the issue is too complex.*

Vu qu'aucune étude de marché n'a été faite, j'hésite à accepter l'offre. *In view of the fact that no market research was done, I am reluctant to accept the offer.*

Je peux en parler puisque j'ai beaucoup d'expérience dans ce domaine. *I can speak about this as I have a lot of experience in this area.*

Comme nous n'avons pas de chiffres précis, il est difficile de savoir. *As we don't have precise figures, it's hard to know.*

On doit examiner la question de plus près puisqu'elle a des implications très importantes. *We must examine this issue more carefully as it has huge implications.*

Du moment où ils ont voté, ils peuvent critiquer. *As long as they've voted, they can be critical.*

Phrases such as **parce que, vu que** etc. are not, of course, restricted to discussing major issues.

On va devoir y aller à pied parce que je n'ai pas pris d'essence. *We'll have to walk there because I haven't put petrol in the car.*

Je veux y aller car j'ai lu que c'est un endroit merveilleux. *I want to go there because I've read that it's a wonderful place.*

Je trouve sa réaction étrange vu qu'il ne me connaît pas. *I find his reaction odd given that he doesn't know me.*

Vu que je n'ai pas encore lu le menu, je ne peux pas commander. *Given that I haven't read the menu yet, I can't order.*

Puisque Laure ne se sent pas bien, je préfère rester à la maison avec elle. *Since Laure's not feeling well, I'd rather stay at home with her.*

Comme la chaleur est insupportable, trouvons un endroit à l'ombre. *As it's unbearably hot, let's find a place in the shade.*

what do *you* think?

À mon avis ... *In my opinion ...*

> **le gouvernement devrait ...** *the government ought to ...*
> **chacun pourrait ...** *every individual could ...*
> **la municipalité doit ...** *the local council must ...*

Give your opinion on some major issues, mixing and matching the above cues with the verbs and topics below. Vary what you say by using **selon moi** *in my view*, or include **je crois** *I believe*/**je pense** *I think*. Try finding alternatives to **le gouvernement, la municipalité** and look up any words that aren't included but that you feel strongly about.

word bank

accepter *to accept*
s'attaquer à *to tackle*
aider *to help*
augmenter *to increase*
se concentrer sur *to focus on*
contribuer à *to contribute to*
prendre des mesures contre *to clamp down on*
éliminer *to eradicate*
ignorer *to ignore*
imposer *to impose*
légaliser *to legalise*
améliorer *to improve*
interdire *to ban*
stimuler *to boost*
protéger *to protect*
recycler *to recycle*
réduire *to reduce*
rejeter *to defeat*
soutenir *to support*
développer *to develop*
tenir responsable *to hold responsible*

la lutte pour/contre *the fight for/against*
la sécurité *security*
l'ordre (m) *law and order*
la cybercriminalité *cybercrime*
le vol d'identité *identity theft*
l'extrémisme (m) *extremism*
le terrorisme *terrorism*
le crime organisé *organised crime*
le trafic de drogues *drug trafficking*
l'environnement (m) *environment*
la durabilité *sustainability*
le changement climatique *climate change*
l'expédition spatiale (f) *space exploration*
l'économie (f) *economy*
les impôts (m) *taxes*
la fraude fiscale *tax evasion*
le chômage *unemployment*
l'aide sociale *benefits*
les droits (m) **de l'homme** *human rights*
l'égalité (f) **des chances** *equal opportunities*
le sexisme *sexism*
le racisme *racism*
l'émigration/l'immigration (f) *emigration/immigration*
le/la migrant(e) économique *economic migrant*

numbers and statistics in conversation

Statistics create the impression that you really know what you're talking about. If you need a reminder of French numbers, go to page 190.

You can introduce your figures with:
C'est un fait que ... *It's a fact that ... It's a given that ...*
Selon les derniers chiffres, ... *According to the latest figures, ...*
Les chiffres révèlent que ... *The figures reveal that ...*

C'est un fait que ça coûte plus de cinq cent mille euros. *It's a fact that it's costing more than 500,000 euros.*
Le Stade de France a une capacité de plus de quatre-vingt mille places. *The Stade de France can hold more than 80,000 spectators.*
Les chiffres révèlent que moins de cinquante personnes ont été blessées. *The figures show that fewer than 50 people have been hurt.*
D'après Jean-Marc, l'entreprise a réalisé un bénéfice de plus de deux millions de livres. *According to Jean-Marc, the company made a profit of over two million pounds.*

To speak about **les pourcentages** *percentages*, use **pour cent** *percent*. Remember that the French for *0.3 zero point three* is 0,3 **zéro virgule trois**.

Ceci contient moins de dix pour cent de matières grasses. *It contains less that 10% fat.*
Il offre jusqu'à vingt pour cent de réduction. *He's offering up to 20% discount.*
Les chiffres indiquent une augmentation de cinq pour cent. *The figures show an increase of 5%.*
La banque prévoit une croissance comprise entre deux virgule cinq et trois pour cent. *The bank is predicting growth of between 2.5% and 3.0%.*

If you want to be bang on trend with facts and figures about France, do what the French do and check in the publication *Francoscopie*, by sociologist Gérard Mermet, who closely monitors French society. He's responsible for coining new words such as **les adulescents** for kidults, **les sexygénaires** for those whose lives start at 60, **l'homo-zappens** for the modern-day man who's forever zapping between the various aspects of his busy lifestyle, and **l'écolonomie** for eco-friendly economy.

Alongside absolute numbers, French has words for approximate numbers.

Je suis ici pour une dizaine de jours. *I'm here for ten days or so.*
J'y suis déjà allé une douzaine de fois peut-être. *I've already been there about a dozen times.*
Rendez-vous dans une vingtaine de minutes. *See you in about twenty minutes.*
On lui donne une trentaine d'années mais en réalité, elle a cinquante-six ans! *She looks about 30 but in fact she's 56!*
On a vu une cinquantaine d'éléphants. *We saw about 50 elephants.*
Il est arrivé une centaine de réfugiés. *About 100 refugees have arrived.*
Il y avait des centaines de supporters en ville. *There were hundreds of fans in town.*
Il y avait un millier de spectateurs. *There were about a thousand spectators.*
Regardez les étourneaux, il y en a des milliers! *Look at the starlings, there are thousands of them!*
Ah beurk! Il y a des milliards de mouches! *Oh yuck! Billions of flies.*

Ordinals, i.e. *first, second, third,* etc. are adjectives, so when they're used with a noun the endings have to agree. There are two ways of saying second: **second(e)** and **deuxième**. Generally **second(e)** is used where there are only two of something and **deuxiè**me where it's second in a list that has more than two items.

Marie en est à son premier mois de grossesse. *Marie's reached the first month of her pregnancy.*
C'est toujours difficile la première fois. *The first time is always hard.*
Ce sont les premiers melons de mon jardin. *These are the first melons from my garden.*
Les premières crêpes ne sont jamais réussies! *The first pancakes are never perfect.*
C'est le fils de son deuxième ou troisième mari? *Is he the son of her second or third husband?*
Pendant la Seconde Guerre mondiale, ... *During the Second World War ...*
C'est son quatre-vingtième anniversaire aujourd'hui. *It's his 80th birthday today.*
Ils sont arrivés trentièmes au rallye. *They came 30th in the rally.*
Elle a perdu ses lunettes pour la énième fois. *She's lost her glasses for the umpteenth time.*

more or less

To express comparatives such as *higher, easier, richer, more interesting, more patient* in French, you use **plus** *more* + the adjective.

Ce puzzle est plus facile. *This puzzle is easier.*
Laure est plus jeune, plus mince et plus riche. *Laure's younger, slimmer and richer.*
Les risques sont plus importants. *The risks are higher.*
Tu es plus patient que moi. *You're more patient than me.*

To say *the biggest, the kindest, the latest, the most intelligent*, you simply add **le/la** in front of **plus**:

C'est le centre commercial le plus grand d'Europe. *It's the biggest shopping mall in Europe.*
Elle est, sans l'ombre d'un doute, la plus gentille des trois sœurs. *She is, without a shadow of a doubt, the kindest of the three sisters.*
J'arriverai à six heures au plus tard. *I'll be there at six at the latest.*

Moins *less* works in the same way.
Tu es moins patient(e) que moi. *You're less patient than me.*
Il est moins riche que son père. *He's less rich than his father.*
Il est le moins charismatique des deux. *He's the least charismatic of the two.*
Ce sont les villes les moins chères de France. *They are the least expensive towns in France.*

Plus and **moins** aren't necessarily followed by an adjective: they can be followed by a number, a noun or an adverb.

Ils ont payé plus d'un million. *They paid more than a million.*
Il est mort il y a plus de six mois. *He died more than six months ago.*
Il vous faudra moins de cinquante euros. *You'll need less than 50 euros.*
Plus de soixante-dix pour cent de la surface de la Terre est recouverte d'eau. *More than 70% of the Earth's surface is covered in water.*

Il y a plus de bruit ici. *There's more noise here.*
Oui, mais il y a moins de moustiques. *Yes, but there are fewer mosquitoes.*

OK, je vais parler plus clairement. *OK, I'll speak more clearly.*
Ils viennent ici moins souvent. *They come here less often. They don't come here as often.*

The French for *better/best* and *worse/worst* don't use **plus** and **moins**. *Better* is **meilleur** when it's an adjective and **mieux** when it's an adverb.

Leurs croissants sont meilleurs; en fait ce sont les meilleurs ici.
Their croissants are better; in fact, they are the best here.
Ils jouent mieux que nous. Leur équipe joue le mieux.
They play *better* than us. *Their team plays the best.*
Le temps est mauvais, pire que prévu. The weather is bad, *worse than expected.*
Il est le pire de tous les candidats. He's *the worst* of all the candidates.

De plus en plus/de moins en moins mean *more and more/less and less*. Le plus/le moins possible means *the most/least possible*.
La situation devient de plus en plus compliquée. *The situation's becoming more and more complicated.*
C'est de moins en moins clair. *It's less and less clear.*
Nous nous trouvons de plus en plus de choses en commun. *We're finding we have more and more things in common.*
Je passe de moins en moins de temps à la piscine. *I spend less and less time at the pool.*
Donnez-nous le plus de détails possibles. *Give us as many details as possible.*
J'y vais le moins souvent possible. *I go there as little as possible.* lit. *the least often*

Many everyday sayings include **plus** and **moins**:

Plus jamais! *Never again!*
En plus, il m'a invité à dîner. *What's more, he invited me for dinner.*
Oui, c'est plus ou moins ça. *Yes, that's more or less it.*
Au moins, je l'aurai rencontré! *At least I'll have met him!*
Pas le moins du monde! *Not in the least!*
tout au moins *at least*
pour le moins *at the very least*

Practise plus and moins with the adjectives from page 33 and page 36 to describe and compare a few people and places. Than is que: Mon père est moins tolérant que moi My father is less tolerant than me.

talking the talk

Nico	Tu aimes cet album, Sophie? C'est génial, comme musique, tu ne trouves pas?
Sophie	Euh … oui …
Nico	À mon avis, ce serait une playlist idéale pour le barbecue. Qu'est-ce que tu en dis?
Sophie	Personnellement, je trouve ça un peu trop déprimant, comme musique, pour un barbecue.
Nico	Ah bon, tu crois? Moi, je ne suis pas vraiment d'accord. C'est calme, reposant.
Sophie	Ben, d'après moi, il faudrait quelque chose d'un peu plus joyeux que ça pour une fête!
	Les invités commencent à arriver … je vais servir des boissons … Oh là là, ça discute dur!
male guest	Pour ma part, je crois profondément que le plus grand problème aujourd'hui est l'immigration.
female guest	Quoi?!
male guest	Eh oui! Nous acceptons bien trop de migrants économiques. Je suis persuadé que notre économie en souffre!
female guest	D'accord, notre économie est fragile …
male guest	En effet!
female guest	… mais, selon vous, tout est à cause des immigrés? Ce n'est pas du tout ça! Je crains que la question soit un peu plus complexe!
male guest	Nous recevons des milliers d'immigrés …
female guest	Tout à fait! Mais ce n'est pas juste de les tenir responsables de nos problèmes, puisqu'eux aussi, ils paient des impôts. Ils contribuent à la société!
male guest	Évidemment, c'est une question d'opinion. Mais, moi, je ne suis pas convaincu que vous compreniez la gravité de la situation.
female guest	Si vous voulez parler de problèmes, parlons du changement climatique, du sexisme, du racisme, des abus des droits de l'homme …

checkpoint 10

1   If you hear someone ask you **à votre avis**, what are you being asked for? What other two phrases can you think of with the same meaning?

2   How would you express *Hear, hear* in French and say you both agree.

3   Which of these phrases would you use to diplomatically agree to disagree:

   Sans aucun doute, Ce n'est pas du tout ça!, C'est une question d'opinion, Tu plaisantes ou quoi? How do you translate the others?

4   List three ways, in addition to **parce que**, of introducing an explanation to support your opinion.

5   What is the infinitive of the verb **sache** in this sentence: **Je ne pense pas qu'il sache nager**?

6   **Une soixantaine de jeunes entre une dizaine et une quinzaine d'années ont participé.** How many youngsters took part and how old were they?

7   What's missing from this mathematical sequence?

   quatrième – douzième – vingtième – ....

8   **Luc est plus jeune que Nathan et a deux ans de plus qu'Alex.** Who's the youngest of the three boys? What's *youngest* in French?

9   Fill the gap to say *hundreds of bees*: .... **d'abeilles**.

10 Write in UK figures **sept virgule cinq pour cent** and **zéro virgule neuf pour cent**.

11 Complete the sentence with the correct form of the verb: **Je suis déçu que votre mari ne .... pas là. est ait soit**

12 *I would like him to go to France with her.* What is special about this sentence in French? How will you translate it?

13 How would you say in French: ... *do you think?* and ... *don't you think?*

14 Think of four different ways of introducing your own personal view on something in French: **..., je crois que c'est possible.**

15 Now say the sentence from question 14 in the negative, meaning you don't believe it's possible. Watch out for the verb in the second part of the sentence!

16 Which two phrases will not be followed by a verb in the subjunctive?

   je crois que, je doute que, je ne pense pas que, j'espère que

onze
inside information

There's no better way of finding out about a place than by talking to the locals. They're the ones with inside information about what's available, how to do something, where to buy the best wine or a replacement charger for your phone, where to go for healthcare and who's who. And they always know the best places to eat.

Tapping into this local knowledge involves asking questions and explaining why you want the information. The language structures you need work in any context: you simply slot in the relevant vocabulary. Don't forget the strategies on pages 54–55 for making sure that people understand you and that you understand their replies.

People will likely respond to your questions using an imperative, which is the structure used to give advice and instructions. You've probably already come across the imperative in basic directions such as **Prenez la première à gauche** *Take the first on the left* or **Allez tout droit** *Go straight on.*

Although a French proverb says **La gourmandise est un vilain défaut** *Indulgence is a sin*, French people tend to prefer another: **Bien boire et bien manger font bien travailler** *Eat well and drink well to work well.* Food is central to French life, and it's much talked about, whether it's sourcing the best items, finding out about what's on offer at the **traiteur** *deli* or shopping for **des produits bio** *organic products* and **des produits locaux** *local produce* at their local **marché bio** *organic market,* asking how to make something, experiencing **la gastronomie** *haute cuisine* or just chatting about the food on your plate or on the menu.

finding out what's available

Il y a *there is/there are* is the most basic French phrase, yet among the most versatile, whether for seeking information or providing it.

You can use it with a noun:

Il y a de la circulation ce matin. *There's a lot of traffic this morning.*
Il y a un problème. *There's a problem.*
Il y a du lait? *Is there any milk?*
Il y a un tas de choses à faire. *There are loads of things to do.*
Il y a des gens que je ne connais pas. *There are people I don't know.*
Il y a un docteur ici? *Is there a doctor here?*
Il y a des escargots au menu aujourd'hui? *Are there snails on the menu today?*

... or with à + the infinitive:

Il y a quelque chose à manger? *Is there anything to eat?*
Qu'est-ce qu'il y a à faire au centre de loisirs? *What is there to do at the leisure centre?*

It's equally useful in other tenses.

future
Il y aura un choix d'entrées. *There will be a choice of starters.*
Il y aura des toilettes? *Will there be toilets?*
Est-ce qu'il y aura d'autres occasions de se revoir? *Will there be other opportunities to meet again?*

conditional
Il y aurait de la place pour moi? *Would there be space for me?*
Est-ce qu'il y aurait des effets secondaires? *Would there be side effects?*

imperfect
Qu'est-ce qu'il y avait comme dessert? *What was there for dessert?*
Il y avait beaucoup de gens. *There were a lot of people.*

perfect
Il y a eu un incendie? *Has there been a fire?*
Il y a eu une tempête en mer. *There's been a sea storm.*
Est-ce qu'il y a eu des retards? *Have there been any delays?*

saying someone or something's missing

To say *there isn't* and *there aren't*, you use **il n'y a pas**, followed by **de/d'**. Don't be tempted to follow it with **un/une** or **du/de la/des**.

Il n'y a pas de place/de temps/d'eau. *There's no room/time/water.*
Il n'y a pas de pain/de confiture. *There is no bread/no jam.*
Il n'y a pas de serviettes. *There aren't any towels.*

Il n'y en a pas can mean *there isn't any (of it), there isn't one (of them)* or *there aren't any (of them)*.

There's another way of expressing a lack of something, using **il manque**:
Il manque quelque chose/quelqu'un. *Something/someone's missing.*
Il manque une personne du groupe. *Someone from the group isn't here.*
La seule chose qui manque, c'est la neige! *The only thing missing is snow!*
C'est parfait: il ne manque rien. *It's perfect: there's nothing missing.*
Il manque deux verres. *We're two glasses short.*

Il manquait une entrée. *There was one starter missing.*
Il manquait les enfants. *The children weren't there.*

... me manque conveys *I'm missing ...* in a physical or emotional sense. **Me** can be replaced by **te, lui, nous, vous** or **leur**, depending on who is lacking something/missing someone (see page 180).
Il me manque une chaussure. *I'm missing one shoe.*
Les mots nous manquent pour vous remercier. *We don't have the words to thank you.*
Alain me manque beaucoup. *I really miss Alain.*
La France te manque? *Do you miss France?*
Elle aimerait rentrer chez elle: sa famille lui manque. *She'd like to go back home: she misses her family.*
Les enfants vous manquent? *Are you missing the children?*

You also use **manquer** to tell someone you're missing them:
Tu me manques. *I miss you* lit. *You are missing to me.*
Tu me manques tellement. *I miss you so much.*
Tu me manques aussi. *I miss you too.*
Vous me manquez tous les deux. *I miss you both.*

finding out how to do something

You can ask how to do just about anything with **On fait comment pour** or **Comment est-ce qu'on fait pour** + the infinitive. The English equivalent is usually *How do I ...? How do you ...? How does one go about ...ing?*

On fait comment pour avoir un permis de pêche? *How do you apply for a fishing permit?*
Comment est-ce qu'on fait pour s'inscrire? *How does one join/subscribe?*
Comment est-ce qu'on pour éteindre l'ordinateur? *How do you turn the computer off?*

Alternatively, you can use **Comment est-ce qu'on** + the third person of a verb, i.e. the one used with **il** and **elle**.

Comment est-ce qu'on utilise ...? *How do you use ...?*
Comment est-ce qu'on allume la télé? *How do we switch on the TV?*
Comment est-ce qu'on change les piles? *How do you change the batteries?*
Comment est-ce qu'on joue aux boules? *How do you play boules?*

Comment ça se ... is also used with the third person of a verb:

Comment ça se dit ... en français? *How do you say it/that in French?*
Comment ça se prononce? *How do you pronounce this?*
Comment ça se mange? *How do you eat it?*
Comment ça se boit, chaud ou froid? *How do you drink it, hot or cold?*

 See how many similar questions you can come up with in just ten minutes. As well as the words on this page, use others that you know. Don't forget to say the questions out loud.

allumer to switch on, annuler to cancel, confirmer to confirm, se connecter à to connect to, se débarrasser de to get rid of, se désinscrire to unsubscribe, éviter to avoid, faire to make, fermer to close, louer to hire, maigrir to lose weight, nettoyer to clean, préparer to prepare

une ampoule blister, un artichaut artichoke, la cafetière coffee maker, la vinaigrette French dressing, l'escargot snail, la gueule de bois hangover, le hoquet hiccups, la lumière the light, la contravention fine, le mot de passe password, la réservation booking, le volet shutter, la vérité truth, la wifi the Wi-Fi

---

asking for advice and information

A simple open question uses a question word (page 27).

Où est la sortie? *Where's the exit?*
À quelle heure ça ouvre? *What time does it open?*
Quel est le score? *What's the score?*

When you want your question to sound less abrupt, you can start with:
Excusez-moi, vous pourriez me dire ... *Excuse me, could you tell me ...*
and when addressing a group of people:
Quelqu'un pourrait me dire ...? *Could anyone tell me ...?*

Vous pourriez me dire ... *Could you tell me ...*
    ... ce qui s'est passé? *... what (has) happened?*
    ... le numéro à appeler? *... what number I need to call?*
    ... quelle est son adresse? *... what his/her address is?*
    ... où est la pharmacie la plus proche? *... where the nearest chemist's is?*
    ... combien de temps ça prend? *... how long it takes?*

Est-ce que quelqu'un pourrait me dire ... or **Quelqu'un pourrait me dire ...**
Could anyone tell me ...
    ... où je peux acheter de l'essence? *... where I can buy petrol?*
    ... comment aller au stade? *... how you get to the stadium?*
    ... pourquoi Alain n'est pas là? *... why Alain isn't here?*
    ... pourquoi ça fait ce bruit bizarre? *... why it's making this funny noise?*
    ... combien de personnes il y avait? *... how many people there were?*
    ... lequel est le meilleur des deux? *... which is the better of the two?*

You need **si** *if, whether* in questions without a question word:
Vous pourriez me dire si Alain est là? *Could you tell me if Alain is there?*
Vous pourriez me dire s'il y a du savon? *Could you tell me whether there is any soap?*
Est-ce que quelqu'un pourrait me dire si l'hôpital est loin d'ici?
Could anyone tell me whether the hospital is a long way from here?
Quelqu'un pourrait me dire s'il y a des nouvelles? *Could anyone tell me if there's any news?*

giving advice and instructions

Official signs use a variety of ways to tell you (not) to do something:

DANGER – DÉFENSE D'ENTRER! *Danger! Do not enter.* lit. *Entry is prohibited.*
PRIÈRE DE NE PAS FUMER. *No smoking.* lit. *You are kindly asked not to smoke.*
NE PAS JETER DE DÉCHETS. *Don't drop litter.*
MERCI D'ÉTEINDRE VOS PORTABLES. *Please switch off your mobiles.* lit. *Thank you for switching off your mobiles.*
VOUS ÊTES PRIÉS DE GARER VOTRE VOITURE AU PARKING. *Please park your car in the car park.* lit. *You are kindly asked to ...*

Many signs use a form of the verb called the imperative.

> **Tir**ez. *Pull.*
> **Pouss**ez. *Push.*
> **Éteign**ez **vos phares.** *Switch off your headlights.*
> **Céd**ez **le passage.** *Give way.*
> **Attach**ez **vos ceintures.** *Fasten your seatbelts.*

The imperative is also the way to give personal advice or instructions. As is clear from the above signs, there's absolutely no difference between the imperative and the present tense verb endings when you're using **vous**.

Appelez le SAMU! *Call the emergency services!*
Prenez ce médicament à jeun. *Take this medicine on an empty stomach.*
Donnez-moi un kilo de cerises, s'il vous plaît. *Give me a kilo of cherries, please.*
Ne perdez pas de vue l'objectif, Sylvain! *Don't lose sight of the goal, Sylvain!*

If it's a reflexive verbs, you add **-vous**:

Amusez-vous bien! *Enjoy yourselves!*
Rappelez-vous ce numéro. *Remember this number.*
Reposez-vous un peu ici. *Have a little rest here.*

If you're telling someone ***not*** to do something, the word order changes and **vous** goes directly before the verb:

Ne vous couchez pas trop tard. *Don't go to bed too late.*
Ne vous inquiétez pas. *Don't worry.*

tu

It's also pretty straightforward to use the imperative with **tu**: you use the same form as the present tense, but remove the final -**s** for -**er** verbs and for verbs that work like **ouvrir** *to open* (page 186).

Fais bien attention. *Do be careful.*
Ne travaille pas trop! *Don't work too hard!*
Ouvre ton cadeau! *Open your present!*
Finis ton dessert! *Finish your dessert!*
Prends ton temps. *Take your time.*
Appelle-moi. *Call me.*

The final -**s** is reinstated when you're using **y** and **en** (see page 181)
Penses-y! *Think about it!*
Parles-en à tes parents. *Speak to your parents about it.*

If it's a reflexive verb, you add -**toi**:
Dépêche-toi. *Hurry up.*
Calme-toi. *Calm down.*
Lève-toi! *Get up!*
Assieds-toi. *Do sit down.*

... unless you're telling someone *not* to do something:
Ne t'inquiète pas. *Don't worry.*
Ne te couche pas trop tard! *Don't go to bed too late!*

Être *to be*, **avoir** *to have* and **savoir** *to know* have irregular imperatives:

	tu	**vous**
être	sois	soyez
avoir	aie	ayez
savoir	sache	sachez

Sois prêt quand j'arriverai. *Be ready for when I arrive.*
Soyez sérieux! Be serious! Sois sage! *Be good! Behave yourself!*
Aie l'air content quand tu la verras! *Look happy when you see her!*
Ayez vos passeports à portée de main. *Have your passports to hand.*

Sache qu'il est hors de question que je rate ton concert! *Know that there's no way I'll miss your concert!*
Sachez qu'il est impossible de revenir en arrière. *Be aware/Know that there's no turning back.*

Aller *to go* is irregular only in the **tu** form, and it loses and regains the -**s** like other verbs: **Va chez le médecin** *Go to the doctor's*; **Vas-y!** *Go (on)!*

everyday instructions

You'll come across the imperative in many everyday phrases:

Excusez-moi. Pardonnez-moi. *Excuse me. Sorry.*
Allez-y, je vous en prie. *Please, do go ahead.*
Fais de ton mieux. *Do your best.*
Profite de la vie! *Seize the moment! Carpe diem.*
Sois patient! *Be patient!*
Garde courage. *Have courage. Be strong.*
Occupe-toi de tes affaires. *Mind your own business.*
Remets-toi vite! *Get well soon!*
Ne fais pas cas de lui. *Take no notice of him.*
Reste-là! *Stay there!*
Tais-toi! *Be quiet! Shut up!*
Ne bouge pas! *Nobody move! Don't move!*
Ne me dérange pas. *Don't disturb me.*
Serre les dents et fais-le! *Come on! Be strong! Grit your teeth and do it!*
Garde les yeux bien ouverts. *Keep your eyes peeled.*
Gardez la monnaie. *Keep the change.*

... and also in recipes:

Assaisonnez avec une bonne pincée de sel, une pincée de poivre et un peu de noix de muscade râpée. *Season with a good pinch of salt, a pinch of pepper and a touch of grated nutmeg.*
Retirez du four, laissez refroidir et saupoudrez de sucre en poudre. *Remove from the oven, leave to cool and dust with caster sugar.*
Faites monter trois blancs d'œufs en neige ferme. *Whisk three egg whites to stiff peaks lit. firm snow.*

You'll also see the infinitive used as an alternative to the imperative in recipes:

Faire revenir le steak de chaque côté pendant quelques secondes. *Fry the steak on each side for a few seconds.*
Beurrer un moule de vingt-quatre cm. *Butter a 24 cm mould.*
Séparer les blancs des jaunes d'œufs. *Separate the egg whites from the yolks.*
Mettre l'huile, le vinaigre et la moutarde dans un bol. *Put the oil, the vinegar and mustard in a bowl.*

talking about food

Food and drink play such a central role in French life that it's well worth having a stock of expressions relating to them.

Vous avez faim? *Are you hungry?*
J'ai faim/J'ai soif. *I'm hungry/thirsty.*
J'ai une faim de loup. *I'm ravenous. I could eat a horse.*
Je mange comme quatre ces temps-ci. *I eat like a pig these days.*
Je n'ai pas beaucoup d'appétit. *I don't feel like eating much.*
Elle mange comme un moineau. *She eats like a bird/sparrow.*
Lui, par contre, mange comme un ogre! *He, on the other hand, eats like a horse!* lit. *like an ogre*
Je meurs de soif. *I'm dying of thirst.*

C'est bon? *Is it good?*
C'est très bon/vraiment délicieux. *It's very good/truly delicious.*
Vous cuisinez vraiment très bien! *You're an excellent cook!*
Je me régale! *I'm really enjoying this!*
Je n'ai jamais mangé une aussi bonne tarte Tatin! *It's the best tarte tatin I've ever eaten!*
J'ai vraiment bien mangé! *I've really eaten well.*
Je ne pourrais plus rien avaler! *I couldn't eat another thing!*
C'est un peu trop fort/épicé pour moi. *It's a bit too strong/spicy for me.*
Ce n'est pas assez sucré/salé. *It's not sweet/salty enough.*
Ça n'a pas vraiment de goût. *It's really bland.*

L'addition, s'il vous plaît! *The bill please!*
C'est moi qui invite! *It's my treat!*
Laissez, c'est pour nous. *It's our treat.*
C'est ma tournée. *I'm paying for this round.*
C'est à mon/notre tour de régler. *It's my/our turn to pay.*
On fait moitié-moitié? *Shall we go halves?*
Chacun n'a qu'à payer sa part. *We could go Dutch. Let's share the cost.*

Some expressions to do with eating and cooking are not to be taken literally!
Je ne suis pas dans mon assiette. *I feel a bit under the weather.* lit. *I'm not in my plate.*
On va devoir mettre les bouchées doubles. *We'll need to work twice as hard.* lit. *We'll need to double what we eat.*
C'est arrivé comme un cheveu sur la soupe. *It came out of nowhere.* lit. *It arrived like a hair on the soup.*

health matters

Talking about how you're feeling physically isn't confined to medical discussions: there are times when it's tactful to explain, for example, why you can't eat something.

Pourquoi tu ne manges pas? Tu ne trouves pas ça bon? *Why aren't you eating? Don't you like it?*
Je suis ... *I'm ...*
> **... diabétique.** *... diabetic.* **... cœliaque.** *... coeliac.*
> **... végétarien(ne).** *... vegetarian.* **... végétalien(ne)** *vegan.*
> **... allergique au gluten/au blé/à toutes sortes de fruits à coque.** *... allergic to gluten/to wheat/to every kind of nut.*
> **... intolérant(e) au lactose.** *... lactose intolerant.*

Je dois faire attention à ce que je mange. *I have to watch what I eat.*
Est-ce qu'il y a des cacahuètes dedans? *Are there peanuts in it?*

Camille n'a rien mangé. Elle ne se sent pas bien? *Camille hasn't eaten anything. Isn't she feeling well?*
Elle se sent très mal. *She feels dreadful.*
Elle a mal à une dent. *Her tooth hurts.*
Elle a de la fièvre/de la température. *She has a temperature.* (more on page 31)
Elle a une migraine. *She has a migraine.*
Elle fait une intoxication alimentaire. *She has food poisoning.*

Vous voulez goûter un peu de ce vin? *Do you want to try this wine?*
Juste une goutte/un doigt. *Just a drop/a smidgen.*
Je ne bois pas d'alcool. *I don't drink alcohol.*
Je prends des médicaments pour ... *I take medication for ...*
> **... la tension.** *... high blood pressure.*
> **... le diabète.** *... diabetes.*
> **... le cœur.** *... a heart condition.*

Je suis enceinte (de cinq mois). *I'm (five months) pregnant.*

Tu n'aimes pas les frites? *Don't you like chips?*
J'adore ça mais je suis au régime. *I love them but I'm on a diet.*
J'ai besoin de perdre cinq kilos avant le mois d'octobre. *I need to lose five kilos by October.*
Ce n'est pas que je n'aime pas mais j'ai trop de cholestérol. *It's not that I don't like them, but my cholesterol is too high.*

Similarly, you might need to explain why you aren't keen or able to join in. Or why someone else isn't.

Tu n'as pas envie de monter jusqu'au château? *Don't you want to go up to the castle?*

J'ai de l'arthrite. *I suffer from arthritis.*

J'ai mal aux genoux quand je monte/descends les escaliers. *My knees hurt when I go up/go down stairs.*

J'ai une tendinite. *I've got tendonitis.*

Je me suis fait mal à la cheville hier. *I hurt my ankle yesterday.*

Je pense que je suis complètement déshydraté(e). *I think I'm really dehydrated.*

Tu ne viens pas à la gym? Qu'est-ce qui ne va pas? *Aren't you coming to the gym? What's up?*

Je me suis claqué un muscle ... *I've pulled a muscle ...*

    ... dans le mollet/dans l'aine. *... in my calf/in my groin.*

Je ne peux pas plier le genou. *I can't bend my knee.*

J'en ai trop fait à l'entraînement hier. *I overdid the training yesterday.*

Je suis crevé(e)/vidé(e)! *I'm shattered!*

J'ai attrapé froid. *I caught a chill.*

Pierre n'est pas là. Il est où? *Pierre's not here. Where is he?*

On l'a emmené à l'hôpital. *He's been taken to hospital.*

Il a fait un malaise ce matin. *He collapsed this morning.*

Il avait une douleur aiguë ... *He had a sharp pain ...*

    ... à la poitrine/au ventre. *... in his chest/in his stomach.*

Il y a eu un accident. *There was/there has been an accident.*

On va à la plage? *Shall we go to the beach?*

J'ai mal à la tête. *My head hurts.*

J'ai la tête qui tourne. J'ai des vertiges. *I feel dizzy.*

Je suis resté(e) trop longtemps au soleil hier. *I stayed out in the sun too long yesterday.*

J'ai pris un mauvais coup de soleil, regarde! *I'm really sunburnt. Look!*

You don't need the words *my, your, his, her* when you're talking about your body:

J'ai mal au dos. *My back hurts.*

Tu as mal au dos? *Does your back hurt? Is your back hurting?*

Il/Elle a mal au dos. *His/her back's hurting.*

wordbank

la nourriture *food*
le repas *meal*
    un repas équilibré *a well-balanced meal*
    un repas gastronomique *a gourmet meal*
    sauter un repas *to skip a meal*
    des amuse-gueules *appetisers, nibbles* lit. *gob-teasers*

un régime (alimentaire), une alimentation
    ... strict(e) ... *a strict diet*
    ... riche en protéines ... *a high-protein diet*
    ... riche en matières grasses ... *a high-fat diet*
    ... faible en glucides ... *a low-carb diet*

La gastronomie française

Did you know that in 2010, UNESCO added French gastronomy to its list of the world's 'intangible cultural heritage'? How can you best experience **les arts de la table** *culinary arts* **à la française**? Splash out on a meal at a **restaurant étoilé**, a restaurant whose chef holds one or several stars given by the **critiques gastronomiques** *food critics* of the famous **Guide Michelin.**

If that's a bit beyond your means, go online and check out **les bonnes tables** *fine dining* where you're staying or just head to **une brasserie** or **une auberge** *inn* (a good quality restaurant, often out of town) and you will get good food at a fraction of the cost.

Parlons bouffe!

Boire and **manger** are not the only words to talk about eating and drinking in French. You might hear the word **la bouffe** *nosh, grub*, as in **On se fait une petite bouffe?** *Shall we eat together?*

The French often use the word **petit** *small, little* not to belittle but, on the contrary, to emphasise the quality of something: **On va se faire de bons petits plats** *We'll treat ourselves to a special meal.*

In France, many special occasions are celebrated with **un gueleton bien arrosé** *boozy feast, slap-up meal*, which might leave you with **une gueule de bois** *hangover* if you're not careful! If the next day you hear about **prendre une bonne cuite** or **être complètement beurré**, it's nothing to do with cooking or buttering something, but all to do with getting blind drunk. And remember, if you're invited for dinner, your host will prefer you to have **un bon coup de fourchette** *a hearty appetite*, lit. *a good way with a fork* than to be **difficile** *a picky eater*. **Alors, bon appétit!**

talking the talk

Nico   Sophie, tes invités vont avoir faim après toutes ces discussions sur l'immigration et l'économie! Tout est prêt pour ce fameux barbecue?

Sophie   Je ne sais pas. Je crois que oui.

Nico   Qu'est-ce qu'il y a à manger? Est-ce qu'il y a des hamburgers?

Sophie   Oui, il y a des hamburgers, du poulet, des merguez, des saucisses ... Voyons ... Qu'est-ce qui manque?

Nico   Il n'y a pas de salade. Il y avait de la salade quelque part, je l'ai vue!

Sophie   Oui, oui, la salade est dans le frigo.

Nico   Les autres invités vont bientôt arriver. Tu leur as dit vers dix-neuf heures, c'est ça? Il y aura beaucoup de monde?

Sophie   Une trentaine de personnes. J'espère qu'il y aura assez de place!

Nico   Dis, Sophie, comment est-ce qu'on allume ce barbecue?

Sophie   Pousse le bouton rouge et ça s'allume automatiquement. Vas-y, mais fais bien attention.

Nico   Génial! Ça marche!

Sophie   Mmm, elles sont bonnes, les saucisses, hein, tu ne trouves pas?

Nico   Euh ... oui, mais ... euh ...

Sophie   Tu ne manges pas? Tu n'as pas faim?

Nico   Ben non, non ... enfin, là, je ne suis pas dans mon assiette ...

Sophie   Ah bon? Mais qu'est-ce qu'il y a? Tu es malade?

Nico   Je ne me sens pas très bien en fait ... Dis, les saucisses, là, qu'est-ce qu'il y a dedans?

Sophie   Ben, du porc ... pourquoi?

Nico   Ah, c'est ça, je suis allergique au porc! Je croyais que c'était du bœuf ... Vite, passe-moi un verre d'eau, je dois tout de suite prendre un médicament.

checkpoint 11

1   How would you adapt **Il y a du vent** to say that it was windy yesterday and that it will be windy tomorrow?

2   Referring to a meal, how would you say *It's the best I've ever eaten*?

3   How do you find out if there will be enough room and if there will be something to eat?

4   In a restaurant or a bar, how would you offer to pay and, if your friend refuses, how would you suggest you share the bill?

5   At the end of a meal, how might you say that you've really eaten well?

6   What do you change in **Il a mal à la poitrine** to say *Her* chest is hurting? And how do you say *She takes medication for high blood pressure*?

7   How do you ask if something contains wheat?

8   Tell a friend to call the emergency services ... and not to call them.

9   Explain that you hurt your knees yesterday.

10 How do you tell a friend you know really well to be ready at 9 a.m. tomorrow morning? What about if you are talking to a group of friends?

11 Starting with *Could anyone tell me* ..., how would you ask in French where the nearest **brasserie** is?

12 How would you urge an elderly person you don't know well to have a rest?

13 If you see **Merci de ne pas fumer dans le parking**, what should you do or not do?

14 What do **Dépêche-toi** and **Tais-toi** mean? How do they change when speaking to two people?

15 Where are you likely to come across the terms **assaisonner, une pincée, saupoudrer, faire monter, beurrer** and **le four**?

16 If you see **Tirez** on a door, do you pull or do you push?

17 How would you tell your friends you're missing them?

douze
keeping in touch

Whether you're keeping in touch with people or with what's going on in the world, the chances are that you'll be doing it via the Internet. To access it on your tablet or smartphone in France, you'll need to ask **Est-ce que vous avez du wifi?** *Do you have Wi-Fi?* and **C'est quoi, le mot de passe?** *What's the password?* Some French people say **le wifi,** others say **la wifi.** In either case, **wifi** is pronounced *weefee*.

Even if you're no technophile, the influence of technology on everyday life is such that it's worth understanding some key terminology in French. This isn't a major hurdle as English words are widely used. That said, you may not instantly recognise some of them when you hear them, as the way they're pronounced is French through and through.

What's interesting for someone learning French is the way the adopted words are used. Their origin might be English but they're governed by the rules of French grammar, making them the perfect illustration of those rules. For instance, the verb *to google* becomes **googler,** taking on the regular **-er** endings.

It is well worth keeping up with new words in French: newly-coined words can appear and disappear very quickly, others stay and even officially enter the dictionary: verbs like **tweeter/twitter** *to tweet* and nouns such as **la twittosphère** *twitter community,* **un youtubeur** or **une youtubeuse** *youtubers.*

le franglais

The number of English words used in French has grown hugely in recent years. The phenomenon is called **le franglais**.

It's very noticeable in many areas like sport, with words like **corner** and **penalty** but also very much in the world of business, **le monde des affaires**:

Je vais checker tout cela et je reviens vers vous par mail. *I'll check all of that and will get back to you by email.*

On organise un brainstorming avec les project managers. *We're organising a brainstorming session with the project managers.*

On va discuter des deadlines pendant la conf call. *We'll talk about deadlines during the conference call.*

Le challenge, c'est de booster les revenus en offrant des options low-cost. *The challenge is to boost returns by offering low-cost options.*

You also come across franglais in the world of fashion, music and media and technology.

Il fait le buzz avec son dernier best-seller. *His latest bestseller is creating a buzz.*

Elle est très glamour mais ça fait un peu has been. Je préfère le look vintage. *She's very glam but it looks a bit dated. I prefer the vintage look.*

Ce soir, en prime time, il y a un remake du biopic de la célèbre star des sixties, Brigitte Bardot. *Tonight, on prime-time TV, they're showing a remake of the biopic of the famous sixties star, Brigitte Bardot.*

... and even relationships:

Il est vraiment hyper speedé depuis son coming out: il squatte chez moi, il dit que c'est cosy. *He's really stressed out since coming out: he's staying over at my place; he says it's cosy.*

Tu l'as rencontré où? À une blind date ou un speed dating? *Where did you meet him? During a blind date or speed dating?*

Non, pendant un team-building, où j'étais invitée avec les happy few. Il était DJ. *No, during a team-building event, where I was invited with the happy few. He was the DJ.*

Le franglais is most in evidence in the world of IT. English words predominate on the internet, particularly among the computer savvy and on social media. Like other borrowed words, they're used according to the rules of French grammar.

Nouns have a gender and articles and respect normal spelling conventions, including in the plural:
le chat, le cloud, le vlogging, l'appli, le hotspot, le streaming, l'emoji, le blog, un slideshow, un pdf, un mail, un troll, une webcam, des tweets, des likes, des posts, etc.

When new verbs are created from English words, they all belong to the -**er** group, e.g: **(t)chatter, crasher, downloader, uploader, googler, liker, taguer, tweeter/twitter, zipper, zoomer.** These newly minted verbs use the endings of regular -**er** verbs and have a past participle ending in -**é**.

Ma fille chatte en ligne pendant des heures. *My daughter chats online for hours.*
Il twitte tous les jours. *He tweets every day.*
Zoome un peu sur son visage. *Zoom in a bit on her face.*
Il m'a tagué sur une photo à la soirée. *He tagged me on a photo at the party.*
Ils ont liké ma page! *They liked my page!*
Mon ordi a crashé ... *My computer's crashed ...*
... pendant que j'uploadais mes photos. *... while I was uploading my photos.*

Chatter or **tchatter** has the specific meaning of *to chat online*: to have a chat face-to-face with someone is **bavarder** or **causer**.

There are attempts to resist the franglais trend and to provide French terminology in all domains, especially business and the Internet, e.g:

le branding = stratégie d'image, un briefing = une réunion préparatoire, un debriefing = une réunion-bilan

Québecois (French Canadians from Quebec) in particular are keen to avoid **franglais** and come up with innovative vocabulary: **le courriel** *email*, **clavarder** *to chat online* (from **bavarder** *chat* on a **clavier** *keyboard*), **une appliquette** *applet*, **une ardoise électronique** *tablet*, **une frimousse** *smiley*, **le pourriel** *spam* (from **pourri** *rotten* and **courriel** *email*), etc.

saying thank you

At the end of a visit come the thanks and the goodbyes.

To say goodbye, use **au revoir** or more casually **salut** *bye, cheers* or even the Italian word **ciao**, which in French is only said on parting (you also hear it quite often repeated twice: **ciao ciao**). Avoid **adieu** *farewell*, which is literary and solemn, except in the south of France where it is used to say both hello and goodbye.

A simple *thank you* is **merci** but you can add to it when you want your thanks to be more enthusiastic.

Merci bien. *Thank you very/so much.*
Merci beaucoup. *Thank you very much.*
Mille mercis. Merci mille fois. *Thanks a million.*
Merci pour tout. *Thanks for everything.*
Encore merci. *Thanks again.*

merci pour or merci de?

When *thank you for* is followed by a noun, you can say **merci pour** or **merci de** — although **merci pour** is more common.
Merci pour ton aide. *Thanks for your help.*
Un grand merci pour votre réponse. *Thank you very much for your reply.*
Merci pour/de votre patience. *Thank you for your patience.*

... but when it's followed by a verb, you must use **de**:
Merci d'être venu. *Thank you for coming.*
Merci de ne pas fumer dans la maison. *Thank you for not smoking in the house.*

There are other ways of expressing your appreciation:
Je te/vous remercie infiniment. *Thank you very much indeed.*
Je ne sais pas comment vous remercier. *I don't know how to thank you.*
Tu es un ange! *You're an angel!*
Je te dois beaucoup. *I owe you big time.*

Je me suis vraiment bien amusé(e). *I've really enjoyed myself.*
Nous avons passé un excellent moment. *We've had a great time.*

Merci rarely passes without a response:
Je t'en prie./Je vous en prie. *You're welcome.*
De rien. Il n'y a pas de quoi. *Don't mention it.*
Tout le plaisir était pour moi. *My pleasure.*

keeping in touch

After the goodbyes and thanks, talk usually turns to staying in touch. Writing letters and emails, and keeping in contact via social media, is excellent practice for your French.

J'ai été ravi(e) de faire votre connaissance/de vous rencontrer. *It's been a pleasure meeting you.*

Nous espérons bien vous revoir l'année prochaine. *We hope to see you again next year.*

Tu vas me manquer. *I'll miss you.* **Vous allez tous me manquer.** *I'll miss you all.*

Restons en contact. *We'll be in touch soon.*

You've already come across the language structures you need:

asking questions: chapters 2 and 11

C'est quoi, votre adresse mail/pseudo Skype? *What's your email address/ Skype name?*

C'est quoi, votre numéro de téléphone? *What's your phone number?*

Tu es sur WhatsApp? *Are you on WhatsApp?*

Comment est-ce que j'installe WhatsApp? *How do I install WhatsApp?*

C'est quoi, la meilleure façon de te joindre? *What's the best way to reach you?*

needs must: chapter 9

Il faut qu'on reste en contact. *We must keep in touch.*

On peut échanger nos coordonnées? *Could we exchange details?*

On pourrait créer un groupe sur Skype/WhatsApp. *We could set up a Skype/ WhatsApp group.*

Alain pourrait partager ses meilleures photos. *Alain could share his best photos.*

future: chapter 8

Je t'appelle dimanche. *I'll call you on Sunday.*

Je te trouverai sur Facebook. *I'll find you on Facebook.*

Je t'envoie tous les infos par sms. *I'll text you all the info.*

On mettra la vidéo sur le cloud. *We'll upload the video to the cloud.*

imperative: chapter 11

Envoie-moi un texto/sms ou un mail. *Send me a text or an email.*

Appelle-moi sur Facetime. *Call me on Facetime.*

N'oublie pas ... *Don't forget ...*

... d'accepter ma demande de contact sur Skype. *... to accept me on Skype.*

... de m'envoyer un mail. *... to write me an email.*

phone calls and emails

If you're planning to phone someone, it's worth knowing the following:

Allô. *Hello.* (only used when speaking on the phone)
Qui est à l'appareil? *Who's calling?*
Ici M. Leblanc. *M. Leblanc speaking. This is M. Leblanc.*
Je ne vous entends pas bien. *I can't hear you very well.*
Je n'ai pas de signal. *I don't have any signal.*
Le signal est faible. *The signal is weak.*
Je n'ai qu'une barre de signal. *I've only got one bar.*
Je n'ai plus beaucoup de batterie. *I haven't got much battery left.*
Mon numéro de portable, c'est ... *My mobile number is ...*
Désolé(e), ce n'est pas le bon numéro. *Sorry, wrong number.*

A question you'll hear often is **Veuillez laisser une message après le signal sonore.** *Please leave a message after the tone.*

Mon adresse mail, c'est ...   Le mot de passe, c'est ...

For these, you need to know how to spell out words (page 21) and you need punctuation marks.

* **astérisque**	, **virgule**
@ **arobase**	# **la touche dièse**
/ **slash, barre oblique**	ABC *upper case* **majuscule**
\ **barre inverse**	abc *lower case* **minuscule**
. **point**	(*in brackets*) **entre parenthèses**
- **tiret**	"*in inverted commas*" **entre guillemets**
_ **tiret bas**	*space* **espace**

Le site, c'est: www (pronounced *doobluh-vay doobluh-vay doobluh-vay*)
point ... or **trois w** (*doubluh-vay*) **point ...** *The site is: www dot ...*

In French, a personal email usually starts with one of the following:
Cher/Chère, **Mon cher/Ma chère**, **Salut** *Hello, Hi,* **Coucou** *Hiya* + the person's name.

You can finish with:
> **À bientôt!** or **À plus/A+!** *See you soon!*
> **Je t'embrasse ...** *Big hug ...* lit. *I embrace you.*
> **Bises ...** or **Bisous ...** *Kisses ...*
> **Amitiés ...** *Best wishes ...* lit. *friendships* (a bit more formal)

shortcuts

Shortcuts originally evolved to make texting easier but are now widely used online, especially on social media sites and in chatrooms.

They follow the same principles in French as they do in English. For example, English transcribes the sound *ate/eight* as 8, so *great* → *gr8*.

French transcribes the sound **(a)in** as **1** and **de** as **2**: à demain → a2m1

The sounds **si** and **ci** are written **6**: **ciné(ma)** → 6né

The sound **ui** is written **8**: **lui** *him* → l8

The aim is to be as brief as possible, while still comprehensible:

> **ke** and **ki** for **que** and **qui**
> **pk pourquoi?** *why?*
> **slt salut** *hi*
> **biz bise** *kiss*
> **eske est-ce que** (in a question)
> **keske qu'est-ce que** *what?*
> **dak d'accord** *OK*
> **qqch quelque chose** *something*
> **qqn quelqu'un** *someone*
> **a12c4 à un de ces quatre** *see you around*
> **2ri1 de rien** *you're welcome*

Other abbreviated forms include:

> **STP s'il te plaît** *please*
> **SVP s'il vous plaît** *please*
> **ALP à la prochaine** *TTFN, bye for now*
> **AMHA à mon humble avis** *IMHO, in my humble opinion*
> **ATT à tout (à l'heure)** *CUL8r, see you later*
> **DQP dès que possible** *ASAP, as soon as possible*
> **MDR mort de rire** *LOL, laughing out loud*
> **NSP ne sais pas** *dunno*
> **PV/en PV en privé** *in private*

wordbank

IT is **l'informatique** (f), and *computer* is **l'ordinateur** (m).

le matériel informatique *hardware*
la tablette *tablet*
l'(ordinateur) portable (m) *laptop*
l'écran *screen*
le câble *cable, wire*
le clavier *keyboard*

la souris *mouse*
l'imprimante (f) *printer*
le casque *headphones*
le clé USB *memory stick*
le chargeur *charger*

le système d'exploitation *operating system*
la mémoire *memory*
le logiciel *program, software*
le nom d'utilisateur *user name*
le mot de passe *password*

le menu *menu*
le curseur/la flèche *cursor/arrow*
la barre d'outils *toolbar*
le fichier *file*
le dossier *folder*
l'icône (f) *icon*

le moteur de recherche *search engine*
le navigateur *browser*
le lien *link*
le fichier joint, la pièce jointe *attachment*
joindre *to attach*

être sur Internet/en ligne *to be online*
le site internet/web *website*
la page web *web page*
le favori, le signet *bookmark*
la boîte de réception *inbox*
l'URL (f) *URL*

connecter *to connect*
se connecter/se déconnecter *to log in/log out*
mettre en marche *to switch on*
rechercher *to search (for)*
naviguer, surfer *to browse/surf*

saisir *to key in*
mettre à jour *to update*
sauvegarder *to back up*
supprimer *to delete*
vérifier les mails *to check e-mail*
mettre à jour, modifier *to edit*

 Create ten sentences in French, combining structures such as On fait comment pour … *or* Comment est-ce qu'on … *with these verbs and nouns: e.g.* How do I turn the printer on? How do I go about uploading this photo? How does this document open? *Or use other verbs you know to say you'd like to check your email, you want/need/ought to send an email, attach/update/edit a file or photo, find a link. Try asking if there's a password and what it is.*

talking the talk

Sophie	Merci mille fois pour toute ton aide, Nico! Tu es un ange!
Nico	Il n'y a pas de quoi. On fait une bonne équipe tous les deux! Je me suis vraiment bien amusé ... même si je n'ai pas pu manger de saucisses!
Sophie	Oui! Moi aussi, je me suis bien amusée. Et ton frère Sébastien, il est vraiment sympa.
Nico	Sébastien? Oui. Ok, je vois.
Sophie	Tu pourrais me donner son numéro de portable? J'aimerais rester en contact avec lui.
Nico	D'accord, je crois que j'ai bien compris.
Sophie	J'aimerais lui poser une question.
Nico	Tu veux sortir avec mon frère, c'est ça?
Sophie	Sortir avec ton frère? Mais non, pas du tout. Mais vu qu'il travaille pour un magazine de mode, je voudrais lui demander s'il peut m'aider à trouver un travail ...
Nico	Alors, tu n'as pas le coup de foudre pour Sébastien? Tu ne veux pas sortir avec lui?
Sophie	Non, je ne veux pas sortir avec lui. Je voudrais seulement rester en contact avec lui, pour des raisons ... professionnelles. Pourquoi? Tu n'es pas jaloux?
Nico	Et si tu restais en contact avec moi? Pour des raisons ... moins professionnelles.
Sophie	Nico, tu m'invites à sortir avec toi?
Nico	Euh, ben ...
Sophie	Appelle-moi demain.
Nico	Allô, Sophie? C'est Nico.
Sophie	Salut!
Nico	Écoute, je voulais t'envoyer mes photos du barbecue par mail ...

Sophie	Ah oui, sympa! Tu as un bon appareil en plus ...
Nico	Oui, mais j'ai téléchargé mes photos, et après ça, mon ordi a crashé.
Sophie	Oh non! Tu avais sauvegardé tes documents?
Nico	Malheureusement non, je suis vraiment idiot.
Sophie	Écoute, tant pis. Les autres vont sûrement mettre leurs photos sur Facebook.
Nico	Oui, sans doute. Euh ... Sophie, je voulais te demander ... je peux t'inviter à dîner ce soir?
Sophie	Mais oui, bien sûr! J'attendais que tu me le demandes!

checkpoint 12

1   When would you want to have **une souris** on your desk?

2   How do you tell someone how pleased you are to have met them?

3   What are **ALP**, **2ri1** and **slt** short for?

4   What do these words represent: **astérisque, arobase, virgule, tiret** and **parenthèses**?

5   Guess which of these are used in French: **le corner, le snowboard, le skater, le shopping, le parking, le camping, le marketing, le jingle, la presse people, le podcast, le spamming**

6   If you're told **Vous n'avez pas fait le bon numéro**, what have you done?

7   How do you think the verb *to email* will be constructed from the French noun **mail**? And how will you say *I'll email you*?

8   What word is missing from **Merci ...... cette magnifique journée** for it to mean *Thank you for the wonderful day*? And what is the word missing here to thank someone for having called you back? **Merci ...... m'avoir rappelé.**

9   Choose the appropriate phrases to thank a close friend: **Merci pour tout!, Je vous remercie infiniment, Mille mercis, Tu es un ange!**

10 How do you ask if there's Wi-Fi available?

11 Using knowledge from this and previous chapters, how would you say *I have lost my mobile* and *We need to buy a battery*.

12 Can you think of three ways to finish a friendly letter, email or text to a close friend?

13 What's the difference between a **texto** and an **sms**?

14 You want to post some photos on Facebook; how would you ask someone how to do it?

15 Ask someone if he/she is going to miss you.

16 Which phrase will you not use in reply to a friend thanking you? What does it mean?
    De rien, Je te dois beaucoup, Je t'en prie, Il n'y a pas de quoi.

grammar terminology

Adjectives are words that describe nouns and pronouns: *good idea*, *strong red wine*, *my fault*, *She's tall*, *It was weird*. In French, unlike English, they change according to what they're describing.

Adverbs add information to verbs, adjectives, other adverbs and whole sentences: *a very good idea*, *He's acting weirdly*, *Luckily he's not here*.

Agreement: A French article or adjective has to agree with, i.e. match, the noun or pronoun it relates to, in terms of gender (masculine or feminine) and number (singular or plural).

Articles are **definite**: *the house, the houses,* or **indefinite**: *a house, an area.*

The **conditional** is the verb form used to say what would or could happen.

Consonants and vowels make up the alphabet: the vowels are **a, e, i, o, u**; the rest are consonants.

The **endings** of words are the final letter(s). In English, a verb ending in *-ed* tells you it happened in the past. In French, endings are much more widespread, with nouns, adjectives and verbs relying on them to convey essential information.

Feminine: See Gender.

Gender: In French, every noun is either masculine (m) or feminine (f). This is its gender, and you need to know a noun's gender because words used with it, such as articles and adjectives, have corresponding masculine and feminine forms in French.

The **imperative** is the verb form used to give instructions or commands: *Wait for me*, *Don't say that*, *Take the first left*.

The **imperfect tense** of a verb is used to describe how things were and to talk about things that happened over a period of time or repeatedly.

Infinitive: French verbs are listed in a dictionary in their infinitive form, ending in **-er, -ir** or **-re.** The English equivalent uses *to*: **travailler** *to work*, **finir** *to finish*, **vendre** *to sell.*

An **intransitive** verb is one that does not have a direct object, e.g. *to arrive, to laugh, to die.*

Irregular nouns, verbs or adjectives don't behave in a predictable way like regular ones and have to be learnt separately.

Masculine: See Gender.

Negatives are words like *not, never, nothing, nobody* and *not ... ever, not ... anybody, not ... anything*.

Nouns are the words for living beings, things, places and abstract concepts: *father, analyst, Siân, giraffe, chair, village, Paris, time, courage*.

Number refers to the difference between **singular** (one) and **plural** (more than one).

The **object** of a verb is at the receiving end. An object can be **direct**: *He sent an email*; or **indirect**, in which case it is often preceded by *to* or *for*: *He sent an email to his friend*.

Ordinal numbers are *first, second, third, fourth,* etc.

The **past participle** of a verb is used with *have* when talking about the past: *I have finished, He has eaten, They had gone*.

The **perfect tense** of a verb is used in French to talk about the past; it is equivalent to the English *I worked* and *I have worked*.

The **person** of a verb indicates who or what is doing something:
1st person = the speaker: *I* (singular), *we* (plural)
2nd person = the person(s) being addressed: *you*
3rd person = who/what is being talked about: *he/she/it/they*

Personal pronouns are words like *I, me, you, we, us, she, her, them*.

The **pluperfect** tense translates *had done something*.

Plural means more than one.

Prepositions are words like *by, in, on, with, for, through, next to*.

The **present tense** of a verb is used to talk about things being done now: *I work, I'm working*.

Reflexive pronouns are **me, te, se, nous, vous, se** used as an integral part of reflexive verbs.

Reflexive verbs in French are made up of two words, the first of which is **se** in the infinitive: **se lever** *to get up*.

Regular nouns, adjectives, verbs etc. conform to a pattern and are entirely predictable.

Relative pronouns are words like *which, who, that*, used to join together parts of a sentence without repeating the noun.

Singular means one, while **plural** means more than one.

The **stem** of a French verb is, for example, what's left when you remove the **-er**, **-ir** or **-re** ending of the infinitive.

The **subject** of a sentence is whoever or whatever is carrying out the verb: *They* have two children, *Anna* reads the paper, *This house* cost a lot of money, *Peace* is possible.

Subject pronouns are *I, we, you, he, she, it, they*.

The **subjunctive** is a form of a verb that's rarely used in English, other than in phrases like *if I were you*, but is widely used in French in defined grammatical circumstances.

Superlative is *the most ...* when comparing several things.

A **syllable** is a unit that contains a vowel and consists of a single sound: *can* has one syllable, *can·ter* has two, while *Can·ter·bu·ry* has four.

Tense refers to when the verb is happening: in the past, present or future. Tenses have names, e.g. present, perfect, imperfect.

A **transitive** verb has a direct object, e.g. *to catch ..., to make ..., to open ...*, whereas an **intransitive** verb does not, e.g. *to arrive, to laugh, to die*.

Verbs relate to doing and being and are identifiable in English because you can put *to* in front of them: *to live, to be, to speak, to play, to think, to have, to need*.

Vowels and consonants make up the alphabet: the vowels are a, e, i, o, u; the rest are consonants.

grammar summary

nouns

All French nouns are either masculine (m) or feminine (f).
The nouns for male people are masculine and females are feminine: **le frère** *brother*, **la mère** *mother*, **le cousin** *male cousin*, **la cousine** *female cousin*, **le copain** *male friend*, **la copine** *female friend*.

A few nouns referring to people can be either masculine or feminine, depending on who you are talking about, for example: **le collègue** *male colleague*, **la collègue** *female colleague*.

There's no foolproof way of working out the gender of other nouns, e.g. *train* is masculine (**le train**), while *car* is feminine (**la voiture**). The table shows some typical masculine and feminine endings, though there are exceptions.

masculine endings		feminine endings	
often ending in a consonant:	or:	often ending in -**e**:	or:
-**c**, -**d**, -**g**, -**k**, -**s**	-**age**	-**ée**, -**ie**	-**ité**
-**non**, -**ron**, -**ton**	-**ège**	-**ance**, -**anse**	-**son**
-**et**	-**isme**	-**ence**, -**ense**	-**tion**
-**ment**	-**eau**	-**ière**	
-**ail**	-**ou**	-**ude**, -**ure**	
-**ier**, -**eur**		-**sse**, -**tte**	
		-**lle**, -**rre**	

Most French nouns add -**s** in the plural: **un café** → **des cafés**; **un train** → **des trains**. There are a few exceptions. Nouns that end in:
- -**s**, -**x** or -**z** don't change: **un/des pays** *country, countries*; **le/les prix** *price, prices*; **un/des nez** *nose, noses*
- -**eau** or -**eu** add -**x**, not -**s**: **un chapeau** *hat* → **des chapeaux**; **un jeu** *game* → **des jeux**
  (a few nouns ending in -**ou** also add -**x**: **un bijou** *jewel* → **des bijoux**)
- -**al** and -**ail** change to -**aux**: **un animal** → **des animaux**; **le travail** *work* → **les travaux**

The added -**s** or -**x** is not pronounced.

A few French nouns have irregular plurals, e.g. **un œil** *eye* → **des yeux** *eyes*; **madame** → **mesdames**; **monsieur** → **messieurs**.

A few nouns that are plural in English are singular in French, e.g. **le jean** *jeans*, **un escalier** *stairs*, and some that are plural in French are singular in English, e.g. **les cheveux** *hair*, **les conseils** *advice*, **les bagages** *luggage*.

articles

In French, the words for *the*, *a* and *some* depend on whether the following noun is masculine or feminine, singular or plural.

		the (singular)	*the* (plural)	*a/an*	*some*
m	*ticket*	le billet	les billets	un billet	des billets
f	*apple*	la pomme	les pommes	une pomme	des pommes

Le and **la** shorten to **l'** when the next word begins with a vowel or a silent **h**: **l'aéroport** (m) *the airport*, **l'hôtel** (m) *the hotel*, **l'orage** (m) *the thunderstorm*, **l'huile** (f) *the oil*, **l'église** (f) *the church*, **l'idée** (f) *the idea*

French uses the definite article more than English does — most noticeably in generalisations such as **Je n'aime pas les poires** *I don't like pears* — but also before:

- abstract nouns: **C'est la vie.** *That's life.*
- countries: **la France, les États-Unis** *USA*
- languages: **le français** *French*, **l'anglais** *English*. **Le, la** or **l'** is used with a language after **apprendre** *to learn* and **comprendre** *to understand*, but not after **parler** *to speak* or **en** *in*: **je comprends le français** but **je parle français, en français.**

Unlike English, French doesn't use **un/une** with nouns denoting occupation or religion:
Je suis médecin. *I'm a doctor.* **Elle est musulmane.** *She's a Muslim.*

adjectives

An adjective is listed in a dictionary in the masculine singular form, e.g. **blanc, canadien, petit, naïf**. Unlike English, the ending of a French adjective varies to match the noun it describes (it is masculine or feminine, singular or plural).

If the masculine adjective ends in **-e**, the masculine and feminine versions are the same, adding an **-s** in the plural:

Le problème est difficile.   **Les problèmes sont difficiles.**
La question est difficile.   **Les questions sont difficiles.**

For adjectives ending in a consonant or **é**, the feminine version generally adds **-e**, while in the plural, both masculine and feminine add **-s**:

Le film est intéressant.   **Les films sont intéressants.**
La suggestion est intéressante.   **Les suggestions sont intéressantes.**

If the masculine adjective ends in **-s** or **-x**, the masculine singular and plural versions are the same: **le vin français/les vins français**
la bière française/les bières françaises

Some adjective endings follow recognisable patterns:

	m/f		m/f
el	**essentiel/essentielle**	c	**blanc/blanche**; **public/publique**
en	**canadien/canadienne**	f	**actif/active**
er	**premier/première**	g	**long/longue**
et	**complet/complète**	x	**délicieux/délicieuse**

Some common adjectives are irregular:
beau/belle *beautiful*; **doux/douce** *soft, gentle*; **faux/fausse** *fake, false*,
frais/fraîche *fresh*; **nouveau/nouvelle** *new*; **vieux/vieille** *old*

position of adjectives

A French adjective usually goes *after* the noun it describes when the two are together, e.g. **un ami français** *a French friend*.
A few very common adjectives and all numbers go before the noun:
beau *beautiful*; **bon** *good*; **grand** *big*; **gros** *big, fat*; **jeune** *young*; **joli** *pretty*;
long *long*; **mauvais** *bad*; **meilleur** *better, best*; **nouveau** *new*; **petit** *small*; **vieux** *old*; **vrai** *real*; **premier** *first*; **second, deuxième** *second*; **troisième** *third*, etc.

possession

Possessive adjectives agree with the gender of what's owned, not the owner. So *his car* is **sa voiture**.

	m sing *	f sing	plural
my	**mon**	**ma**	**mes**
your (**tu**)	**ton**	**ta**	**tes**
his/her	**son**	**sa**	**ses**
our	**notre**	**notre**	**nos**
your (**vous**)	**votre**	**votre**	**vos**
their	**leur**	**leur**	**leurs**

* and feminine singular before a vowel or silent **h**

Leurs portables sont dans ton sac? *Are their mobiles in your bag?*
Notre oncle connaît son frère. *Our uncle knows his/her brother.*

French doesn't use -'s to indicate possession:

J'aime bien l'idée de Sophie. *I like Sophie's idea.*

C'est le livre de sa copine. *It's his/her (girl)friend's book.*

this, that

Ce/cette/cet *this, that,* **ces** *these, those:*

- goes before the noun and agrees with it: **ce bar, cette conversation, ces clés**
- has a special masculine singular form used before a vowel or silent **h: cet homme, cet été**

Add **-ci** *this* or **-là** *that* for emphasis:

ce menu-ci *this menu,* **cette voiture-là** *that car*

Celui-ci and **celui-là** mean *this one, that one.*

Celle-ci and **celle-là** are the feminine versions.

Je vais prendre celui-ci. *I'll take this one.* (masculine item)

Je préfère celle-là. *I prefer that one.* (feminine item)

Ceux-ci/ceux-là are the masculine plural forms and **celles-ci/celles-là** are the feminine plurals:

Je préfère ceux-ci. *I prefer these (ones).* (m)

adverbs

French adverbs never change their form. They often end in **-ment** (equivalent to *-ly* in English). It's commonly added to the feminine form of an adjective to make it into an adverb: **heureusement** *luckily,* **rapidement** *quickly,* **seulement** *only.*

A few adverbs are formed from a masculine adjective instead, e.g. **vraiment** *really,* **absolument** *absolutely.*

Some very common adverbs don't end in **-ment**, for example: **très** *very,* **trop** *too,* **plutôt** *rather,* **assez** *quite,* **un peu** *a bit,* **si** *so,* **vite** *quickly.*

comparisons

You add **plus** *more* and **moins** *less* to adjectives and adverbs to compare two or more things: **plus froid** *colder,* **plus intéressant** *more interesting,* **moins cher** *less expensive,* **moins vite** *less quickly.*

Than is **que: Le livre est plus intéressant que le film.** *The book is more interesting than the film.*

Le/la/les + plus/moins means *the most* or *the least:* **la langue la plus difficile** *the most difficult language,* **les pays les moins riches** *the least wealthy/rich countries*

prepositions

Some prepositions have a direct equivalent in English: they tell you when or where something happened:

when: **après** **le match** *after the match*, **avant** **mon départ** *before my departure*, **dans** **cinq minutes** *in five minutes*, **vers** **minuit** *towards, around midnight*

where: **sur** **la table** *on the table*, **sous** **le bureau** *under the desk*, **devant** **la gare** *in front of the station*, **derrière** **ma maison** *behind my house*, **dans** **mon sac** *in my bag*, **entre** **la poste et la banque** *between the post office and the bank*

Some French prepositions correspond to more than one English usage.

à   *at* **à la maison** *at home*, **à six heures** *at six o'clock*

        in **J'habite à Londres.** *I live in London.*

        to (with cities, towns, villages and small islands) **Nous allons à Paris.** *We're going to Paris.*

à combines with **le** and **les** to make a new word:

     à + le → au: au cinéma *to the cinema*; **à + les → aux: aux États-Unis** (m pl) *to the USA*

de   *of* **une photo de mon mari** *a photo of my husband*

        from, out of **un message de Marie** *a message from Marie*, **sortir du cinéma** *to go out of the cinema*

de also combines with **le** and **les** to make a new word:

     de + le → du; de + les → des

de + definite article can mean:

- *some*: **du pain, de l'huile et des tomates** *some bread, some oil and some tomatoes*. In French, the articles are used even when English might leave them out.
- *of the*: **le site web du restaurant, l'anniversaire de l'actrice, les photos des vacances**

Some French expressions have **de** built in, e.g. **près de** *near to*, **à côté de** *next to*: **près de la mer** *near the sea*, **à côté du marché** *next to the market*.

subject pronouns

The French subject pronouns **je, tu, il, elle, on, nous, vous, ils** and **elles** show who or what is carrying out the verb.

Je shortens to **j'** before a vowel or an **h**: **j'aime, j'habite**.

There are two words for *you*, each of which uses a different verb ending:
tu: when talking to one person who is a friend or relative, or a child.

Young people often use **tu** with each other from the start, but it's best avoided in formal situations.

vous: when talking to one person you don't know very well, or who is older than you. It's also the word to use when talking to more than one person.

Il and **elle** both mean *it*, as well as *he* or *she*; use **il** to stand for a masculine noun and **elle** for a feminine noun.

On is used a lot in spoken French to mean *we*, *they* or *you* (people in general). It takes the same verb endings as **il** and **elle**.

object pronouns

When the object of a verb (the person or thing affected) is a pronoun and not a named person/thing, it can be direct (e.g. *me*, *him*, *us*) or indirect (e.g. *to me*, *to him*, *to us*). In French, only the words for *him/her/it/them* have different direct and indirect forms:

direct		indirect	
me	*me*	**me**	*to me*
te	*you*	**te**	*to you*
le, l'	*him/it*	**lui**	*to him*
la, l'	*her/it*	**lui**	*to her*
nous	*us*	**nous**	*to us*
vous	*you*	**vous**	*to you*
les	*them*	**leur**	*to them*

Object pronouns normally go in front of the relevant verb:
Je voudrais le voir. *I'd like to see it/him.*
Je ne les aime pas. *I don't like them.*
Elle m'a téléphoné ... *She phoned me* (lit. *phoned to me*) ...
Nous pouvons vous accompagner? *Can we come with you?*

But they go after an imperative: **Envoie-lui un texto.** *Send (to) him a text.*

other pronouns

Emphatic pronouns **moi, toi, lui, elle, nous, vous, eux, elles** are used:
- for emphasis: *Moi*, j'aime le bleu, mais *lui*, il préfère le rouge. *I prefer the blue one, but **he** prefers the red one.*
- after a preposition: **avec moi** *with me*, **pour nous** *for us*, **contre eux** *against them*

Y is a pronoun often translated as *there*. It comes before the verb and is used

- to replace a place: **Tu connais la Suisse? Oui, j'y suis allé l'année dernière.** *Do you know Switzerland? Yes, I went there last year.*
- to replace a thing (never a person) introduced by **à, au, à l', à la** or **aux**: **Tu penses aux conséquences?** *Are you thinking of the consequences?* **Oui, j'y pense.** *Yes, I'm thinking about them.*

En is a pronoun meaning *of it/them* or *some/any*. It also comes before the verb.
Vous avez combien de frères? J'en ai trois. *How many brothers have you got? I've got three (of them).*
Vous avez des suggestions? Oui, j'en ai. *Have you got any suggestions? Yes, I have some.*
Qu'est-ce que vous en pensez? *What do you think of it?*

It also replaces a thing (never a person) with expressions ending in **de**, such as **avoir besoin de** *to need*, **avoir envie de** *to want*:
Tu as besoin de la voiture? Non, je n'en ai pas besoin. *Do you need the car? No, I don't need it.*

Qui and **que** are pronouns meaning *who, whom, which, that*. Both can be used for people and for things. **Qui** is used when it's the subject of the following verb, and **que** when it's the object.
C'est l'hôtel qui est en face de la gare. *It's the hotel that is opposite the station.*
J'ai une cousine qui travaille à l'hôpital. *I have a cousin who works at the hospital.*
Voici le bar que je préfère. *Here's the bar that I prefer.*
C'est l'homme politique que j'admire le plus. *He's the politician that I admire most.*

verbs

In French, there are three main groups of verbs, ending in **-er, -ir, -re** in the infinitive (the form that appears in the dictionary). The **-er, -ir, -re** ending changes in a predictable, regular way according to:
1) subject: *who/what* is carrying out the verb,
2) tense: *when* it takes place.

There are sets of endings for each of the following:
present tense: *happens, is happening*; also after **depuis**: *has been happening* since a particular time or for a period of time
future tense: *will happen, is going to happen*
conditional: *would happen (if)*
imperfect tense: *was happening, used to happen, happened repeatedly or regularly*
perfect tense: *happened, has happened, did happen*

pluperfect tense: *had happened*
subjunctive: *happens, happened* based on the speaker's feelings, opinions, tastes rather than solid fact
imperative: commands and instructions for **tu, vous, nous**
past participle: *happened*, after *had, have, will have, would have* in past tenses

The next three pages set out these various endings for **regular** verbs in each of the three groups, i.e. those that follow the standard pattern. Pages 185–187 show how many widely used verbs deviate from these patterns: these are classed as **irregular**.

Pattern for regular verbs ending in -er

infinitive   **travailler** *to work*

	present	future	conditional
je	travaille	travaillerai	travaillerais
tu	travailles	travailleras	travaillerais
il/elle/on	travaille	travaillera	travaillerait
nous	travaillons	travaillerons	travaillerions
vous	travaillez	travaillerez	travailleriez
ils/elles	travaillent	travailleront	travailleraient

	imperfect	perfect
je/j'	travaillais	ai travaillé
tu	travaillais	as travaillé
il/elle/on	travaillait	a travaillé
nous	travaillions	avons travaillé
vous	travailliez	avez travaillé
ils/elles	travaillaient	ont travaillé

	present subjunctive
je	travaille
tu	travailles
il/elle/on	travaille
nous	travaillions
vous	travailliez
ils/elles	travaillent

past participle   travaillé
imperative   travaille, travaillons, travaillez

Verbs ending in -ger and -cer

In the **nous** form of the present tense and in all forms of the imperfect, verbs ending in **-ger** preserve the soft **g** sound by adding an **-e** before **-ons** (present) and **-ai, -ais, -ait, -aient** (imperfect): **nous mangeons, je mangeais** Similarly verbs ending in **-cer** change the **-c** to a **-ç: nous commençons, je commençais**

Pattern for regular verbs ending in -re

infinitive   **vend**re *to sell*

	present	future	conditional
je	vends	vendrai	vendrais
tu	vends	vendras	vendrais
il/elle/on	vend	vendra	vendrait
nous	vendons	vendrons	vendrions
vous	vendez	vendrez	vendriez
ils/elles	vendent	vendront	vendraient

	imperfect	perfect
je/j'	vendais	ai vendu
tu	vendais	as vendu
il/elle/on	vendait	a vendu
nous	vendions	avons vendu
vous	vendiez	avez vendu
ils/elles	vendaient	ont vendu

	present subjunctive
je	vende
tu	vendes
il/elle/on	vende
nous	vendions
vous	vendiez
ils/elles	vendent

past participle   vendu
imperative   vends, vendons, vendez

Pattern for regular verbs ending in -ir

infinitive **fin**ir *to finish*

	present	future	conditional
je	**fin**is	**fin**irai	**fin**irais
tu	**fin**is	**fin**iras	**fin**irais
il/elle/on	**fin**it	**fin**ira	**fin**irait
nous	**fin**issons	**fin**irons	**fin**irions
vous	**fin**issez	**fin**irez	**fin**iriez
ils/elles	**fin**issent	**fin**iront	**fin**iraient

	imperfect	perfect
je/j'	**fin**issais	ai **fin**i
tu	**fin**issais	as **fin**i
il/elle/on	**fin**issait	a **fin**i
nous	**fin**issions	avons **fin**i
vous	**fin**issiez	avez **fin**i
ils/elles	**fin**issaient	ont **fin**i

	present subjunctive
je	**fin**isse
tu	**fin**isses
il/elle/on	**fin**isse
nous	**fin**issions
vous	**fin**issiez
ils/elles	**fin**issent

past participle **fin**i

imperative **fin**is, **fin**issons, **fin**issez

agreement of past participle

When the perfect tense is made with **être**, the ending of the past participle agrees with the subject, by adding **-e**, **-s** or **-es**:

Mon grand-père est né en Irlande. *My grandfather was born in Ireland.*
Ma grand-mère est née en France. *My grandmother was born in France.*
Ma copine est partie hier. *My girlfriend left yesterday.*
Mes parents sont restés en Algérie. *My parents stayed in Algeria.*
Les femmes sont allées au théâtre. *The women went to the theatre.*

Generally, there's no agreement with **on** but some people do make the agreement when it's clear who **on** refers to:

Paul: Mes frères et moi, on est allés au café. *My brother and I went to the café.*
Léa: Les filles, on est passées par la mauvaise porte! *Girls, we went through the wrong door!*

For verbs taking **avoir**, the past participle only has to agree with a direct object pronoun:

Où est la voiture. Je l'ai laissée sur le parking. *Where's the car? I left it in the car park.*
Paul: Le football m'a toujours intéresé. *I've always been interested in football.*
Léa: Ses idées m'ont toujours intéresée. *I've always been interested in his/her ideas.*

irregular verbs

Not all verbs follow the regular patterns. **Être** *to be,* is irregular in all tenses while many other widely used verbs are irregular in one, some or all their tenses.

present

aller *to go*: je vais, tu vas, il/elle va, nous allons, vous allez, ils/elles vont
avoir *to have*: j'ai, tu as, il/elle a, nous avons, vous avez, ils/elles ont
boire *to drink*: je bois, tu bois, il/elle boit, nous buvons, vous buvez, ils/elles boivent
connaître *to know*: je connais, tu connais, il/elle connaît, nous connaissons, vous connaissez, ils/elles connaissent
devoir *to have to*: je dois, tu dois, il/elle doit, nous devons, vous devez, ils/elles doivent
dire *to say*: je dis, tu dis, il/elle dit, nous disons, vous dites, ils/elles disent
écrire *to write*: j'écris, tu écris, il/elle écrit, nous écrivons, vous écrivez, ils/elles écrivent
être *to be*: je suis, tu es, il/elle est, nous sommes, vous êtes, ils/elles sont

faire *to do, to make*: je fais, tu fais, il/elle fait, nous faisons, vous faites, ils/elles font

ouvrir *to open*: j'ouvre, tu ouvres, il/elle ouvre, nous ouvrons, vous ouvrez, ils/elles ouvrent

partir *to leave*: je pars, tu pars, il/elle part, nous partons, vous partez, ils/elles partent

pouvoir *to be able to*: je peux, tu peux, il/elle peut, nous pouvons, vous pouvez, ils/elles peuvent

prendre *to take*: je prends, tu prends, il/elle prend, nous prenons, vous prenez, ils/elles prennent

savoir *to know*: je sais, tu sais, il/elle sait, nous savons, vous savez, ils/elles savent

venir *to come*: je viens, tu viens, il/elle vient, nous venons, vous venez, ils/elles viennent

voir *to see*: je vois, tu vois, il/elle voit, nous voyons, vous voyez, ils/elles voient

vouloir *to want to*: je veux, tu veux, il/elle veut, nous voulons, vous voulez, ils/elles veulent

couvrir *to cover*, **découvrir** *to discover*, **offrir** *to offer* and **souffrir** *to suffer* behave like **ouvrir**

sortir *to go out*, **mentir** *to lie* and **sentir** *to feel* behave like **partir**

apprendre *to learn* and **comprendre** *to understand* behave like **prendre**

revenir *to come back* and **devenir** *to become* behave like **venir**

future and conditional

The following have irregular stems for the future and conditional, onto which you add the regular endings.

	future	conditional
aller *to go*	j'irai	j'irais
avoir *to have*	j'aurai	j'aurais
devoir *to have to*	je devrai	je devrais
être *to be*	je serai	je serais
faire *to do, to make*	je ferai	je ferais
pouvoir *to be able to*	je pourrai	je pourrais
venir *to come*	je viendrai	je viendrais
voir *to see*	je verrai	je verrais
vouloir *to want to*	je voudrai	je voudrais

imperfect

être *to be*: **j'étais, tu étais, il/elle était, nous étions, vous étiez, ils/elles étaient**

All other verbs form their imperfect from the **nous** part of the present tense: remove **-ons** and replace it with the imperfect endings, e.g.

	nous in present	imperfect
avoir *to have*	av**ons**	**j'avais**
faire *to do, to make*	fais**ons**	**je faisais**
voir *to see*	voy**ons**	**je voyais**

perfect

Many common verbs have an irregular past participle, including the following (see also page 67):

	past participle		past participle
avoir *to have*	eu	**mourir** *to die*	mort
boire *to drink*	bu	**naître** *to be born*	né
dire *to say*	dit	**offrir** *to offer*	offert
écrire *to write*	écrit	**ouvrir** *to open*	ouvert
être *to be*	été	**prendre** *to take*	pris
faire *to do, to make*	fait	**venir** *to come*	venu
lire *to read*	lu	**voir** *to see*	vu
mettre *to put*	mis		

impersonal verbs

Most verbs are 'personal', i.e. they change their form depending on the person doing them: **je vais, nous allons, ils vont.**

A few very useful verbs are 'impersonal'. These don't refer to anyone in particular and they have only one form in each tense: the third person singular or **il** form. For example:

- **il y a** *there is/there are*: **Il y a un problème.** *There is a problem.*
- **Il pleut** *It's raining*, **Il faisait chaud** *It was hot* and other weather expressions
- **il faut**, which means *I/you/we must need to* and is generally followed by an infinitive: **Il faut continuer.** *I/you/we must carry on.*

- **Il est important/(im)possible/facile/difficile/interdit + de + infinitive:**
  Il est important de faire du sport. *It's important to exercise.*
  Il est difficile de comprendre son accent. *It's difficult to understand his/her accent.*
  Il est interdit de fumer. *Smoking is forbidden.*

verbs followed by an infinitive

Some key verbs can be followed immediately by an infinitive:

devoir *to have to*: **Vous devez partir.** *You must leave.*

pouvoir *to be able to*: **Nous pouvons étudier ensemble.** *We can study together.*

savoir *to know*: **Je sais danser.** *I know how to dance.*

vouloir *to want to*: **Tu veux visiter la ville?** *Do you want to look round the town?*

aimer *to like*: **J'aime bien travailler ici.** *I like working here.*

espérer *to hope*: **J'espère apprendre aussi l'espagnol.** *I hope to learn Spanish too.*

Certain verbs need **à** before the following infinitive, e.g:

apprendre à *to learn (to)*: **J'apprends à jouer du piano.** *I'm learning to play the piano.*

commencer à *to begin (to)*: **Je commence à avoir faim.** *I'm beginning to feel hungry.*

Others need **de**, e.g:

avoir envie de *to want (to)*: **J'ai envie de faire la grasse matinée.** *I want to have a lie-in.*

conseiller de *to advise (to)*: **Je vous conseille d'arriver de bonne heure.** *I'd advise you to get there early.*

negatives

To make a negative statement, **ne ... pas** goes around the verb:
Je ne parle pas espagnol. *I don't speak Spanish.*

In the perfect tense, it goes around the part of **avoir** or **être** that comes before the past participle:
Je n'ai pas vu votre collègue. *I haven't seen your colleague.*

With reflexive verbs, **me, te, se,** etc. go before the verb inside **ne ... pas:**
Normalement, je ne me couche pas tôt. *Normally I don't go to bed early.*
Je ne me suis pas couché tôt hier. *I didn't go to bed early yesterday.*

Ne is also used with negative words like **jamais** *never*, **rien** *nothing*,
personne *nobody*, **plus** *no longer, any more*, **ni ... ni** *neither ... nor*, **que** *only*:
Je ne regarde jamais les feuilletons. *I never watch soaps.*

Elles ne fument plus. *They don't smoke any more.*

Il n'aime ni le thé ni le café. *He likes neither tea nor coffee.*

In the perfect tense verb, **ne ... plus, ne ... rien** and **ne ... jamais** go around the part of **avoir** or **être** that comes before the past participle:

Je n'ai rien acheté. *I bought nothing. I didn't buy anything.*

But **ne ... personne** and **ne ... que** go around the past participle too:

Je n'ai lu que la première page. *I've only read the first page.*

questions

Questions can be formed with a question word:

Qui? *Who/Whom?*

Où? *Where?*

Quand? *When?*

Comment? *How?*

Pourquoi? *Why?*

Que ...? *What ...?*

Qu'est-ce que ...? *What?*

Quel(le) ...? *Which ...?*

Combien de ...? *How much ...? How many ...?*

They can also be formed by making your voice go up at the end of a statement so that it sounds like a question or by adding **est-ce que** before a statement or after a question word:

Est-ce que vous aimez la musique classique? *Do you like classical music?*

Quand est-ce que vous partez? *When are you leaving?*

Quel *which? what?* is a question word used with a noun. It changes to **quelle** when the noun is feminine; the plural is **quels** (m pl) or **quelles** (f pl).

Lequel? *which one?* can replace **quel** + noun. It has the same forms as **quel**.

Vous avez lu son mail? – Lequel? *Did you read his/her email? – Which one?*

Il y a des chips nature ou au fromage: lesquelles tu préfères? *There are plain or cheese-flavoured crisps: which do you prefer?*

numbers

numbers 1–99

0	**zéro**	11	**onze**
1	**un**	12	**douze**
2	**deux**	13	**treize**
3	**trois**	14	**quatorze**
4	**quatre**	15	**quinze**
5	**cinq**	16	**seize**
6	**six**	17	**dix-sept**
7	**sept**	18	**dix-huit**
8	**huit**	19	**dix-neuf**
9	**neuf**	20	**vingt**
10	**dix**		

Un changes to agree with its noun, like *a/an*: **un garçon, une fille**

21	**vingt-et-un**	28	**vingt-huit**
22	**vingt-deux**	29	**vingt-neuf**
23	**vingt-trois**	30	**trente**
24	**vingt-quatre**	40	**quarante**
25	**vingt-cinq**	50	**cinquante**
26	**vingt-six**	60	**soixante**
27	**vingt-sept**		

The numbers 31–69 repeat the pattern 21–29: **cinquante-trois** *53*, **soixante-neuf** *69*

Un changes to **une** in numbers followed by a feminine noun: **quarante-et-une voitures** *41 cars*; **cinquante-et-une étoiles** *51 stars*

70 is literally *sixty-ten*, and 71–79 are counted as *sixty-eleven, sixty-twelve ... sixty-nineteen*:

70	**soixante-dix**	75	**soixante-quinze**
71	**soixante-et-onze**	76	**soixante-seize**
72	**soixante-douze**	77	**soixante-dix-sept**
73	**soixante-treize**	78	**soixante-dix-huit**
74	**soixante-quatorze**	79	**soixante-dix-neuf**

80 is literally *four-twenties*. This combines with 1–19 for the numbers 80–99:

80	**quatre-vingts**	90	**quatre-vingt-dix**
81	**quatre-vingt-un**	91	**quatre-vingt-onze**
82	**quatre-vingt-deux**	92	**quatre-vingt-douze**
83	**quatre-vingt-trois**	93	**quatre-vingt-treize**
84	**quatre-vingt-quatre**	94	**quatre-vingt-quatorze**
85	**quatre-vingt-cinq**	95	**quatre-vingt-quinze**
86	**quatre-vingt-six**	96	**quatre-vingt-seize**
87	**quatre-vingt-sept**	97	**quatre-vingt-dix-sept**
88	**quatre-vingt-huit**	98	**quatre-vingt-dix-huit**
89	**quatre-vingt-neuf**	99	**quatre-vingt-dix-neuf**

80 is the only number to have an **s** on **vingts**.
81 and 91 don't include **et** before **un**, as smaller numbers do.

numbers 100 +

100	**cent**	175	**cent soixante-quinze**
101	**cent un**	200	**deux cents**
102	**cent deux**	201	**deux cent un**
110	**cent dix**	220	**deux cent vingt**
150	**cent cinquante**	500	**cinq cents**

In the plural, **cent** *a hundred* adds an -s only in round hundreds: 300 **trois cents**, but 310 **trois cent dix**; 700 **sept cents**, but 701 **sept cent un**

Thousands are separated either by a space or a full stop: 7 000 or 7.000.

1 000	**mille**	100 000	**cent mille**
1 100	**mille cent**	500 000	**cinq cent mille**
1 500	**mille cinq cents**	1 000 000	**un million**
2 000	**deux mille**	2 000 000	**deux millions**
10 000	**dix mille**	1 000 000 000	**un milliard**

Mille *a thousand* doesn't change in the plural: 2 000 **deux mille**, 5 500 **cinq mille cinq cents**, but **un million** *a million* and **un milliard** *a billion* have the regular plurals **millions** and **milliards**.

French uses a comma where English has a decimal point:

L'inflation actuelle en France est de zéro virgule dix pour cent. *Inflation is currently at 0.10% in France.*

La Banque prévoit une croissance de zéro virgule trois pour cent au premier trimestre. *The Bank is predicting growth of 0.3% in the first quarter.*

first, second, third, etc.

Ordinal numbers (*first, second, third*, etc.) are formed by adding **-ième** to the cardinal number (*one, two, three*) minus its final vowel, apart from **premier/ première** *first*:

1st	**premier/première**	**1er** (m), **1ère** (f)
2nd	**deuxième/second(e)**	**2e**
3rd	**troisième**	**3e**
4th	**quatrième**	**4e**
5th	**cinquième**	**5e**
6th	**sixième**	**6e**
7th	**septième**	**7e**
8th	**huitième**	**8e**
9th	**neuvième**	**9e**
10th	**dixième**	**10e**

The **er** of **premier** changes to **ère** for **première**. *First* in 21, 31, 41, etc. is **unième**: **vingt et unième** *21st*, **cent et unième** *101st*.

There are two ways of saying *second*: **second(e)** and **deuxième**. Generally **second(e)** is used where there are only two of something and **deuxième** where it's second in a list that has more than two items.

Cinquième adds **u** before **ième** and the **f** in **neuf** becomes **v** in **neuvième**.

Ordinal numbers agree in gender and number with their noun — although only **premier** and **second** have separate feminine forms:
la première semaine *the first week*
le premier mois *the first month*
la Seconde Guerre mondiale *the Second World War*
les troisièmes auditions *the third auditions*

answers to checkpoints

checkpoint 1 page 24

1 Excuse(z)-moi, Pardon! or Je suis désolé(e); *2* vous; *3* madame; *4* Je suis ...;
5 beaucoup, infiniment; *6* Je t'en prie, Je vous en prie, Il n'y a pas de quoi,
De rien; *7* commiserate; *8* Excusez-moi; *9* my stepson, my son-in-law;
10 À demain/On se retrouve demain, À samedi/On se retrouve samedi,
On se retrouve dans dix minutes; *11* Je vous présente (or Voici) ma cousine
Anna; *12* They both mean *are*. Es is the verb after tu, when you are talking to
a person you know well, êtes is the verb after vous, for when you are talking
to someone you don't know well, or to more than one person. *13* night time;
14 fille (= daughter). In rare cases, tante (= aunt) might be younger than you.
15 Asseyez-vous. Faites comme chez vous. *16* Bonjour, Monsieur le Maire/
Madame le Maire. *17* Brown: bay air oh doobluh-vay enn, Smith: ess emm ee
tay ash, Jones: jhee oh enn uh ess, Green: jhay air deux uh enn; *18* Vous êtes
d'où? *19* that you call them tu instead of vous; *20* Ce n'est pas grave.

checkpoint 2 page 40

1 J'apprends le français. J'étudie le français; *2* non, c'est ça; *3* Comment est-ce
qu'on dit farm en français? *4* une piscine, un restaurant, un terrain de jeux, un
court de tennis, etc. *5* qui, pourquoi, quel, quand, où, comment, combien;
6 (Est-ce que) je peux vous aider? *7* Je n'ai pas soif. Tu as/Vous avez froid?
Elle a raison. J'ai mal à la tête. *8* Mon oncle est divorcé. My uncle is divorced.
Mes amies sont galloises. My (girl)friends are Welsh. Ma cousine est blonde.
My cousin is blonde. Mon voisin est très travailleur. My neighbour is very
hard-working. Ma copine est un peu paresseuse. My (girl)friend is a bit lazy.
9 je pensais, j'aimais; *10* bavard, généreux, poli, fidèle = describe someone's
personality; grand, gros, mince, petit = describe someone's appearance;
montagneux means mountainous (it cannot describe a person); *11* nasty,
mean; *12* Où se trouve le camping? *13* j'ai peur; *14* ensemble; *15* énorme/
minuscule, tranquille/animé, vieux/neuf, ensoleillé/ombragé, propre/sale

checkpoint 3 page 52

1 agriculteur/ferme, maître-nageur/piscine, médecin/hôpital, professeur/
école, vendeur/magasin; the person left over is a cook: cuisinier; *2* no;
3 depuis/ans; *4* archéologue, météorologue; rheumatologist,
ophthalmologist, radiologist; *5* un agent immobilier; *6* Cela ne fait aucune
différence; *7* Je suis au chômage. *8* Ma fille fait un apprentissage. *9* un
employé; an employee is a person, the others are all words for work, job;
10 the health sector/an office; *11* Quelle est ta/votre fonction? *12* tu vends,

vous aimez, nous choisissons, vous cherchez, tu finis, nous travaillons;
13 head of factory, factory supervisor, plant manager; *14* nous gagnons; *15* Je suis responsable du site web. (I'm in charge of/responsible for the web site.)

checkpoint 4 page 64

1 Je n'ai pas compris. *2* Tu me comprends./Vous me comprenez?/(Est-ce que) tu suis/vous suivez? *3* good; *4* Quelle bonne idée! *5* Comment dit-on crisis en français? *6* trop: trop difficile; *7* ennuyeux – the others are all positive; *8* d'abord is used to start a conversation/argument, pour conclure is to end it; *9* positive: quel plaisir, quel soulagement; negative: quel dommage, quelle déception, quelle bêtise; *10* Est-ce que tu peux/vous pouvez me l'écrire?/ Est-ce que tu pourrais/vous pourriez me l'écrire? *11* bref, mais; *12* Est-ce que vous pouvez/pourriez parler plus lentement, s'il vous plaît? *13* par exemple; *14* to say 'What a fool!' *15* all of them; *16* c'est-à-dire; *17* Est-ce que tu peux/ pourrais répéter, s'il te plaît? *18* à vrai dire; *19* ouf; *20* Je l'ai sur le bout de la langue.

checkpoint 5 page 76

1 rêvé, maigri, répondu; *2* Je suis retourné; *3* Avant-hier; *4* J'ai perdu mon porte-monnaie. *5* avoir: vivre, manger, courir; être: naître, rester, mourir, monter; *6* L'année dernière, nous avons fait une croisière et nous sommes restés cinq jours en mer. *7* Je viens (juste) d'appeler la police. *8* Vous êtes allée où hier? *9* il a satisfait, il a stupéfait; *10* a short while ago; in a little while, shortly; *11* boire, devoir, avoir, lire, pouvoir, savoir, voir; *12* déjà: Vous êtes déjà allée en Corse? *13* how you two met; *14* the first is perfect (we have planned; I went/have gone out), the second pluperfect (we had planned; I had gone out); *15* il y a; *16* j'avais dormi, ils étaient partis, vous vous étiez ennuyés?, nous n'avions pas mangé

checkpoint 6 page 86

1 de temps en temps; d'habitude, habituellement, normalement, généralement; *2 i)* pluperfect, *ii)* imperfect; *3* être; *4* étions; *5* replace travaillons with travaillions and prend with prenait (both imperfect); *6* J'ai rencontré Amélie quand j'avais douze ans. *7* Julie était en train de lire quand je suis arrivé. *8* depuis; *9* avait; *10* quand j'étais petit(e)/enfant; quand j'étais étudiant(e); *11* est allé/allait; *12* quand; *13* Il y avait beaucoup de monde au cinéma. *14* use être en train de; *15* imperfect: voulait; *16* perfect: a arrêté; est partie; *17* J'aimais travailler à mon compte. *18* c'étaient; C'étaient mes amis de Paris.

checkpoint 7 page 98

1 ortie is a plant, the others are all insects; 2 Nous aimons bien/beaucoup/ vraiment la chambre or La chambre nous plaît bien/beaucoup/vraiment; 3 Est-ce que les jeux vidéo les intéressent? 4 Je n'aime pas le fromage. 5 no; 6 je déteste (I hate); 7 j'ai aimé; 8 wines (les vins m): préférés; a region (une région): préférée; a museum (un musée): préféré; music (la musique): préférée, films (les films m): préférés; photos (les photos f): préférées; 9 Je n'aime pas du tout (I don't like at all); je n'aime pas trop is I don't much like; 10 tu préfères, vous préférez; 11 J'aime (bien/beaucoup) le jazz/le jazz me plaît (bien/beaucoup). 12 vraiment, du tout; 13 toujours; 14 Je voudrais de l'eau. 15 meilleur; 16 assez, beaucoup, énormément 17 Je n'aime pas beaucoup passer l'aspirateur, je préfère faire du jardinage.

checkpoint 8 page 118

1 jeudi, samedi; mai, juin, juillet; 2 viendrai is future: I will come; viendrais is conditional: I would come; 3 joyeux or bon anniversaire; joyeux Noël; bon rétablissement; bon voyage; bon weekend; 4 Vous voudriez venir fêter/faire le réveillon de Noël chez nous?/Ça vous dit de venir fêter Noël chez nous? 5 malheureusement; 6 rendez-vous; pile or précises; 7 À toi/vous de même. 8 lundi is this Monday whereas le lundi is every Monday; 9 visiterai = visiterais; 10 C'est vraiment dommage. 11 étais; If you were less busy, we'd go for a stroll around the village. 12 Il faisait/Il a fait froid; C'était pluvieux. 13 le premier mai; 14 Je vous attendrais si je pouvais. 15 during the rush hour; 16 Bonne chance!; Bon courage! 17 Désolé(e), je ne peux pas. Et si nous allions/on allait faire de la voile à midi le lendemain/le trente-et-un mai?/On pourrait aller faire de la voile ...

checkpoint 9 page 132

1 The first means you have to change trains and the second that you can change trains (but don't have to). 2 what you want/would like to do: j'aimerais, nous voulons, j'ai envie de, je voudrais; what you have to/must do: nous devrions, je dois, j'ai besoin de, il faut; je pourrais = I could; 3 Julien doit partir et il veut prendre une photo de groupe. 4 Désolé, je dois partir très tôt. 5 Je ne veux pas vous déranger mais je peux vous poser une question/puis-je vous poser une question? 6 (Est-ce que) vous voulez/Vous voudriez visiter Bordeaux? 7 I like doing sport, I would like to do some sport, I ought to do some sport; 8 Je voudrais/j'aimerais apprendre, je devrais apprendre, je dois apprendre, je veux apprendre, j'ai besoin d'apprendre, j'ai envie d'apprendre; 9 Qu'est-ce qu'il faut faire? 10 je n'ai pas pu; j'aurais dû; 11 (Est-ce que) vous avez envie d'aller/Ça vous dirait d'aller à la fête du vin? 12 Je te dois un bon repas. 13 Ils n'ont pas voulu voyager. 14 Je ne sais pas faire de la plongée. 15 Vous n'auriez pas dû.

checkpoint 10 page 146

1 for your opinion; selon vous/d'après vous; *2* Bien dit! Bravo! Nous sommes entièrement d'accord! *3* C'est une question d'opinion; Undoubtedly, Nothing of the sort, Are you kidding or what? *4* car, puisque, comme; *5* savoir – sache is the present subjunctive; *6* about 60; around 10-15 years old; *7* vingt-huitième: 4 + 8 = 12 + 8 = 20 + 8 = 28; *8* youngest = Alex; le plus jeune; *9* des centaines; *10* 7.5%; 0.9%; *11* soit; *12* you need to use a verb in the subjunctive; Je voudrais qu'il aille (subjunctive) en France avec elle; *13* à ton/votre avis?; tu ne trouves pas/vous ne trouvez pas?, tu ne penses pas/vous ne pensez pas? *14* Moi; Personnellement; Pour ma part; En ce qui me concerne; *15* (Moi; Personnellement; Pour ma part; En ce qui me concerne), je ne crois pas que ce soit (subjunctive) possible. *16* je crois que, j'espère que

checkpoint 11 page 160

1 il y avait du vent hier/il y aura du vent demain; *2* Je n'ai jamais mangé un aussi bon repas!/C'est le meilleur repas que j'aie jamais mangé. *3* Il y aura/ Est-ce qu'il y aura assez de place et quelque chose à manger? *4* C'est moi qui invite/C'est à mon tour de régler; On fait moitié-moitié. *5* J'ai vraiment bien mangé. *6* Elle a mal à la poitrine; Elle prend des médicaments pour la tension. *7* Est-ce qu'il y a du blé dedans? *8* Appelle le SAMU! N'appelle pas le SAMU! *9* Je me suis fait mal aux genoux hier. *10* Sois prêt(e) à neuf heures demain matin; Soyez prêt(e)s ...; *11* Est-ce que quelqu'un pourrait me dire; Quelqu'un pourrait me dire où est la brasserie la plus proche? *12* Reposez-vous! *13* You shouldn't smoke in the car park. *14* Hurry up, Be quiet/Shut up; Dépêchez-vous, Taisez-vous; *15* in a recipe; *16* you pull; *17* Vous me manquez

checkpoint 12 page 171

1 When it is a computer mouse. *2* J'ai été ravie de faire votre connaissance/ de vous rencontrer. *3* ALP = à la prochaine; 2ri1= de rien, slt = salut; *4* * @ , - ( ) *5* They are all used! *6* You have called a wrong number. *7* mailer; Je te/ vous maile or Je vais te/vous mailer. *8* pour; de; *9* All but Je vous remercie infiniment, which is more formal. *10* Est-ce que vous avez/Il y a du wifi? *11* J'ai perdu mon portable; Nous devons acheter/Nous avons besoin d'acheter une batterie. *12* À bientôt! or À plus/A+, Je t'embrasse, Bises or Bisous; *13* None; they both means a text. *14* Comment est-ce que je mets/ uploade des photos sur Facebook? *15* Est-ce que je vais te manquer? *16* Je te dois beaucoup; I owe you big time.

answers to verb practice

verb practice 1 page 39

1   a suis (I am divorced.); b sommes (We are not English.); c est (Christine is very stubborn.); d sont (David and his brother are twins.); e êtes (How long are you here for?); f est (The hotel is clean and quiet.); g suis (I'm not very talkative.); h est (Mr Bassani is not married.); i sont (Your children are lovely.); j es (Are you engaged?)

2   a ai, a (I have blue eyes but my father has grey eyes.); b a (Franck is not sleepy.); c a (How old is Camille?); d avons (My wife and I are lucky.); e as (Are you 19 or 20?); f avez (Is it right that you have three children?); g ont (They have a little flat in town.); h avez (Aren't you thirsty?)

3   a Elle est/Est-elle/Est-ce qu'elle est canadienne ou américaine? b (Est-ce que) Martine et Mathilde sont heureuses/contentes? c (Est-ce que) l'hôtel a une piscine? d Marc est gay, non/c'est ça? e (Est-ce que) tu as soif?/As-tu soif?/(Est-ce que) vous avez soif?/Avez-vous soif? f (Est-ce qu')il y a un court de tennis?

verb practice 2 page 51

1   a ajoutes; b changent; c trouvez; d dure; e posons; f pleure; g parlez; h aime; i détestent; j danses

2   a choisis; b finissent; c réussit; d vieillis; e vendons; f descendez; g perd; h attends

3   a s'; b s'; c nous; d vous; e te; f me; g se

verb practice 3 page 75

1   a as parlé; b êtes sortis; c a perdu; d suis tombé(e); e ont choisi; f avons attendu; g ont vendu; h a envoyé; i est rentrée

2   a avais parlé/had talked; b étiez sortis/had gone out; c avait perdu/had lost; d étais tombé(e)/had fallen; e avaient choisi/had chosen; f avions attendu/had waited; g avaient vendu/had sold; h avait envoyé/had sent; i était rentrée/had come back

3   admis, commis, permis, promis; compris, appris, surpris; décrit, prescrit, dit, prédit; souri, suffi; réduit, séduit, traduit, cuit, construit, détruit; méconnu, reconnu; atteint, éteint, joint, plaint

4 Hier, j'ai travaillé jusqu'à midi. Je suis allé(e) en ville après le déjeuner. J'ai vu Martin. J'ai fait les courses. J'ai trop dépensé! J'ai envoyé un mail à William et j'ai laissé un message à maman. Pauline est arrivée à six heures. Pauline venait de partir quand papa a téléphoné.

verb practice 4 page 85

1 *a* voulais; *b* avions; *c* connaissait; *d* regardait; *e* prenais; *f* allaient; *g* était; *h* faisiez

2 *a* il prenait; *b* j'allais faire, *c* je me levais ... il faisait; *d* ma fille avait, *e* vous préfériez; *f* Thierry vérifiait, *g* nous allions; *h* ils jouaient; *i* vous diniez; *j* Lucie et Anne habitaient

3 *a* J'étais, nous étions/on était, suis tombé(e) = I was with Lucas; We were in the town centre when I fell over on the pavement. *b* elle est née, elle habitait, avaient = She was born in 1984; as a child, she lived in Grasse, in Provence, where her parents had a perfume shop. *c* tu es allé(e), a rencontré, travaillait = Did you go/Have you been to the place where your mother met your father when he was still working in Senegal?

verb practice 5 page 117

1 *a* commenceras/you will start; *b* iront/they will go; *c* prendrez/you will take, *d* finira/it will finish; *e* mettrons/we will put; *f* tiendra/we will hold; *g* devrai/I will have to, *h* fera/he will do; *i* pourrons/we will be able to; *j* viendra/she will come; *k* serai/I will be; *l* auras/you will have

2 *a* commencerais/you would start; *b* iraient/they would go; *c* prendriez/you would take; *d* finirait/it would finish; *e* mettrions/we would put; *f* tiendrait/we would hold; *g* devrais/I would have to; *h* ferait/he would do; *i* pourrions/we would be able to; *j* viendrait/she would come; *k* serais/I would be; *l* aurais/you would have

3 *a* future/it will depend; *b* perfect/I (have) prepared myself; *c* perfect/he (has) phoned; *d* conditional/they would study; *e* future/we will decide; *f* future/she is going to come back; *g* imperfect/they preferred; *h* present/you intervene; *i* perfect/they went/have gone; *j* imperfect I ate/used to eat/was eating

4 *a* pleut; *b* j'avais; *c* donnez; *d* j'irais; *e* pouvait; *f* aiderai

verb practice 6 page 131

1 vouloir: wanted to, would like to; pouvoir: could, may, can, used to be able to; devoir: ought, was supposed to, must, should have, had to, used to have to

2 *a* il doit; vous devez; *b* nous voulons; tu veux; *c* elles doivent; je dois; *d* ils peuvent; je peux; *e* on veut; vous voulez; *f* tu peux; nous pouvons; *g* tu dois; vous devez; *h* vous pouvez; on peut; *i* je veux; ils veulent

3 imperfect: je devais, tu devais, il/elle devait, nous devions, vous deviez, ils/elles devaient; je pouvais, tu pouvais, il/elle pouvait, nous pouvions, vous pouviez, ils/elles pouvaient; je voulais, tu voulais, il/elle voulait, nous voulions, vous vouliez, ils/elles voulaient
conditional: je devrais, tu devrais, il/elle devrait, nous devrions, vous devriez, ils/elles devraient; je pourrais, tu pourrais, il/elle pourrait, nous pourrions, vous pourriez, ils/elles pourraient; je voudrais, tu voudrais, il/elle voudrait, nous voudrions, vous voudriez, ils/elles voudraient

conte de fées page 82

There was once a king so great, so loved by his people, so respected by all his neighbours and allies, that he could be said to be the happiest of all monarchs.

answers to questions on how to use a dictionary page 102

1 all of them except sardine
2 nouns: animal, travail, corail; adjectives: familial, blanc, joyeux, beau; verbs: perdre, comprendre

vocabulary builder

Nouns are followed by their gender **m, f** or **m/f.**
Adjectives are listed with their masculine singular ending (page 176). The feminine ending is included for ones that don't simply add **-e**, e.g. **f -euse.**
Verbs are in the infinitive; irregular past participles **pp** are included.

A
able: to be able to pouvoir (pp pu)
abortion avortement (m)
about à peu près, environ, vers
absolutely absolument, tout à fait
abstract abstrait
absurd absurde
to accept accepter
accident accident (m)
to accompany accompagner
according to selon, d'après
accountant comptable (m/f)
to ache avoir mal
acidic acidulé
active actif/active
activity activité (f)
actor acteur
actress actrice
actually en fait
to add ajouter
addition (in) en plus
address adresse (f)
to admit admettre (pp admis)
to adore adorer
adult adulte (m/f)
advance (in) à l'avance, d'avance
adventurous aventureux (f -euse)
advert annonce (f), publicité (f)
advice conseil (m)

to advise conseiller
affectionate affectueux (f -euse)
afraid: to be afraid avoir peur
after après
afternoon après-midi (m)
afterwards après, ensuite
age âge (m)
aged âgé
aggressive agressif (f -ive)
ago il y a
to agree être d'accord
agreed d'accord
agriculture agriculture (f)
airport aéroport (m)
alcohol alcool (m)
all tout; not at all pas du tout
all the best amitiés (f pl), bon courage
allergic allergique
allergy allergie (f)
almond amande (f)
almost presque
alone seul
along le long de
already déjà
also aussi
although bien que
always toujours
amazed étonné
amazing formidable, extraordinaire
American américain
among parmi
amusing drôle, amusant
ancient ancien(ne)
and et

angry en colère, fâché
animal animal (m)
ankle cheville (f)
ant fourmi (f)
anxious anxieux (f -euse)
anybody quelqu'un
anyway de toute façon
to appear apparaître (pp apparu)
appetiser amuse-gueule (m)
apple pomme (f)
apple tree pommier (m)
appointment rendez-vous (m)
apprenticeship apprentissage (m)
appropriate approprié
approximately à peu près, environ
architect architecte (m/f)
architecture architecture (f)
area région (f)
arm bras (m)
to arrive arriver
art dessin (m)
arthritis arthrite (f)
artistic artistique
arts arts (m pl)
as comme
as usual comme d'habitude
to ask demander
asthma attack crise (f) d'asthme
at last enfin
athlete athlète (m/f)
atmosphere ambiance (f)

to attach joindre (pp joint)
to attack agresser, attaquer
attic grenier (m)
attractive mignon(ne)
aunt tante (f)
Australian australien(ne)
available disponible
avocado avocat (m)
to avoid éviter

B
B&B chambre (f) d'hôte
back dos (m), fond (m)
bad mauvais
badminton badminton (m)
bag sac (m)
baker's boulangerie (f)
balanced équilibré
balcony balcon (m)
bald chauve
bank banque (f)
bank card carte (f) bancaire
banker banquier/banquière
banknote billet (m)
bar bar (m)
barbecue barbecue (m)
bargain affaire (f), aubaine (f)
basketball basket (m)
bath baignoire (f)
to bathe se baigner
bathroom salle (f) de bains
battery pile (f), batterie (f)
to be être (pp été)
to be able pouvoir (pp pu)
to be born naître (pp né)
to be called s'appeler
to be careful faire attention (pp fait)
beach plage (f)
beard barbe (f)
to beat battre

beautiful beau/bel(le)
beauty beauté (f)
because parce que
because of à cause de
to become devenir (pp devenu)
bed lit (m); single bed lit simple; double bed lit double; to go to bed se coucher
bedroom chambre (f)
bee abeille (f)
beef bœuf (m)
before avant
to begin commencer
to believe croire (pp cru)
belt ceinture (f)
bench banc (m)
to bend plier
beneficial bienfaisant
benefit avantage (m)
to benefit from profiter de
benefits allocations (f pl) sociales
best le meilleur (adj), le mieux (adv); best wishes meilleurs vœux
better meilleur (adj), mieux (adv)
between entre
bicycle vélo (m), bicyclette (f)
big grand
bike vélo (m); mountain bike vélo tout terrain (VTT)
bill facture (f)
billiard room salle (f) de billard
billions milliards (m pl)
bin poubelle (f)
binoculars jumelles (f pl)
biologist biologiste (m/f)
bird oiseau (m)
birth naissance (f); date of birth date (f) de naissance
birthday anniversaire (m)

bisexual bisexuel(le)
bit morceau (m)
bit (a) un peu
black noir
to bleed saigner
bleeding saignant
bloke type (m), mec (m)
blonde blond
blood sang (m)
blood pressure tension (f) artérielle
blue bleu
boat bateau (m)
bodybuilding culturisme (m), musculation (f)
bold audacieux (f -euse)
book livre (m)
to book réserver
boot botte (f)
border frontière (f)
bored: to get bored s'ennuyer
boring ennuyeux
born né
to borrow emprunter
boss chef (m), patron(ne)
both tous les deux
to bother déranger
bottle bouteille (f)
bowls boules (f pl)
box office guichet (m)
boy garçon (m)
brave courageux
brazen audacieux (f -euse)
bread pain (m)
to breathe respirer
bridge pont (m)
brief bref/brève
bright lumineux (f -euse)
brilliant super, génial
to bring apporter
to bring in rentrer
Britain Grande-Bretagne (f)
British britannique
Brittany Bretagne (f)
broken cassé
brother frère (m)
brown marron, brun

browser navigateur (m)
bruise bleu (m), contusion (f)
brunette brune
building bâtiment (m)
building contractor entrepreneur (f -euse) en bâtiment
bungee jumping saut (m) à l'élastique
burglary cambriolage (m)
burly costaud
bus autobus (m)
bus station gare (f) routière
bus stop arrêt (m)
business entreprise (f)
businessman homme d'affaires
businesswoman femme d'affaires
busy: to be busy with s'occuper de
but mais
butter beurre (m)
button bouton (m)
to buy acheter

C
café café (m)
cake gâteau (m)
calendar calendrier (m)
to call appeler; to be called s'appeler
call centre centre (m) d'appels
camera appareil photo (m)
campsite camping (m)
canny astucieux (f -euse)
capital city capitale (f)
captivating passionnant
car voiture (f)
to carry porter
cartoon bande (f) dessinée/BD, dessin (m) animé
case étui (m), cas (m); in any case en tout cas

cashpoint distributeur (m) de billets
cast distribution (f)
castle château (m)
cat chat (m)
catastrophic catastrophique
cautious prudent
to celebrate fêter
celebration fête (f)
central central
central heating chauffage (m) central
centre centre (m)
century siècle (m)
CEO PDG (m/f)
certainly bien sûr, certainement
championship championnat (m)
change changement (m)
to change changer, échanger
change (money) monnaie (f)
to charge recharger
charity organisation (f) caritative
charity work travail (m) bénévole
charming charmant
to chat bavarder, causer
to chat online chatter, tchatter
chatty bavard
to check vérifier
cheeky impudent
cheese fromage (m)
chef chef de cuisine
chemical engineer ingénieur chimiste (m/f)
chemist pharmacien (m)
chemist's pharmacie (f)
cherry cerise (f)
chest poitrine (f)
chicken poulet (m)
child enfant (m/f)
chilled frais
chilly frais

chimney cheminée (f)
chiropodist podologue (m/f)
chocolate chocolat (m)
choice choix (m)
to choose choisir
Christmas Noël (m)
church église (f)
cider cidre (m)
cinema cinéma (m)
city ville (f)
civil partnership (in a) en union civile; pacsé
class classe (f)
classmate camarade (m/f) de classe
clean propre
to clean nettoyer
to clear up ranger
clearly manifestement
clever intelligent, habile, astucieux
cliff falaise (f)
climate climat (m)
climate change changement (m) climatique
to climb monter, escalader
climbing escalade (f)
clingy moulant
to close fermer
clothes vêtements (m pl)
cloud nuage (m)
cloudy nuageux
clove (of garlic) gousse (f)
clumsy maladroit
coast côte (f)
coconut noix de coco (f)
coeliac cœliaque
coffee café (m)
coincidence coïncidence (f)
cold froid; to be cold avoir froid
cold (illness) rhume (m)
collar col (m), collier (m)
colleague collègue (m/f)
colour couleur (f)

to come venir (pp venu)
to come back rentrer, revenir (pp revenu)
comfort confort (m)
comfortable confortable
commercial commerçant
to communicate communiquer
company société (f)
compartment compartiment (m)
compass boussole (f)
compatible compatible
completely complètement, totalement
complicated compliqué
composer compositeur (m)
computer ordinateur (m)
computer scientist informaticien(ne)
computing informatique (f)
concert concert (m)
to conclude conclure
conference (academic) colloque (m)
confidence confiance (f)
confident assuré
to confirm confirmer
congested bondé
to congratulate féliciter
congratulations félicitations (f pl)
consultant conseiller/ère
to contact contacter
to contain contenir (pp contenu)
contents contenu (m)
continent continent (m)
to continue continuer
contract contrat (m)
convenient commode
conversation conversation (f)
to cook cuire (pp cuit), cuisinier, faire (pp fait) la cuisine

cook cuisinier/ère
cooked cuit
cookery cuisine (f)
corner coin (m)
Corsica Corse (f)
to cost coûter
cot lit (m) d'enfant
cotton coton (m)
to cough tousser
country pays (m)
country(side) campagne (f)
couple couple (m)
course cours (m), stage (m)
course (of) bien sûr, naturellement
cousin cousin (m), cousine (f)
covered couvert
to crash percuter
crazy fou/folle
credit card carte de crédit (f)
crockery vaisselle (f)
to cross traverser
crossroads carrefour (m)
crossword mots croisés (m pl)
to crush écraser
cupboard placard (m)
curious curieux (f -euse)
curly frisé
customs officer douanier/ère
to cut couper
to cycle faire du vélo
cycle track piste cyclable (f)

D
to dance danser
dance la danse (f)
dangerous dangereux
to dare oser
dark foncé (colour), sombre
dark-haired brun(e)
darling chéri/chérie

date date (f); date of birth date de naissance
to date dater
dated vétuste
daughter fille; daughter-in-law belle-fille
dawn aube (f)
day jour (m), journée (f)
deaf sourd
dear cher/chère
to decide décider (de)
to decorate repeindre
deep profond
defence défense (f)
to defrost dégivrer
degree (temp) degré (m), (academic) diplôme (m)
dehydrated déshydraté
delay retard (m)
delegate délégué (m)
deli traiteur (m)
delicate délicat
delicious délicieux (f -euse)
delighted ravi
democracy démocratie (f)
denim jean (m), en denim (adj)
dentist dentiste (m/f)
department département (m)
deposit arrhes (f pl)
depression dépression (f)
deputy adjoint
to describe décrire (pp décrit)
desert désert (m)
to deserve mériter
designer créateur (m)
dessert dessert (m)
detail détail (m)
diabetes diabète (m)
diabetic diabétique
to die mourir (pp mort), décéder
diet régime (m)
different différent
difficult difficile
dilapidated délabré

dining room salle à manger (f)
dinner dîner (m); to have dinner dîner
dinner jacket smoking (m)
diplomatic discret (f -ète)
director directeur/directrice
dirty sale
disappointed déçu
disappointing décevant
disappointment déception (f)
disaster catastrophe (f)
to discover découvrir (pp découvert)
discreet discret (f -ète)
discrimination discrimination (f)
to discuss discuter
disgusting dégoûtant
dish plat (m)
dishwasher lave-vaisselle (m)
diversity diversité (f)
diving plongée (f)
divorced divorcé
DIY bricolage (m)
to do faire (pp fait)
to do stupid things faire des bêtises
doctor médecin (m/f), docteur (m)
dog chien (m)
dogsbody homme (m)/bonne (f) à tout faire
dolphin dauphin (m)
doubt doute (m)
dozen douzaine (f)
to draw (art) dessiner, (sport) faire (pp fait) match nul
draw (tie) égalité (f), match (m) nul
dreadful affreux (f -euse)
dream rêve (m)
to dream rêver
dressed: to get dressed s'habiller

drink boisson (f), pot (m)
to drink boire (pp bu)
to drive conduire (pp conduit)
driving licence permis (m) de conduire
drizzle crachin (m)
drop goutte (f)
drug drogue (f)
drug addict toxicomane (m/f)
drunk ivre
dry sec/sèche, aride
dryer sèche-linge (m)
duck canard (m)
duration durée (f)
during pendant
to dust épousseter
duty devoir (m)

E
each chaque
each person chacun
eagle aigle (m)
ear oreille (f)
early tôt, en avance
to earn gagner
easily facilement
east est (m)
Easter Pâques (m)
easy facile
to eat manger, (slang) bouffer
ecology écologie (f)
economist économiste (m/f)
economy économie (f)
editor rédacteur (m), rédactrice (f)
education éducation (f), enseignement (m)
effective efficace
egg œuf (m)
elderly âgé
electric électrique
elegant élégant
email address adresse (f) mail
emergency urgence (f)

employee employé (m), employée (f)
employment emploi (m)
to empty vider
end bout (m), fin (f)
engaged fiancé
engineer ingénieur (m/f)
England Angleterre (f)
English anglais
to enjoy oneself s'amuser
enormous énorme
enough assez; that's enough ça suffit
enough: to be enough suffire (pp suffi)
to enter entrer
entirely entièrement
environment environnement (m)
equal opportunities égalité (f) des chances
equality parité (f)
equipped équipé
escalator escalator (m)
especially surtout
essential essentiel(le)
estate agency agence (f) immobilière
estate agent agent (m/f) immobilier
euthanasia euthanasie (f)
eve veille (f)
evening soir (m), soirée (f)
event événement (m)
every chaque
every day tous les jours
everyone tous, tout le monde
exactly exactement, précisément
to exaggerate exagérer
exam examen (m)
example exemple (m); for example par exemple
to exceed dépasser
excellent excellent
exceptional exceptionnel(le)
excess excès (m)

to exchange échanger
excursion excursion (f)
to excuse excuser; excuse me excusez-moi
exercise exercice (m), activité (f) physique
exhibition exposition (f)
to exit sortir
exit sortie (f)
expensive cher/ chère
to explain expliquer
explanation explication (f)
to explore explorer
exquisite exquis
extremism extrémisme (m)
eye œil (m); pl yeux

F
fabric tissu (m)
facility facilité (f)
fact fait (m); in fact en fait
factory usine (f)
to faint s'évanouir
faithful fidèle
to fall tomber
to fall asleep s'endormir
false faux/fausse
family famille (f)
famished (to be) avoir une faim de loup
famous célèbre, connu
fan supporter (m/f)
to fancy (doing) avoir (pp eu) envie de
fantastic super, génial, fantastique
far loin
farm ferme (f)
farmer agriculteur/ agricultrice
farmhouse ferme (f)
fashion mode (f)
fashion designer styliste (m/f)
fat gros(se)
father père (m)
father-in-law beau-père (m)

favourite préféré
fear peur (f); to be afraid avoir peur
to fear craindre (pp craint)
to feed donner à manger à
to feel like avoir envie de
festival fête (f)
fiancé(e) fiancé(e)
file fichier (m)
film film (m)
finally finalement
finance finance (f)
to find trouver
to find out découvrir (pp découvert)
finger doigt (m)
to finish finir, terminer
fire feu (m), incendie (f)
fire fighter pompier (m/f)
fireplace cheminée (f)
first premier (f -ière)
first (of all) d'abord
first name prénom (m)
to fish pêcher
fishing pêche (f)
fit: to get/keep fit se remettre en forme
fitness remise en forme (f)
flask gourde (f)
flat appartement (m)
flight vol (m)
floor plancher (m)
floor (storey) étage (m)
flour farine (f)
flu grippe (f)
fly mouche (f)
fog brouillard (m)
foggy brumeux
to fold plier
folder dossier (m)
to follow suivre (pp suivi)
food nourriture (f)
food poisoning intoxication (f) alimentaire
foot pied (m); on foot à pied

football foot(ball) (m)
footballer footballeur/ footballeuse
footpath sentier (m)
for pour, depuis
foreman contremaître (m)
forest forêt (f)
to forget oublier
former ancien(ne)
fortunately heureusement
foster family famille (f) d'accueil
frank franc/ franche
frankly franchement
fraud fraude (f)
free gratuit, libre
freedom liberté (f)
freelance (to be) être indépendant, travailler à son compte
to freeze geler
freezer congélateur (m)
French français (adj)
French (language) français (m)
french window porte-fenêtre (f)
Frenchman Français (m)
French-speaking francophone
Frenchwoman Française (f)
fridge frigo (m), réfrigérateur (m)
friend ami (m), amie (f), copain (m), copine (f)
friendly sociable
friendship amitié (f)
to frighten faire peur à
frog grenouille (f)
from de, à partir de
front: in front of devant
frozen (IT) bloqué, gelé
fruit fruit (m)
fruity fruité
full complet (f -ète)
full time à plein temps

fundamentalism fondamentalisme (m)
funeral enterrement (m)
funny drôle
furthermore d'ailleurs

G
gale tempête (f)
gallery galerie (f)
gambling jeu (m)
game jeu (m)
gap year année (f) de césure
garden jardin (m)
to garden faire du jardinage (pp fait)
garden centre pépinière (f), jardinerie (f)
garlic ail (m)
garment vêtement (m)
gas gaz (m)
gay gay
generous généreux (f -euse)
Geneva Génève; Lake Geneva Lac Léman
gentle doux/douce
to get obtenir (pp obtenu)
to get bored s'ennuyer
to get dressed s'habiller
to get off (a vehicle) descendre
to get up se lever
gifted doué
gig concert (m)
girl fille (f)
girlfriend petite amie (f)
to give donner
glasses lunettes (f pl); sun glasses lunettes de soleil
global warming réchauffement climatique (m)
glossy glacé
glove gant (m)
gluten gluten (m)
to go aller
to go down descendre

to go for a walk se promener, faire une promenade
to go home rentrer
to go out sortir
to go to bed se coucher
to go up monter
goal (sport) but (m), objectif (m)
golf golf (m)
golf course terrain (m) de golf
good bon(ne)
goodwill bon vouloir (m)
to google googler
gourmet gastronomique
government gouvernement (m)
grandchildren petits-enfants (m pl)
granddaughter petite-fille (f)
grandfather grand-père (m)
grandmother grand-mère (f)
grandparents grands-parents (m pl)
grandson petit-fils (m)
graphic designer graphiste (m/f)
grateful reconnaissant
great génial, classe, super
Great Britain Grande-Bretagne (f)
green vert
grey gris
group groupe (m)
to grow old vieillir
to grow/grow up grandir
grown-up adulte (m/f)
growth croissance (f)
guide guide (m/f)
gym salle (f) de gym

H
to haggle marchander
hair cheveux (m pl)
hairdresser coiffeur (m), coiffeuse (f)

hairstyle coiffure (f)
half (of amount, object) moitié (f)
half (time, numbers, measurement) demi
half past et demie
half-way à mi-chemin
hall salle (f)
hand main (f)
handsome beau/bel(le)
handy pratique
to hang up raccrocher
hangover gueule (f) de bois
to happen arriver, se passer
happiness bonheur (m)
happy heureux (f -euse)
hardly à peine
hardworking travailleur (f -euse)
harsh rigoureux (f -euse)
hat chapeau (m)
to hate avoir horreur de, détester
to have avoir (pp eu)
to have to devoir (pp dû), il faut (pp fallu)
hayfever rhume (m) des foins
hazelnut noisette (f)
head tête (f)
head (chief) chef (m/f)
headache mal (m) à la tête
headlight phare (m)
health santé (f)
health and safety l'hygiène et la sécurité
to hear entendre
heart cœur (m)
hearth foyer (m)
to heat chauffer
heating chauffage (m)
heatwave canicule (f)
heavenly paradisiaque
heavy lourd
hedge haie (f)
hello bonjour, (on phone) allô

helmet casque (m)
to help aider
help aide (f)
Help! Au secours!
helpful serviable, utile
here ici
here you are voici, voilà
to hesitate hésiter
high haut
hike/hiking randonnée (f)
hill colline (f)
hire location (f)
to hire louer
historic historique
history histoire (f)
hoax canular (m)
to hold tenir (pp tenu)
holiday séjour (m),
vacances (f pl)
holiday camp colonie de
vacances (f)
homework devoirs (m pl)
honest honnête, sincère
to hope espérer
horrendous horrible
horrible horrible
horse cheval (m)
horse riding équitation (f)
hospital hôpital (m)
hot chaud; to be hot
avoir chaud
hotel hôtel (m)
hour heure (f)
house maison (f); at the
house of chez
housewife femme au
foyer (f)
how comment
how much, how many
combien (de)
however pourtant,
cependant
HR ressources humaines
(f pl)
huge vaste, énorme
human rights les droits
(m pl) de l'homme
humid humide
hunger faim; to be

hungry avoir faim
to hurry se dépêcher
to hurt faire mal
to hurt oneself se faire mal
husband mari (m)

I
i.e. c'est-à-dire
idea idée (f)
ideal idéal
identity identité (f)
identity card carte (f)
d'identité
if si
ill malade
illegal illégal, clandestin
immaculate impeccable
immediately tout de suite
impetuous impétueux
(f -euse)
important important
imposing imposant
impossible impossible
impressive
impressionnant
impulsive impulsif (f -ive)
in à, en, dans
incredible incroyable
independent
indépendant
industrial industriel(le)
industrial estate zone (f)
industrielle
information
renseignements (m pl)
inhabitant habitant (m)
to injure blesser
in-laws beaux-parents
(m pl)
insensitive insensible
inside intérieur (m)
to install installer
institute institut (m)
insurance assurance (f)
intelligent intelligent
interesting intéressant
intern stagiaire (m/f)
international
international
to interrupt interrompre

to intervene intervenir
(pp intervenu)
interview entretien (m),
entrevue (f)
intolerant intolérant
to introduce présenter
investor investisseur
(f -euse)
invitation invitation (f)
to invite inviter
Ireland Irlande (f)
Irish irlandais
iron fer à repasser (m)
to iron repasser
irresponsible
irresponsable
island île (f)
IT informatique (f)
IT system système (m)
informatique

J
jacket veste (f)
jealous jaloux
jeans jean (m sing)
job travail (m), métier
(m), emploi (m), poste
(m), boulot (m)
to joke plaisanter
joke blague (f)
journalist journaliste
(m/f)
journey voyage (m)
to jump sauter
jumper pull (m)
just juste

K
keen enthousiaste
to keep garder, maintenir
(pp maintenu)
to keep fit garder la
forme
kettle bouilloire (f)
key clé (f)
key (IT) touche (f)
to key in saisir
keyboard clavier (m)
killjoy rabat-joie (m)
kind gentil/gentille,
aimable

kind-hearted généreux (f -euse)
kindness gentillesse (f)
kingdom royaume (m)
kiss bisou (m)
to kiss embrasser; to air-kiss faire la bise, faire un bisou
kit bag sac (m) de sport
kitchen cuisine (f)
knee genou (m)
to know (fact) savoir (pp su); (person, place) connaître (pp connu)

L
label étiquette (f)
lack manque (m)
lactose lactose (m)
ladder échelle (f)
laid-back décontracté
lake lac (m)
lamp lampe (f)
language langue (f)
laptop ordinateur portable (m)
large grand
last dernier (f -ière)
to last durer
late tard, en retard
to laugh rire (pp ri)
laundry lessive (f), linge (m)
law loi (f)
lawn pelouse (f)
lawyer avocat(e)
lazy paresseux (f -euse)
leaflet dépliant (m)
to learn apprendre (pp appris)
to leave (behind) laisser
to leave (depart) partir
left (on/to the) (à) gauche
leg jambe (f)
leisure centre centre (m) de loisirs
lemon citron (m)
to lend prêter
length longueur (f)
lesbian lesbienne

less moins
to let laisser, louer
letter lettre (f)
level niveau (m)
to lie in faire la grasse matinée
life vie (f)
lifeguard maître-nageur (f -euse)
lift ascenseur (m)
to light allumer
light lumière (f)
light (qualifying a colour) (colour) clair, (weight) léger (f -ère)
to like aimer
like (as) comme
linen lin (m)
list liste (f)
to listen écouter
litter déchets (m pl)
little petit
little (a) un peu
to live habiter, vivre (pp vécu)
live performance spectacle (m) en direct
lively animé
living room salon (m), séjour (m)
to load charger
to loathe avoir horreur de
local local
to lock fermer à clé
to log in se connecter
to log out se déconnecter
logical logique
long long/longue
longer: no longer ne ... plus
to look after (occupy oneself with) s'occuper de
to look at regarder
to look for chercher
to look like ressembler à
to look up rechercher
to lose perdre
loss perte (f)
loss report déclaration (f) de perte

lot (a) beaucoup
to love aimer, adorer
love (in love) amoureux
lover amant (m), amateur/amatrice
to lower baisser
loyal fidèle
luck chance (f); to be lucky avoir de la chance
lunch déjeuner (m); to have lunch déjeuner
luxurious luxueux (f -euse)
luxury luxe (m)

M
mad fou/folle
mad: to be mad about avoir une passion pour
made fabriqué
magnetic magnétique
main principal
maintenance entretien (m)
to make faire (pp fait)
manager directeur
manageress directrice
map carte (f), plan (m)
marathon marathon (m)
married marié
married: to get married se marier
marshy marécageux (f -euse)
martial arts arts martiaux (m pl)
marvellous merveilleux (f -euse)
to match coordonner
match (sport) match (m), partie (f)
maybe peut-être
meal repas (m)
mean méchant
to mean vouloir dire
meat viande (f); cold meats charcuterie (f)
mechanic mécanicien (m), mécanicienne (f)
media médias (m pl)
medication médicament (m)

medium moyen (adj)
to meet rencontrer, se retrouver
meeting réunion (f), rendez-vous (m)
message message (m)
microwave oven micro-ondes (m)
midday midi (m)
middle-class bourgeois
migraine migraine (f)
migration migration (f)
mild doux/douce
milk lait (m)
mineral water eau minérale (f)
minimum wage SMIC (m)
minister ministre (m/f)
minute minute (f)
to miss (e.g. train) rater
to mistake: make a mistake se tromper
misunderstanding malentendu (m)
mix mélanger
mobile phone portable (m)
model modèle (m), mannequin (m)
moderate modéré
modern moderne
money argent (m)
month mois (m)
more plus; more and more de plus en plus
morning matin (m)
mosquito moustique (m)
most (le/la) plus; at most au plus
mother mère (f)
mother-in-law belle-mère (f)
motor racing course (f) automobile
motorbike moto (f)
mountain montagne (f)
mountain bike vélo (m) tout terrain (VTT)
mountaineering alpinisme (m)

mountainous montagneux (f -euse)
mouse souris (f)
mouth bouche (f)
to move bouger
to move house déménager
to mow tondre
mud boue (f)
muddy boueux (f -euse)
to mug agresser
mug grande tasse (f)
muscular musclé
museum musée (m)
music musique (f)
musician musicien (m), musicienne (f)
must: to have to il faut (pp fallu), devoir (pp dû)
myself moi-même

N
naive naïf/naïve
naked nu
name nom (m); first name prénom (m)
nanny nourrice (f)
narrow étroit
nasty méchant
national national
nationality nationalité (f)
natural naturel
nature reserve réserve (f) naturelle
naughty méchant, vilain
near près (de), proche (adj)
nearby tout près
neck cou (m)
need besoin (m); to need avoir besoin de
neglected mal (entre)tenu
neighbour voisin
neither ... nor ne ... ni ... ni
nettle ortie (f)
never ne ... jamais
nevertheless toutefois, cependant

new nouveau/nouvelle, neuf/neuve
news nouvelles (f pl)
news agency agence (f) de presse
newspaper journal (m)
next prochain
next to à côté de
nice aimable, gentil, sympa, agréable
night nuit (f)
nightmare cauchemar (m)
nobody, no-one ne ... personne
noise bruit (m)
noisy bruyant
north nord (m)
nose nez (m)
nosy curieux (f -euse)
nothing ne ... rien
novel roman (m)
now maintenant
now and then de temps en temps
number numéro (m)
nurse infirmier (m), infirmière (f)
nut fruit (m) à coque

O
o'clock heure (f)
obese obèse
obliged obligé
obvious évident
obviously évidemment
occasionally de temps en temps
ocean océan (m)
odd bizarre, curieux (f -euse)
to offer offrir (pp offert)
office bureau (m)
office worker employé(e) de bureau
officially officiellement
often souvent
oil huile (f)
OK d'accord, OK

old vieux/vieille, ancien(ne)
olive olive (f)
online en ligne
only seulement, ne ... que
to open ouvrir (pp ouvert)
opening times horaires (m pl) d'ouverture
opera opéra (m)
opinion avis (m); in my opinion à mon avis
opposite contraire (m)
opposite en face de (adv)
optimistic optimiste
to order commander
organic bio
to organise organiser
organiser organisateur (m), organisatrice (f)
original original
other autre
outside extérieur (m)
outskirts alentours (m pl), environs (m pl)
outspoken franc/franche
oven four (m)
over there là-bas
overseas outre-mer
to overtake doubler, dépasser
overtime heures (f) supplémentaires
to owe devoir (pp dû)
owner propriétaire (m/f)
oyster huître (f)

P
to pack faire la valise
pain douleur (f)
painful douloureux (f -euse)
painkiller analgésique (m)
to paint peindre (pp peint)
pair couple (m), paire (f)
pancake crêpe (f)

parachuting parachutisme (m)
paragliding parapente (m)
parents parents (m pl)
park parc (m)
to park garer
part partie (f)
part time à mi-temps
partly en partie
partner compagnon (m), compagne (f)
party fête (f), soirée (f)
to pass, go past passer
passport passeport (m)
password mot (m) de passe
pasta pâtes (f pl)
patient patient
pavement trottoir (m)
to pay payer
to pay attention faire attention
peace paix (f)
peace (and quiet) calme (m), tranquillité (f)
peaceful tranquille
peanut cacahuète (f)
to peel éplucher
people gens (m pl); a lot of people beaucoup de monde
pepper poivre (m)
perfect parfait
perfection perfection (f)
perfectly parfaitement
perhaps peut-être
permit permis (m)
person personne (f)
personal personnel
pessimistic pessimiste
pet animal (m) de compagnie
petrol essence (f)
pharmacist pharmacien (m), pharmacienne (f)
phone appareil (m), téléphone (m)
to phone appeler, téléphoner

phone number numéro (m) de téléphone
photo photo (f)
to photograph photographier
photographer photographe (m/f)
physical physique
picnic piquenique (m)
picture tableau (m), peinture (f)
picturesque pittoresque
pie tarte (f)
piece morceau (m)
pilot pilote (m/f)
pinch pincée (f)
pink rose
pitch terrain (m)
pity dommage (m); it's a pity c'est dommage
place endroit (m), lieu (m)
plain plaine (f)
to plan compter
to play jouer
play (drama) pièce (f)
play area terrain (m) de jeux
pleasant agréable
please s'il te/vous plaît
to please plaire (pp plu)
pleased heureux/heureuse
pleased to meet you enchanté
pleasure plaisir (m)
plumber plombier (m/f)
plump dodu
pocket poche (f)
poem poème (m)
police police (f)
police officer agent (m/f) de police
police station commissariat (m) (de police)
policy politique (f)
polite poli
politician homme/femme politique

politics politique (f)
polluted pollué
pollution pollution (f)
pony poney (m)
pool piscine (f)
poor pauvre
popular populaire
port port (m)
possible possible
post office bureau (m) de poste
postman facteur (m)
potholing spéléologie (f)
to pour verser
power pouvoir (m)
PR relations publiques (f pl)
practical pratique
to practise pratiquer, travailler
to prefer préférer
pregnant enceinte
to prepare préparer
present cadeau (m)
press agency agence (f) de presse
press officer attaché (m) de presse
pretty joli, mignon(ne)
to prevent empêcher
price prix (m)
priest prêtre (m)
printer imprimante (f)
private privé
problem problème (m)
to produce produire
product produit (m)
profit bénéfice (m)
to promise promettre (pp promis)
promise promesse (f)
property propriété (f)
to protect protéger
to provide fournir
provided that pourvu que
psychological psychologique
public public (f -ique)
to pull tirer

pullover pull (m)
puncture crevaison (f)
pure pur
purse porte-monnaie (m)
to push pousser
to put mettre (pp mis)
puzzle puzzle (m)

Q
quality qualité (f)
quarter quart (m)
question question (f)
queue queue (f)
to queue faire la queue
quickly vite, rapidement, à toute vitesse
quiet tranquille

R
rabbit lapin (m)
racism racisme (m)
radio radio (f)
railway chemin de fer (m)
rain pluie (f)
to rain pleuvoir (pp plu)
rape viol (m)
to rape violer
rapid rapide
rarely rarement
rash impétueux (f -euse)
rash (skin) rougeurs (f pl)
rather plutôt
to reach atteindre (pp atteint)
to read lire (pp lu)
reader lecteur (m)
ready prêt
real véritable
really absolument, super, vraiment
reason raison (f)
to receive recevoir (pp reçu)
recently récemment
recipe recette (f)
to recommend recommander, conseiller
recyclable recyclable
to recycle recycler
red rouge

to reduce réduire (pp réduit)
reduction réduction (f), tarif (m) réduit
refugee réfugié(e)
to refuse refuser
regional régional, du terroir
to regret regretter
regularly régulièrement
relative parent (m)
to relax se reposer
relaxation relaxation (f)
reliable fiable
relief soulagement (m)
to relieve soulager
to remain rester
to remember se rappeler de
to remind rappeler
remote isolé
to renew renouveler
renovated rénové
to rent louer
repair shop/garage atelier (m) de réparation
to repeat répéter
reply réponse (f)
to reply répondre
report (incident) faire une déclaration
research recherche (f)
researcher chercheur (m), chercheuse (f)
to reserve réserver
residential résidentiel(le)
resort station (f)
responsible responsable
to rest se reposer
restaurant brasserie (f), restaurant (m)
to restore restaurer
result résultat (m)
retail vente (f)
retired retraité
to return rentrer, retourner
rheumatism rhumatismes (m pl)

rich riche
rich (food and drink) moelleux (f -euse)
to ride (horse) faire du cheval (pp fait)
ridiculous ridicule
right droit (m)
right (correct) bon(ne); to be right avoir raison
right (on/to the) (à) droite; (pol) de droite
to risk risquer
river rivière (f)
road rue (f), routière (adj)
roadhog chauffard (m/f)
robust robuste
role rôle (m), domaine (m)
room pièce (f), place (f), chambre (f), salle (f)
room temperature (at) chambré
rose rose (f)
rough accidenté
rucksack sac (m) à dos
rude impoli
rudeness impolitesse (f)
rugby rugby (m)
rugged accidenté
to run courir
run-down délabré
running course (f), jogging (m)
rural rural
rush hour heure (f) de pointe

S
sabbatical year année (f) sabbatique
sad triste
to sail faire de la voile
sailing voile (f)
salad salade (f)
sale solde (m); at sale price en solde
sales (business) ventes (f pl)
sales assistant vendeur (m), vendeuse (f)

salmon saumon (m)
salt sel (m)
salty salé
same même
sand sable (m)
sandy sablonneux (f -euse)
satisfying satisfaisant
saucepan casserole (f)
to save up faire des économies
to say dire (pp dit)
scenery paysage (m)
school école (f), collège (m)
score (game) score (m)
Scotland Écosse (f)
Scottish écossais
scruffy débraillé
sea mer (f)
to search for rechercher
seaside bord (m) de la mer
to season assaisonner
season ticket carte (f) d'abonné, carte d'abonnement
seat place (f)
seatbelt ceinture (f)
second deuxième, second
second-hand d'occasion
security sécurité (f)
security guard agent (m) de sécurité
to see voir (pp vu)
to see again revoir (pp revu)
see you soon à bientôt
selfish égoïste
to sell vendre
sell-by date date (f) de péremption
semi-detached house maison (f) jumelle
to send envoyer
sensible raisonnable
sensitive sensible
separate séparé

serious grave, sérieux (f -euse)
seriously sérieusement
to serve servir
several plusieurs
to sew faire de la couture (pp fait)
sexism sexisme (m)
shade ombre (f)
shaded à l'ombre, ombragé
to shake secouer, agiter, trembler
to shake hands serrer la main
to share partager
shattered crevé, vidé
sheet drap (m)
shirt chemise (f)
shop magasin (m)
short court, petit
shortcut raccourci (m)
shoulder épaule (f)
to show montrer
show spectacle (m)
shower douche (f); to have a shower se doucher
shower (of rain) averse (f)
shrewd astucieux (f -euse)
shy timide
side côté (m)
side effects effets secondaires (m pl)
signal signal (m)
silk soie (f)
since depuis
sincere sincère
to sing chanter
singer chanteur (m), chanteuse (f)
single célibataire
sister sœur (f)
to sit (oneself) down s'asseoir
situated situé
situated: to be situated se trouver

size taille (f) (clothes), pointure (f) (shoes)
skating patinage (m)
to ski faire du ski
to skid déraper
skiing ski (m)
skinny maigre
to skip sauter
skirt jupe (f)
to sleep dormir
to sleep in faire la grasse matinée
sleepy: to be sleepy avoir sommeil
sleeve manche (f)
slice tranche (f)
slim mince
to slim maigrir
slowly lentement
small petit
to smile sourire
to smoke fumer
snail escargot (m)
snobbish snob (m/f)
to snow neiger
so ainsi, alors, donc, si, tellement
sofa bed canapé-lit (m)
software company société (f) de logiciels
some des, quelques
somebody quelqu'un
something quelque chose
sometimes quelquefois, parfois
somewhat plutôt
son fils (m); son-in-law beau-fils, gendre
song chanson (f)
soon bientôt
sorry désolé, navré
sort sorte (f)
south sud (m)
south of France Midi (m)
spa station (f) thermale
space espace (m)
spacious spacieux (f -euse)

to speak parler
specialised spécialisé
speciality spécialité (f)
spectator spectateur (m), spectatrice (f)
speech discours (m)
speech therapist orthophoniste (m/f)
to spell épeler
to spend (money) dépenser
to spend (time) passer
spicy épicé
spider araignée (f)
spinach épinards (m pl)
spoilsport rabat-joie (m/f)
sport sport (m)
sports centre complexe sportif (m), centre sportif (m)
sporty sportif (f -ive)
spotless impeccable
square place (f); carré (adj)
squash (game) squash (m)
stable écurie (f)
stadium stade (m)
stage scène (f)
stairs escalier (m)
to start commencer
starter entrée (f)
state état (m)
station gare (f)
to stay rester, loger
stay séjour (m)
to steal voler
stepdaughter belle-fille (f)
stepson beau-fils (m)
to stir remuer
stockbroker courtier (m), courtière (f)
stomach ventre (m)
stone pierre (f)
to stop arrêter, s'arrêter
storey étage (m)
stormy orageux (f -euse)

story histoire (f)
straight hétéro (m/f)
straight ahead tout droit
strange étrange
street rue (f)
stressed stressé
stressful stressant
strict sévère
to strike faire grève (pp fait)
strong fort
stubborn têtu
student étudiant (m), étudiante (f)
to study étudier
stupid bête
stupidity bêtise (f)
sturdy costaud
subject sujet (m)
to suffer souffrir (pp souffert)
to suggest proposer
suit costume (m)
to suit aller, convenir (pp convenu)
to sulk faire la tête
summer été (m)
sun soleil (m)
sun cream crème solaire (f)
to sunbathe bronzer
sunburn coup (m) de soleil
sunglasses lunettes (f pl) de soleil
sunny ensoleillé
sunny interval éclaircie (f)
superb superbe
supermarket supermarché (m)
supernatural surnaturel(le)
supervisor chef de service
sure sûr
surgery cabinet (m) médical
surname nom (m) de famille

surprise surprise (f)
survey sondage (m)
sustainability durabilité (f)
to swallow avaler
swap échange (m)
sweet sucré, (person) mignon(ne)
to swim nager, se baigner
swimming natation (f)
swimming instructor maître-nageur (m), maître-nageuse (f)
swimming pool piscine (f)
to switch off éteindre
to switch on allumer, mettre en marche (pp mis)
Switzerland Suisse (f)
system système (m)

T
table table (f)
tablet (IT) tablette (f)
tablet (med) comprimé (m)
tactful discret (f -ète)
to take prendre (pp pris)
to take (people) emmener
to take down descendre
to take out sortir
to take part participer
talented doué
tall grand
taste goût (m)
to taste déguster, goûter
tasting dégustation (f)
tattoo tatouage (m)
tax impôt (m), taxe (f)
taxi driver chauffeur (m)/ chauffeuse (f) de taxi
teacher professeur (m/f)
team équipe (f)
tedious ennuyeux (f -euse)
television télévision (f)
to tell dire (pp dit), raconter

temperature température (f), fièvre (f)
tennis tennis (m)
tennis court court (m) de tennis
terrace terrasse (f)
terrible terrible, affreux
terrorism terrorisme (m)
than que
to thank remercier
thank you merci
that ça, cela, ce, cet, cette
that one celui-là (m), celle-là (f)
theatre théâtre (m)
theft vol (m)
then après, ensuite, puis
therapy thérapie (f)
there là; over there là-bas
there is, there are il y a
there you are voilà
therefore ainsi, alors, donc
these/those ces
thin maigre, mince, fin
thing chose (f), objet (m)
thingy machin (m), truc (m), bidule (m)
to think penser
thirst soif; to be thirsty avoir soif
this ce, cet, cette; this is voici
this one celui-ci (m), celle-ci (f)
thoughtless irréfléchi, inconsidéré
thousands milliers (m pl)
thrilling passionnant
throat gorge (f)
thunderstorm orage (m)
tick tique (f)
ticket billet (m)
to tidy ranger
time temps (m), (of day) heure (f), (occasion) fois (f); from time to time de temps en temps
time: on time à l'heure
tiny minuscule

tired fatigué
tiredness fatigue (f)
toast toast (m)
today aujourd'hui
together ensemble
tomato tomate (f)
tomorrow demain
tongue langue (f)
too aussi; too (much/many) trop (de)
tooth dent (f)
top sommet (m), top (m)
torch lampe (f) de poche
tourism tourisme (m)
tourist touriste (m/f)
tourist office office du tourisme (m), syndicat d'initiative (m)
touristy touristique
towards vers
towel serviette (f)
town ville (f); town centre centre-ville (m)
trade commerce (m)
trade-union syndicat (m)
trade-unionist syndicaliste (m/f)
tradition tradition (f)
traditional traditionel(le)
traffic circulation (f)
traffic lights feux (m pl)
tragic tragique
train train (m)
trainee stagiaire (m/f)
trainer entraîneur (m/f)
trainers (footwear) baskets (f pl)
transgender transgenre
to translate traduire (pp traduit)
to travel voyager
travel agent agent (m) de voyages
treatment cure (f), traitement (m)
to trip trébucher
trouble trouble (m), ennuis (m pl)
trousers pantalon (m)

true vrai
to trust avoir confiance en
trustworthy fiable
truth vérité (f)
to try (on) essayer
t-shirt tee-shirt (m)
tummy ache mal (m) au ventre
to turn tourner
to turn off éteindre (pp éteint)
to turn on allumer
twins jumeaux/jumelles

U
ugly laid
unbearable insupportable
uncle oncle (m)
under sous
to understand comprendre (pp compris)
underwater sous-marin (adj)
unemployed au chômage
unemployment chômage (m)
unexpected imprévu
unfortunately malheureusement
United Kingdom Royaume-Uni (m)
United States États-Unis (m pl)
university université (f)
unless à moins que
to unload décharger
unmissable incontournable
unpleasant désagréable
until jusqu'à
unusual insolite
up to jusqu'à
to update mettre (pp mis) à jour
urban urbain
USA États-Unis (m pl)
to use utiliser
useful utile

user name nom (m) d'utilisateur
usual habituel(le); as usual comme d'habitude
usually d'habitude, normalement, généralement
U-turn: to do a U-turn faire demi-tour

V
to vacuum passer l'aspirateur
vacuum cleaner aspirateur (m)
vegan végétalien(ne)
vegetarian végétarien(ne)
very très, super
very much beaucoup
view vue (f)
village village (m)
vineyard vignoble (m)
visit visite (f)
to visit visiter, fréquenter
visitor visiteur (m)
voice voix (f)
volleyball volley (m)
volunteer volontaire (m/f)
to vote voter

W
to wait (for) attendre
waiter serveur (m)
waitress serveuse (f)
to wake (oneself) up se réveiller
Wales pays de Galles (m)
to walk marcher; to go for a walk se promener
walk promenade (f); to go for a walk faire une promenade
walk round faire le tour de
walking shoe chaussure (f) de marche
wallet portefeuille (m)
to wallpaper tapisser
to wander round flâner, faire (pp fait) un tour

to want vouloir (pp voulu), avoir envie de
war guerre (f)
warm chaud
to wash laver
washable lavable
washing lessive (f), linge (m)
washing machine machine (f) à laver
washing-up vaisselle (f)
wasp guêpe (f)
to watch regarder
water eau (f)
water skiing ski nautique (m)
water sports sports nautiques (m pl)
waterproof imperméable
way chemin (m)
weak faible
to wear porter
weather temps (m)
weather forecast météo (f), prévisions (f pl) météorologiques
web page page (f) web
website site (m) internet/web
wedding anniversary anniversaire (m) de mariage
week semaine (f)
weekend weekend (m)
to weigh peser
weight poids (m)
welcome! bienvenue!
welcoming accueillant
well bien, alors, enfin
well-being bien-être (m)
well-equipped bien équipé
well-kept bien (entre)tenu
Welsh gallois
west ouest (m)
wet room salle d'eau (f)
what? qu'est-ce que? quoi?

whatsit machin (m), truc (m), bidule (m)
wheat blé (m), froment (m)
wheelchair fauteuil (m) roulant
when quand
where où
whereas tandis que
which que, qui
which one? lequel?/laquelle?
white blanc/blanche
white coffee café (m) au lait
who qui
whole entier (f -ère); on the whole dans l'ensemble
why pourquoi
widowed veuf (m)/veuve (f)
width largeur (f)
wife femme (f)
Wi-Fi wifi (m or f)
wind vent (m)

window fenêtre (f)
windsurfing: to go windsurfing faire de la planche à voile
wine vin (m)
winter hiver (m)
to wish souhaiter
wish vœu (m); best wishes meilleurs vœux
with avec; with pleasure volontiers
to withdraw retirer
without sans
woman femme (f)
to wonder (to ask oneself) se demander
wonderful magnifique, merveilleux (f -euse)
wooded boisé
woods forêt (f)
wool laine (f)
word mot (m)
to work travailler
work travail (m)
to work (function)

fonctionner, marcher
to work hard (slang) bosser
world monde (m), mondial (adj)
to worry s'inquiéter
worse pire
worst le/la pire
to write écrire (pp écrit)
wrong: to be wrong avoir tort

Y
year an (m), année (f)
yellow jaune
yesterday hier
yet encore
yoga yoga (m)
young jeune
youth hostel auberge (f) de jeunesse

Z
zip fermeture (f) éclair
zipped zippé